PROTESTANT THOUGHT
AND NATURAL
SCIENCE

John Dillenberger

PROTESTANT THOUGHT AND NATURAL SCIENCE

A Historical

Interpretation

NASHVILLE Abingdon Press NEW YORK

PROTESTANT THOUGHT AND NATURAL SCIENCE

Copyright © 1960 by John Dillenberger

Reprinted by arrangement with Doubleday & Company, Inc.

PRINTED AND BOUND BY THE
PARTHENON PRESS AT NASHVILLE,
TENNESSEE, UNITED STATES OF AMERICA

To Paul Lehmann and Paul Tillich
my teachers, former colleagues, and friends

Contents

CONTENTS

CONTENTS

Acknowledgments

The following have kindly granted permission to quote the relevant passages in the text of this manuscript: Oxford University Press, from E. Cassirer, *Rousseau, Kant and Goethe* (1945); Editorial Board, Smith College Studies in History, from Grant McColley (trans. and ed.) *The Defense of Galileo of Thomas Campanella* (1937); Encyclopædia Britannica, from *Great Books of the Western World* (volume XXVI, 1952); University of California Press, from " Mathematical Principles of Natural Philosophy," in *Great Books of the Western World* (volume XXXIV, 1952); Routledge, from E. A. Burtt, *The Metaphysical Foundations of Modern Physical Science* (1951); G. Bell, from H. Butterfield, *The Origins of Modern Science* (1949); Huntington Library Publications, from Paul Kocher, *Science and Religion in Elizabethan England* (1953); Harvard University Press, from T. S. Kuhn, *The Copernican Revolution* (1957); University of California Press, from Galileo, *Dialogue Concerning the Two Chief World Systems* (1953); T. and T. Clark, from F. Schleiermacher, *The Christian Faith* (1928); Harper and Brothers, from J. W. Kennedy (ed.), *Henry Drummond, an Anthology* (1953); Manchester University Press, from Roy Pascal, *The German Sturm and Drang* (1953); McGraw-Hill Book Company, Inc., from I. Newton, *Opticks* (1931); The University of North Carolina Press, from Arnold Williams, *The Common Expositor* (1948); Doubleday and Company, Inc., from Galileo, *Letter to Grand Duchess Christina*, in *Discoveries and Opinions of Galileo*, by Stillman Drake; The Clarendon Press, Oxford, from I. Newton, as quoted by F. S. Marvin, *The Living Past* (1931); Routledge, from de Broglie, *The Revolution in Physics* (1954); Gerald Holton and the *American Journal of Physics*, from G. Holton, "Johannes Kepler's Universe: Its Physics and Metaphysics," *American Journal of Physics* (May 1956); Random House, Inc., from *English Philosophers from Bacon to Mill* (1939) and *The Origin of Species and the Descent of Man*.

Introduction

This volume is not a history of the conflicts between theology and science nor of the harmony between the two. It is however, an attempt to penetrate behind the concrete issues, of which we all are aware in some form or another, to the underlying problems which exercised the major parties in the debates. These problems are the deeper issues which seldom appeared openly in the debates. Hence, this volume consists of chapters in historical interpretation.

The span covered in this volume is Protestantism from the Reformation to the present. This extensive sweep is justified in that the fundamental aim is to reopen problems in a wider perspective and to stimulate fresh and more detailed work in many areas. While I have done new historical work in some areas as the basis for contending for a fresh interpretation, I am aware of the extensive work of others, particularly the excellent monographs which exist on special periods and problems. When I have been dependent on them, I hope my indebtedness has been duly noted. It may be added that the works of E. A. Burtt, Marjorie Nicolson, Basil Willey, and Herbert Butterfield have been most helpful in the area of the relation of science to other cultural movements.[1] They have more adequately raised the questions with which theologians also had to deal than have most other writers, including theologians. By and large, the general books in the

[1] For example, Basil Willey, *The Seventeenth Century Background* (1934); *The Eighteenth Century Background* (1940); *Nineteenth Century Studies* (1949); H. Butterfield, *The Origins of Modern Science* (New York, 1953). In addition to such books as *Newton Demands the Muse* and *A Voyage to the Moon*, Marjorie Nicolson has written a number of essays on the influence of scientific discoveries, such as the telescope, microscope, and the new astronomy, on the literature of the period. These have been collected and published in a paperback volume, entitled *Science and Imagination* (Ithaca: Great Seal Books, 1956).

field have been written either by those who were suspicious of theology or by those who were interested in a religion which had lost its classical form. In the first category belong such older works as those by A. D. White and John William Draper. In spite of the fact that the work by A. D. White was reissued as late as 1955, there is no reason to regard it as an acceptable scholarly book today, much less as an adequate interpretation.[2] In the second category belong such contemporaries as C. A. Coulson and Charles Raven. It is not my purpose, however, to concern myself with the extent to which either man stands in a more classical Christian tradition. My concern is rather to note that their own views of science and religion make it impossible for them to see that there were genuine issues behind some of the controversies. Hence, they think too much of the unfortunate conflicts and recite instances of harmony which are as difficult to accept theologically as are the bitter conflicts.

Both types of writers have ignored the issues which arose for those who held a more classical view of Protestant thought. This does not mean that the obscurantist and dogmatic views of theologians and scientists, whenever found, are defensible. But it does mean that one must attempt to see the issues more keenly than has heretofore been the case. Since these issues are developed in the text, they will not be summarized here. But it is possible to say that the fundamental problem underlying all the issues is the relative authority and interpretation of Nature and Scripture in theological matters.

It will be only too obvious that this book is written from a viewpoint. But that viewpoint is significant only because it demands the consideration of issues which have been pushed aside or have been unrecognized. It does not dictate the answers; in fact, there are no answers in this book. The hope is only that certain lines may have been laid down which may prove fruitful in avoiding former mistakes and in precipitating further exploration. For those who are helped by theological guideposts, it may be said that the position assumed

[2] Andrew D. White's two volumes, *A History of the Warfare of Science with Theology in Christendom*, first published in 1895, were republished as recently as 1955 by George Braziller, New York, in a single volume. The volume by Draper is *History of the Conflict between Religion and Science* (New York, 1896).

throughout this volume is neither to the right of Barth nor to the left of Tillich. This is another way of saying that no single interpretation is assumed, but that Protestant orthodoxy, forms of Protestant liberalism, and fundamentalism, are rejected. These movements erred because they either defied the new science or capitulated to its ethos. The problems in this volume make sense only from a theological perspective other than those alternatives. This must be said at the outset, since a theological position cannot be developed but must be assumed throughout this study.

The book is divided into two major sections, the first consisting of eight chapters and the second of two, in order to distinguish the approach in each. No more needs to be said concerning the first section than that the aim is to give a fairly extensive coverage of the major issues. But the second section, which is entitled " Notes on New Directions," has demanded definite principles of selection. If one were to treat the contemporary literature as extensively as the literature in the previous section, the book would be twice as long as it now is. Moreover, it would be a different book than is intended. The first part represents a unit of history. The second part represents new directions in theology and in science, and those only with reference to the problems which have emerged in the first part. Hence, a severe restrictive principle of selection has been employed. The second part exists only to note the changes which have taken place in theology and science in the last half-century, and what these changes may and may not imply for the relation of the two disciplines. The unity of the book consists in issues which run throughout. But the treatment in the two areas is designedly different. In my own estimation, the substance of the book is in the first part. The second part is a viewing of the problems of the first part in the light of new, significant developments. For this reason, a good deal of literature and some crucial developments which do not bear on the themes pursued here, have been excluded. Even the significant writings of Barbour, Coulson, Heim, Hesse, M. Holmes Hartshorne, Howe, Mascall, Pollard, Polanyi, Raven, Schilling, Smethurst, Whitehouse, and others, only indirectly enter into this volume. The impact of the ethos of science upon the social sciences—a problem on which there has been much discussion—has been ignored, even though a total picture would demand its inclusion. Particular problems and developments in contemporary biology have been ignored. While many problems might have taken a different turn if biology had come into prominence, vis-à-vis physics and astronomy, the fact is that it did not become an area of decisive influence apart from Darwinism. Moreover, while developments in biology may become more important in the future, the situation is not now such that it can be singled out for attention. Whitehead and process philosophy have also been excluded from this study, largely because neither can be said to have become a decisively new direction in theology or in the philosophy of science. At present, insights from this area have been incorporated into more traditional theological positions.

The last part of the volume has been restricted to three areas of concern. First, theologians such as Barth, Bultmann, and Tillich have been selected because they represent the theological revolution in our time. Second, the revolution in contemporary science, particularly in physics, has been set forth. Both revolutions are delineated with reference to the new situation which has emerged and to the history of the problem in the first part. Third, an analysis is made of contemporary problems in the light of their antecedent history.

Much has been made in recent years of the notion that the Western advance in science occurred on Christian soil, and would not have developed as it has on a Greek basis or on an Eastern basis. Such a statement is hard to document or to refute. The flowering of science did occur in the context of Christian history. In the West the idea of matter as created, independent, and positive came partly out of a Christian baptism of Greek views. In this sense the statement is correct, and it can be said that an overly other-worldly Christianity was itself the fruit of Greek views. But many of the philosophical sources for the new science were also Greek. Moreover, there is a difference between stating that Western science flourished on Christian soil and stating that it would not have developed in another context. Those who maintain the latter claim more than can be currently substantiated. Since the present study does not deal with this issue directly and has provided no new evidence for assessing the statement, no further attention has been given to this problem.[3]

The incentive for writing these chapters was provided by the invitation to give the Thomas White Curric lectures at Austin Theological Seminary, Austin, Texas. These lectures were given in February, 1959. While the text is more extensive than the lectures, it was originally written as the basis for the lectures. Hence, the content essentially coincides. I could not pass this opportunity to express my appreciation to the Committee administering this lectureship for the kind invitation to deliver these lectures. Nor should I want to neglect expressing my gratitude for the hospitable and friendly week in Austin.

But the interest in the problem antedates the preceding invitation. Students in seminars at Columbia, Harvard, Drew, and the Pacific School of Religion, will recall the concern and detect areas in which they too have worked. The response of various members of the Duke Divinity School faculty to a lecture I gave in which some of the theses of this volume were first publicly tested did much to encourage me to complete the project. Likewise, the invitation to lecture with Dean Harold Schilling at the Danforth seminar on Religion and Science at Pennsylvania State University provided a context for more extensive work and exploration. But the occasion for actually carrying through much of the research and initial writing came through an award from the American Association of Theological Schools together with a Sabbatical from Harvard. As a result, the academic year, 1957-1958 was spent in Heidelberg, Germany.

In addition to Dean Schilling, with whom I have for some time discussed mutual problems in this field and who has read the manuscript and offered suggestions, I should also like to thank my colleague, Gordon Harland, for searching questions, many wise suggestions of a substantive nature, and untangling so many of my complicated and obscure sentences. Another colleague at Drew, John Ollom of the

[3] For a discussion of the general thesis, see particularly M. B. Foster, " The Christian Doctrine of Creation and the Rise of Modern Natural Science," *Mind*, 43 (1934), 446-68; A. N. Whitehead, *Science and the Modern World*; John Baillie, *Natural Science and the Spiritual Life*.

Physics Department, has been most helpful at a number of crucial points. With my former colleague, Edward A. Dowey, Jr., now of Princeton Theological Seminary, I once shared a seminar on this subject and through the years we have discussed and debated many of the issues involved. I am grateful to him, too, for many helpful suggestions which have improved the manuscript. Many people have borne the more technical side of the work. Mrs. Sumner Shir and Mrs. Robert Douglas spent many hours typing sections from ancient tomes not readily available. The staffs of various libraries—Columbia, Harvard, and Heidelberg, particularly—have aided in making hard-to-obtain materials more readily available. From beginning to end, the obvious helpfulness of my wife which has entered into every page and stage of the project cannot be measured. But finally, as everyone knows, I must assume responsibility for what is here set down.

JOHN DILLENBERGER

Drew University
Madison, New Jersey
February, 1960

PART ONE

CHAPTERS IN HISTORICAL

ANALYSIS

I

Copernicus and the Reformation on the Continent

The main contours of the Biblical picture of the world appeared as satisfactory as any other until well into the sixteenth century. This was true even for those who were not enamoured of the Christian way of living and thinking. Moreover, a Biblical picture of the world had a distinct advantage in a culture which claimed a Christian understanding of life. It seemed only appropriate that the accepted view of the *nature* of reality should coincide with the *picture* of reality. Such a mutual reinforcing was theologically convenient and psychologically secure.

But the Church had not come to this point without some difficulty. Cosmas Indicopleustes, a sixth-century merchant turned monk, had insisted on the literal accuracy of all Biblical passages. According to a literalistic interpretation of Isaiah 40:22, he insisted that the earth was flat. But even those with more flexible minds defended preconceived pictures of the world because certain theological assumptions appeared inseparable from them. For example, neither Lactantius nor Augustine had accepted the notion of inhabited antipodes. That there were people living on the opposite side of the earth was considered to be impossible because there was no way in which the ancestors of Adam could have crossed the ocean to live there, and obviously all

21

inhabitants of the earth were the direct lineal descendants of Adam. For still others, human life on the antipodes would have demanded another crucifixion, since life there could have had no connection with life here. Hence the belief that there was life on the antipodes was dismissed because it was considered absurd on theological grounds. In subsequent periods, it may be noted in passing, one encounters opposition to the contention that there might be life on other planets because that would demand innumerable crucifixions.

At the end of the first third of the sixteenth century, however, certain conclusions were inevitable. The earth was known to be round —it had been sailed around—and explorers had seen life on the antipodes. Still, in spite of such accomplishments, no serious challenge to the Biblical picture was felt. On the contrary, it was believed that at long last a picture of the earth and the heavens in which the scientific and Biblical understandings were harmonized was about to be realized. To be sure, more exact mathematical observations and calculations were needed for the sake of an accurate calendar, but this seemed merely a matter of detail, certainly not a question involving fundamental reorientation.

The picture of the universe was essentially as follows: the Ptolemaic system which had originated in Hellenic soil and which subsequently acquired Aristotelian form, had been brought into close relationship with the Biblical picture. In that process a number of transformations had taken place. The Biblical picture of the world had been maintained in its essentials but certain definite Biblical passages, such as Isaiah 40 had to go by the board. Aristotle, too, had been altered at a number of crucial points. His affirmations of the eternity of the world and his denial of immortality had been rejected. His understanding of nature had been accepted but it was given Christian baptism. Theologians and humanists differed between each other and among themselves with reference to the details and proper interpretation of Aristotle, but there was little debate concerning his authority in the domain of nature and science. Philosophers and theologians were basically at one in their understanding and observation of nature.

The general picture of the universe was clear. At its centre was the immobile planet—Earth. It was composed of earth and water, the two lowest of the four elements. Hell was at the centre of the earth and at the greatest distance from the heavens. The abandoning of the notion of a flat earth resulted in certain modifications, but the conception of the world was not basically altered. The world picture was still essentially hierarchical in the spatial as well as in the philosophical and theological sense. Hell was still spatially farthest removed from the realm of pure heaven, and the inhabited earth was still appropriately situated between the two. Beyond the earth was a series of spheres, usually about eight in number. These contained the planets, including the moon and the sun. The planets moved in perfect circular form around the fixed earth, though not with the earth necessarily the perfect centre of each circle. The planets were primarily made up of the noble element, fire. Beyond the spheres was the *primum mobile*, a different type of sphere, responsible for the whirling of the planets in their orbits around the earth and for the movement of all the spheres about the earth. Beyond the *primum mobile* was the *empyrean* heaven, immobile but encasing the universe—the incorruptible dwelling place of God and the eventual abode of the redeemed.

Such a world could be visualized. Its meaning could also be discerned. Space and destiny coincided in this world that so fruitfully mixed Ptolemaic, Aristotelian and Biblical assumptions. The whole universe ministered to the earth, and the domain of nature assured the significance of man and of the drama of redemption. At long last it was both philosophically and scientifically clear that the Christian drama was woven into the very texture of history and nature. A total coherent view had emerged in which everything had its place and its purpose. A picture so magnificent and so satisfying could not easily be abandoned.

While this view of the world gave a special status to the Christian understanding, it was comprised more of philosophical than of scientific and Biblical concepts. It was grounded in many metaphysical assumptions—such as the notion of the four elements, the immutability of the heavens, the necessity of circular motion, the subtilty of the heavens and of the baser earth, the tendency for things to seek their appropriate place with reference to the heavens and earth, the centrality and immobility of the earth. Only for the latter—the centrality and immobility of the earth—could Biblical passages be marshalled, such as the reference to Joshua commanding the sun to stand still, and additional passages from Job and the Psalms. In this total picture the Biblical and strictly scientific elements were indeed meagre.

Nevertheless, it was a formidable view of the universe. It had been developed and refined through the centuries and it found universal acceptance. This picture of the world was so integral to the ends and purposes of life that it became a matter of urgency to solve outstanding problems associated with that picture. One of the most urgent needs was that of securing a simple, over-all mathematical explanation for the various planetary movements. The traditional cycles and epicycles needed to be placed into one comprehensive and consistent mathematical system. But, at most, this was felt to be an internal problem demanding no basic alteration.

It is of the utmost significance that Copernicus be understood in this setting. According to his own testimony, Copernicus sought for such mathematical unity. Not finding it in traditional mathematics, he reread the philosophers to see if there might be other suggestions concerning the movements of the planets and spheres which would assist him in the solution of this mathematical problem. This unusual procedure proved to be profitable, for it was in such study that he discovered the suggestion of the movement of the earth. Copernicus described his problem and discovery as follows:

Accordingly, when I had meditated upon this lack of certitude in the traditional mathematics concerning the composition of movements of the spheres of the world, I began to be annoyed that the philosophers, who in other respects had made a very careful scrutiny of the least details of the world, had discovered no sure scheme for the movements of the machinery of the world, which has been built for us by the Best and Most Orderly Workman of all. Wherefore I took the trouble to reread all the books by philosophers which I could get hold of, to see if any of them even supposed that the movements of the spheres of the world were different from those laid down by those who taught mathematics in the schools. And as a matter of fact, I found first in Cicero that Nicetas thought that the Earth moved. And afterwards I found in Plutarch that there were some others of the same opinion: I shall copy out his words here, so that they may be known to all: " Some think that the earth is at rest: but Philolaus the Pythagorean says that it moves around the fire with an obliquely circular motion, like the sun and moon. Herakleides of Pontus and Ekphantus the Pythagorean do not give the earth any movement of locomotion, but rather a limited movement of rising and setting around its centre, like a wheel."[1]

It was through experimenting with this philosophical suggestion that Copernicus was able at length to achieve a unified picture and ultimately he came to this conclusion:

And so, having laid down the movements which I attribute to the Earth farther on in the work, I finally discovered by the help of long and numerous observations that if the movements of the other wandering stars are correlated with the circular movement of the Earth, and if the movements are computed in accordance with the revolution of each planet, not only do all their phenomena follow from that but also this correlation binds together so closely the order and magnitudes of all the planets and of their spheres or orbital circles and the heavens themselves that nothing can be shifted around in any part of them without disrupting the remaining parts and the universe as a whole.[2]

Copernicus claimed too much; he had certainly not solved all the mathematical problems. But if greater mathematical harmony, unity, and simplicity was a desirable goal, then Copernicus had made a signal contribution. The attractiveness of his proposal lay in its mathematical symmetry and in that it seemed more adequately to explain planetary motion than did the Ptolemaic system. He allegedly reduced the number of planetary cycles from approximately eighty to thirty-four.[3]

[1] N. Copernicus, *On the Revolutions of the Heavenly Spheres, Great Books of the Western World* (Chicago: Encyclopædia Britannica, Inc., 1952), Vol. XVI, p. 508.
[2] Ibid., p. 508.
[3] The book is not consistent with reference to the precise number of cycles.

The reversal of the positions of the earth and of the sun was not particularly significant from a mathematical standpoint. Nevertheless, a mathematical problem within an accepted theory had issued in a new theory of the universe. For those schooled in the Aristotelian Christian tradition, this new conception had drastic consequences. In this tradition, the earth occupied a unique position among the planets. It was, to be sure, a place of corruption, but above all, it was the place of God's redemptive work. It was the abode of man, the special object of God's concern. But now it appeared that the earth was no longer a special place. One could no longer distinguish between the earth and the planets.

It appeared that the crowning work of God with reference to man no longer had a special spatial setting, automatically bearing witness to God's intention. The cherished identity of purpose and place was called into question. This identity was the central issue rather than the supposed insignificance of man attending the dislodging of the earth from the centre of things. This is not to deny that there were aspects of the Copernican position which made man uneasy. But they were of a different order. One of these implied that the stars of the eighth sphere were so distant as to border on infinity with the consequence that the closely knit and compact universe was gone, and man was exposed to the dread of infinity in spatial terms. This was the real significance of the removal of the earth from its traditional central place.

There were thus three major reasons why the new theory of the universe would create problems among theologians. First, it seemed to run counter to those Biblical passages which assumed the centrality of the earth and the movement of the sun. Second, it dislodged the comfortable interrelation of space and destiny. Third, it confronted man with the anxiety engendered by infinity.

But the new theory did not make easy progress among fellow scientists either. Most of the arguments which Copernicus used could also be turned against him. Certainly he had no genuine proof. Not only was there an absence of new and startling discoveries; the very suggestion of the mobility of the earth and the more central position of the sun violated whatever observations people did know. It must always be remembered that only later did new instruments, such as the telescope, bring new observations to the support of the Copernican position. Professor Burtt has written :

. . . It is safe to say that even had there been no religious scruples whatever against the Copernican astronomy, sensible men all over Europe, especially the most empirically minded, would have pronounced it a wild appeal to accept the premature fruits of an uncontrolled imagination, in preference to the solid inductions, built up gradually through the ages, of men's confirmed sense experience. . . . Contemporary empiricists, had they lived in the sixteenth century, would have been first to scoff out of court the new philosophy of the universe.[4]

The Copernican suggestion appeared almost universally to be another philosophical view which did not have the advantages of the older system. For some it looked like the revival of an ancient and already discredited philosophical view. Initially the choice presented itself as one between the Aristotelian–Ptolemaic system with its Christian frame of meaning and purpose, and the mathematical philosophy represented by Copernicus with its joy in comprehensive unity and simplicity of numerical proportion. It was not a choice between one science and another, or between one philosophy and a scientific view; it was a choice between philosophies, between the Aristotelian-Ptolemaic or the Neo-Platonic-Pythagorean. The former had been reconciled with the Christian drama. The latter, with its combination of mystical and quantitative adoration of mathematics, ignored the purposes of God and history and appeared irreconcilable with Christianity.

Much has been written about the manner in which theologians rejected Copernicus. But in any final assessment of the grounds for either acceptance or rejection of his views, it is of the utmost importance to pay close attention to dates. As early as 1525, Copernicus evidently had some fame, though his major work did not appear until

[4] E. A. Burtt, *The Metaphysical Foundations of Modern Physical Science* (Revised ed.; New York: The Humanities Press, 1951), p. 25.

1543. The book, *De Revolutionibus Orbium Caelestium*, was not widely accepted by astronomers in the decades immediately following its publication. This was the case in spite of the appearance of a new star in the Constellation Cassiopeia in 1572 and the tracing of the orbit of the comet of 1577. Both of these suggested that the traditional scientific conceptions were inadequate. However, genuine evidence for the basic Copernican position had to await the work of Kepler and Galileo in the early seventeenth century. Before that time, acceptance or non-acceptance could not be decided on what were later understood to be scientific grounds. Professor Butterfield dates the breaking down of the Aristotelian-Ptolemaic system from the time of Galileo, but adds also that there appeared no satisfactory alternative system until the time of Newton's *Principia* in 1687. The period from Galileo to Newton was one in which

. . . though the more modern of the scientists tended to believe in the movement of the earth from this time, the general tendency from about 1630 seems to have been to adopt the compromise system of Tycho Brahé. In 1672 a writer could say that the student of the heavens had four different world-systems from which to choose, and there were men who even talked of seven.[5]

It is important to remember three periods whenever we consider the history of scientific advance. First is the period from Copernicus to Galileo. During this time there was no more compelling reason to accept than to reject the Copernican view. The balance was perhaps slightly on the side of rejection. This can be said even if one discredits the strong bias of the Aristotelians in favour of the older position. The second period is that between Galileo and Newton. Here it was still possible to entertain alternative positions, though the weight of the evidence was certainly in the direction of the Copernican view. The third period is that of the Newtonian world-view. The genius of Newton had brought into being a unified conception of the universe. This position too had its problems; nevertheless, now the basic Copernican position was scientifically irrefutable. Not a little misunderstanding

[5] H. Butterfield, *The Origins of Modern Science* (New York: The Macmillan Co., 1953), p. 55.

could have been avoided if both scientific and theological historians had paid close attention to the chronological order of the scientific periods.

B: SCIENCE IN THE CONTINENTAL REFORMATION

It is historically unjustifiable for scientists or theologians to present a single picture of opposition to the new science, ranging all the way from Luther to the middle of the eighteenth century. To put Luther and Calvin in the same category as Gerhard or Voetius is to say that a scientist who rejected Copernicus in the middle of the sixteenth century is to be considered on the same grounds as one who rejected him in the third or sixth decades of the seventeenth century.

It is equally important to delineate the context of theological inquiry. When that is done, it will become clear that the collection of passages from theological writings, frequently wrested out of their setting, does violence to a proper understanding of what was going on. In what follows, different theological perspectives will be discussed and related to the precise scientific period in which they occurred.

The classical Reformation figures, including Luther, Calvin, and Melanchthon belong to the period in which there was no compelling reason for accepting the Copernican system. Were it not for the fact that they discussed the nature of astronomical theories in positive terms, and at the same time were negative concerning Copernicus, no further word would be necessary on the subject. Nevertheless, it is highly instructive to see what their general attitude toward science was, the conception they held, and what specifically they had to say about Copernicus. All this can be understood, however, only as it is seen in relation to the manner in which they interpreted Scripture. It will be useful therefore to clarify their hermeneutical principles and then proceed to a consideration of their scientific notions and views on Copernicus.

It is necessary to distinguish between what the Reformers considered to be the basis of Biblical interpretation and authority, and what they thought about the text of Scripture. For Luther and Calvin, Scripture took authority from its Christological centre. It witnessed to Christ. The acts of God in Christ became known and were received in the faith engendered through the Biblical records. Hence, the authority of the Bible was derived from the content of its message. The priority of Christ, its centre, was maintained.[6]

When Luther suggested that all passages and books of the Bible were not on the same level and needed to be judged by whether or not they bore witness to or conformed to Christ, he enunciated a basic principle of interpretation. As Luther put it, in perhaps too simple a form: the Bible is the cradle in which Christ is laid. By such a statement he wanted to stress the limits to which Biblical interpretation might go and to affirm the basis from which the words were to be understood and received.

The authority of the Bible was not primarily the information which it supplied. Its meaning could only be apprehended in a vital Christologically centred faith. Hence, only as the Spirit and the text were so conjoined as to create and nourish faith did the Bible become the Word of God in the full sense. Insofar as the Bible and the Word of God were identified, it was because the Bible was known to be the living Word through the confirming activity of the Holy Spirit.

Calvin's basic conception was no different. The Scripture was Christologically interpreted. The difference was that he did not so readily accept levels in Scripture and hence occasionally strained certain texts in order to give them evangelical meaning. But this was simply a variation in a commonly held position. Calvin as much as Luther also stressed the living Word. Only through the work of the Spirit were both the content and the authority of the Bible attested to us. This is clearly articulated in the seventh chapter of the first book of *The Institutes*. It is true that in the following chapter he listed what he considered to be lesser confirmations of the authority of Scripture. These include reference to prophecy having been fulfilled and corro-

[6] See the excellent article by Paul Lehmann, " The Reformers' Use of the Bible," *Theology Today* (October, 1946), pp. 328-44.

boration of Biblical truth through miracles. While these aspects became central in the later defence of the Bible, this should not blind us to the subsidiary role which they had in Calvin.[7]

It is true of course that the Reformers were creatures of their day with respect to accepting the total words of the Bible as true. It would not have occurred to them to suggest that the hermeneutical principle freed them from what we today call the notion of the infallibility of the text. But it is important to note that the text free from error (except for linguistic or copy errors) was not the centre of their attention. God was considered to be the author of the Bible because He spoke through it.

The Reformers' spiritual interpretation of Scripture and the subsidiary role of the infallibility of the text cannot be overemphasized. It stands in sharp contrast to the orthodox interpretation which followed, where the accuracy and scientific truth of the Biblical text was the focus of attention. The Reformers did stress the literal or plain meaning of the text, namely—what the text said. But what was said could not be equated simply with the information which was provided. The plain meaning of the text was still its theological meaning. The stress on the literal or clear meaning of the text was a weapon against the allegorical interpretation carried on by Rome, an affirmation that the meaning of a text could not be stretched beyond what it actually said. For instance, Luther insisted upon the six days of creation, not for literalistic reasons, but because Hilary and Augustine so easily spun allegories on the basis of Genesis. For Luther, Genesis dealt with the visible world, not a world of fancies.[8] For Luther and Calvin the infallibility of Scripture was not a cardinal theological point to be consciously defended in order for Scripture to be Scripture. They insisted upon an interpretation which did not stray from the plain meaning of the text in order to keep interpretation in line with what the author of Scripture intended. When subsequently the accent shifted to the inerrant text as the *proof* of the message, the Bible was

[7] For a reinterpretation of Calvin's view of Scripture over against the traditional ones, see the relevant section of the excellent study by E. A. Dowey, Jr., *The Knowledge o God in Calvin's Theology* (New York: Columbia University Press, 1952).
[8] *Weimar Ausgabe*, 42, 4, 26. Hereafter cited as WA.

no longer understood from its Christological centre. That centre had been protected by Luther and Calvin through their insistence on the plain and grammatical meaning of the text. Later, text, inspiration and revelation were identified. Instead of insistence on the plain meaning of the text, the central focus was on the infallibility of the divine book. The literal meaning of a biblical passage had been changed into a theory of literalism.

This distinction was not made by the Reformers, for they were not faced by this question. But in the light of subsequent developments in Protestant Orthodoxy, it becomes important for our discussion that we make a clear distinction. In what follows, the literal will refer to the plain meaning of the text in a Christologically orientated understanding, while literalistic will refer to the stress upon the inerrant text as the central point of Biblical authority.

Let us now refer to the Reformers. Luther and Calvin interpreted the Bible in respect to scientific matters in such a way as to make possible the acceptance of new theories. Luther distinguished between the disciplines, insisting that each must have its own sphere and end, but not extend beyond it. Astronomy and Scripture therefore must both be viewed according to their own art.[9] That the sun gives light to the moon and the stars was a matter for astronomers to consider,[10] but that the light from the moon represents a matter of God's care for men was a theological affirmation.[11] Calvin specifically followed an ancient tradition when he suggested that Moses frequently spoke according to the obvious way of comprehending and had no intention of speaking scientifically about the stars. Commenting on the fifteenth and sixteenth verses of the first chapter of Genesis, Calvin wrote as follows:

> For Moses here addresses himself to our senses, that the knowledge of the gifts of God which we enjoy may not glide away. Therefore, in order to apprehend the meaning of Moses, it is to no purpose to

[9] WA 42, 36, 6.
[10] Calvin agreed but added that the moon was not a dark body. John Calvin, *Commentaries on the First Book of Moses called Genesis*, trans. John King (Grand Rapids: Wm. B. Eerdmans Publishing Co., 1948), I, 86.
[11] WA 42, 31.

soar above the heavens; let us only open our eyes to behold this light which God enkindles for us in the earth. By this method . . . the dishonesty of those men is sufficiently rebuked, who censure Moses for not speaking with greater exactness . . . Moses wrote in a popular style things which, without instruction, all ordinary persons, endued with common sense, are able to understand; but astronomers investigate with great labour whatever the sagacity of the human mind can comprehend . . . Moses . . . rather adapts his discourse to common usage.[12]

Certainly such distinctions provided considerable freedom from theological and Biblical dictation in astronomical matters.

Astronomy, in fact, was viewed as a positive science by both Luther and Calvin. Luther specifically made a distinction between astronomy and astrology; he affirmed the former and rejected the latter.[13] He was at once amused and distressed by Melanchthon's interest in astrology.[14] For Luther, astrology was not a science. It could not be confirmed by demonstration.[15] Moreover, it was nothing less than idolatry, and hence stood in violation of the first commandment.[16] This is true in spite of the fact that one can gain the false impression from his Lectures on Genesis, that Luther defended astrology in a limited way.[17] But the context, as the translator of Luther's Works has seen, demands that astrologia be understood as astronomy.[18] It must also be recalled that the Lectures on Genesis were partially changed by editors to bring them into line with the views of Melanchthon and therefore cannot altogether be relied on in these matters.[19] There is, however, no reason to doubt that Luther did concede that there might be some truth in astrological predictions. But the statement is circumscribed and set into the context in which Luther denied that astrology could be maintained among the sciences.[20] Luther did not deny that the stars could conceivably have some influence upon the

[12] Calvin, op. cit., pp. 85, 86, 87.   [13] Tischreden, 4, No. 4705. Hereafter TR.
[14] TR 2, No. 1480; 3, No. 2892b and 2952b.   [15] TR 4, No. 4705.
[16] TR 1, No. 1026.   [17] WA 42, 24.
[18] Martin Luther, Luther's Works trans. George V. Schick (St. Louis: Concordia Publishing House, 1958), I, p. 31.
[19] See page xi of the Introduction to Vol. I of Luther's Works.
[20] Luther's Works, I, p. 45; WA 42, 33, and 34.

lives of men. But he was certain that we could not have any knowledge of this influence.

Calvin wrote in a similar vein. Suffice it here to note two corroborating items. First, he wrote a book against astrology, *Admonition against the Astrology that is called Judicial* (1549). Secondly, he spoke positively of astronomy:

> This study (astronomy) is not to be reprobated, nor this science to be condemned, because some frantic persons are wont boldly to reject whatever is unknown to them. For astronomy is not only pleasant but also very useful to be known; it cannot be denied that this art unfolds the admirable wisdom of God. Wherefore, as ingenious men are to be honoured who have expended useful labour on this subject, so they who have leisure and capacity ought not to neglect this kind of exercise. Nor did Moses truly wish to withdraw us from this pursuit in omitting such things as are peculiar to the art; but because he was ordained a teacher as well of the unlearned and rude as of the learned, he could not otherwise fulfil his office than by descending to this grosser method of instruction.[21]

But on one level Luther and Calvin had reservations concerning the place and use of the sciences. Luther was afraid that science might so extend its interest in the natural processes of nature to the point where it no longer understood these forces as being under the control of the ever-active sovereign will of God. He was fearful that an undue concentration upon natural explanations would obscure the ultimate ground of things. While he thus accepted many philosophical assumptions which came from Aristotle, as for example, the four elements, he was unwilling to tarry long at such points. He considered the traditional spheres a useful help to the human imagination in learning of the movements of the heavens. But he refused to accept the traditional spheres as being necessarily true, let alone the explanatory outlines given by the astronomers.[22] Nor could Luther engage in scientific speculations about Biblical passages. He accepted the Mosaic notion that there was water above the firmament, but he imme-

---

[21] Calvin, op. cit., pp. 86-87. See also *Institutes of the Christian Religion*, I. v. 2. and 5; I. xiv. 21.
[22] WA 42, 21.

diately added that he did not understand it.[23]   Such acceptance of a Biblical passage was not so much insistence upon the Biblical text as it was a concern for a theological understanding of the work of the Creator. This was at all times the central concern. He felt that science and philosophy could easily obscure the significance of such affirmations by absorption in the elaboration of details. Hence, he accepted only such scientific and metaphysical explanation which helped or at least did not hinder a theological understanding.

Calvin's reservation about science was similar to that of Luther. He feared that an excess of curiosity in science would take attention away from the Creator. Ordinary curiosity in the observation of nature was not discouraged. Nature was to be investigated in order to enrich and enliven one's adoration of God; a disinterested scientific approach would weaken one's awareness of the lively control and directing activity of God within the natural order. Such a development would be destructive of a true knowledge of God. It would affirm His existence while obscuring the vital relationship He has with His world. Such deism, he prophetically discerned, would sap the springs of authentic faith. Hence, the aim of all true science could be no other than that of showing forth the marvellous works of Him who is the source and meaning of one's life. He feared that the astronomers would proclaim the wisdom of the Creator in static terms. But such terms missed the real wisdom of God. God's wisdom could be apprehended only in a vital knowledge of His marvellous deeds in directing nature and in His redeeming work in Christ.

Part of the suspicion of science is further related to the definite conviction that the understanding and activity of God could not be contained in the available cosmology. Luther was not interested in the crystalline sphere in the accepted cosmology because it tended to confine God. He rejected the notion that God was confined to heaven when heaven was conceived in restricted, spatial terms. On the other hand, Luther rejected the notion that God filled the world as one filled a sack with straw. In contrast to both these views, he believed

[23] WA 42, 20 and 24. Calvin, by contrast, reviewed the alternatives and decided that Moses meant clouds.

that God could neither be grasped nor measured. In commenting on the phrase, " the right hand of God," Luther stated that God was not like a body or a stool which could be observed to be in one place and therefore not in another.[24] Instead, the right hand of God referred to the almighty power and presence of God; He could not be located and yet was present at all places simultaneously.[25] For Luther, God was apart from all, over all, and present to all things. He was around all, through all, below and above, behind and before; nothing was so small that He was not smaller; nothing so great, that He was not greater.[26] God was supernatural and unsearchable but apprehended in His disclosure to us.

While Calvin affirmed that the finite body ascended to heaven, he too, interpreted " sitting at the right hand of God " as reigning in power, majesty, and glory. Further, commenting on the phrase, " Our Father who art in heaven " in the Lord's Prayer, Calvin wrote:

. . . It is not hastily to be inferred, that he is included and circumscribed within the circumference of heaven, as by certain barriers. For Solomon confesses, that ' the heaven of heavens cannot contain ' him. And he says himself, by the prophet, ' The heaven is my throne, and the earth is my footstool.' By which he clearly signifies that he is not limited to any particular region, but diffused throughout all space. But because the dullness of our minds could not otherwise conceive of his ineffable glory, it is designated to us by the heaven, than which we can behold nothing more august or more majestic. Since, then, wherever our senses apprehend any thing, there they are accustomed to fix it, God is represented as beyond all place, that when we seek him we may be elevated above all reach of both body and soul. Moreover, by this form of expression, he is exalted above all possibility of corruption or mutation; finally, it is signified, that he comprehends and contains the whole world, and governs the universe by his power. Wherefore, this is the same as if he had been said to be possessed of an incomprehensible essence, infinite magnitude or sublimity, irresistible power, and unlimited immortality. But when we hear this, our thoughts must be raised to a

[24] WA 23, 133, and 134.   [25] WA 23, 143.   [26] WA 26, 339.

higher elevation when God is mentioned; that we may not entertain any terrestrial or carnal imaginations concerning him, that we
may not measure him by our diminutive proportions, or judge of
his will by our affections.[27]

In the light of the preceding, it is possible to say that Luther and
Calvin had a positive view of science in a theological setting. Two
things need, however, to be recalled before looking at what they had
to say of Copernicus. First, they had not tied themselves to a literalistic view of Scripture. Their Christological view of Scripture could
have enabled them to abandon using Biblical texts as scientific explanations of phenomena. Second, they had not in fact accepted the
current cosmology in such a way that their theological understanding
was tied to it. Hence, there was nothing in their theological thinking
necessitating the rejection of new scientific explanations. In principle,
change was possible. Yet both rejected the views associated with
Copernicus. We have now to ask the reasons for this rejection.

Luther's apparent rejection of Copernicus was not as simple as
most commentators in the history of science lead us to believe. One
usually hears only two things: that Luther dismissed Copernicus with
the words, " the fool would upset the whole art of astronomy," and
that he defended the passage in Joshua, where it is declared that the
sun stood still.[28] One is tempted to say that the designation " fool " is
comparatively mild when used by Luther for an enemy. But that is
hardly to the point. It would be more relevant to point to some
textual criticism concerning this phrase, " the fool would upset the
whole art of astronomy." Heinrich Bornkamm reminds us that the
phrase first appeared in the Aurifaber notes of Luther's Table-Talk,
while the same general passage without this particular phrase is found
in the earlier Lauterbach materials of June, 1539.[29] Both Aurifaber
and Lauterbach included the notes of others in their Table-Talk com-

[27] J. Calvin, Institutes of the Christian Religion, Allen translation, (Philadelphia), III. xx.
40. See also IV. xvii. 18.
[28] TR 1, 855.
[29] Heinrich Bornkamm, " Kopernikus im Urteil der Reformatoren," Archiv für Refor-
mations-Geschichte, 40 (1943), pp. 171-83. See TR 1, 855 (Aurifaber); TR 4, 4638 (Lauterbach).

pilations, and in this instance, we know that Aurifaber definitely did. Also, Lauterbach, who does not have the sentence, is generally more reliable.[30] It is certainly believable that Luther made such a statement; it is also possible that it comes from the hand of a later editor, who for reasons of opposition to Copernicus, or on the basis of hearsay, may have incorporated it. In any case, it should be borne in mind that the only reference to Copernicus on the part of Luther came not from his own hand but from notes taken by students who ate with him. But let us suppose that either or both of the passages are true. The conversation dates from 1539 and at best is testimony that Luther had heard of the views of Copernicus four years before the publication of the latter's major work. It is certainly no more than the off-hand remark of a volatile man. It cannot be justly used to substantiate the claim that Luther was about to undertake a crusade against the new science, or that he was responsible for Protestant opposition to it, as is implicit in countless books on the history of science. In fact, the relevant *Table-Talk* material was not available until 1566, twenty years after his death.

Calvin, like Luther, also believed in the correctness of the Ptolemaic system. In commenting on Psalm XIX, he assumed the movement of the sun; but he added that in describing the details of such movement, David was not writing scientifically but in terms of God's accommodation.[31] In commenting on Psalm XCIII, Calvin wrote in precise Ptolemaic form :

> The heavens revolve daily, and, immense as is their fabric, and inconceivable the rapidity of their revolutions, we experience no concussion—no disturbance in the harmony of their motion.[32]

In this, as in other passages, Calvin wrote in a calm manner. The Ptolemaic system was assumed and there is no evidence that he was

---

[30] Wilhelm Norlind, " Copernicus and Luther: A critical Study," *Isis*, 44 (1953), pp. 273-76.

[31] John Calvin, *Commentary on the Book of Psalms* (Edinburgh, 1845), I, 315-16. Accommodation refers to the way in which God condescends to human capacities and forms, in order that He can make Himself known to man. This is not said from the standpoint of greater ease of understanding on the part of man, but on the basis of God's self-chosen act.

[32] Ibid., (1847), IV, 6-7.

defending it from vehement attacks. Although he was writing later than Luther, Copernicus was not mentioned.[33]

In spite of the Ptolemaic assumptions of Luther and Calvin, they did not defend the old astronomy in the light of a developed conception of the inerrancy of Scripture. Rather, the new science was not yet widely accepted. In so far as they knew of it, it exhibited a spirit which would prove difficult to harmonize with a Biblical understanding. But Biblical passages were not yet used in and of themselves as proof texts in the defence of the astronomical theories. That was a later development.

In contrast to Luther and Calvin, Melanchthon consciously identified himself with a definite conception of science, particularly of the cosmos. But this was determined more by philosophical than by what we would call scientific considerations. We have already indicated that it was difficult, if not impossible, to distinguish philosophical and scientific matters in this period. In any case, the source of Melanchthon's rather definite views was three-fold. In the first place, he was a humanist and therefore concerned with classical thought. The humanists had not challenged the traditional conception of nature. On the whole they had accepted it. Hence, Melanchthon was almost inevitably bound to traditional ideas of nature. In the second place, certain consequences were inherent in the fact that Melanchthon was entrusted with the responsibility for the educational side of the new Protestant movement. His curricular programme revived Aristotelian conceptions on a number of fronts, particularly in the study of nature. He assumed responsibility both for an increased interest in the study of Aristotle and for the dissemination of works of an Aristotelian outlook. He had Sacrobosco's introduction to astronomy, a definitely Aristotelian work, republished. In fact, with reference to the study of nature, Melanchthon considered Aristotle the greatest of all time. In the third place, on theological grounds Melanchthon was interested in the unity of the sciences for the sake of both

[33] White, op. cit., p. 127. Apparently referring to a comment on the first verse of the 93rd Psalm in Calvin's Commentary on Genesis, A. D. White quotes a passage in which Copernicus is mentioned by name. I have been unable to find the passage in Calvin and doubt that it exists.

university and church. He attributed the low state of religion to the decay of the sciences. He believed that Aristotelian metaphysics provided a definite unity to all studies and relegated all disciplines to their rightful place.[34] The prestige and integrity of theology as the queen of the sciences depended upon such unity.

Melanchthon himself provided us with such a unified picture in his *Initia Doctrinae Physicae*. Here the Aristotelian-Ptolemaic conception was dominant and assumed without question.[35] The traditional Aristotelian arguments against the movement of the earth were used, including the old objection that if the earth moved, everything would break into pieces. The usual Biblical passages were also cited, such as Psalms 45, 69, 78, Proverbs 1:4, and of course the Joshua passage about the sun standing still. These arguments may not have been central to his concerns. But nevertheless, the views of Copernicus certainly did not fit into his total philosophical-theological picture. They would have destroyed both philosophical unity and Biblical understanding.

The significance of the philosophical issue is quite apparent. Melanchthon believed that Copernicus had revived outmoded philosophical views which had already been discredited in the ancient world. Melanchthon was acquainted with Aristarch of Samos, whose third-century B.C. pre-Copernican views had already been rejected in antiquity.[36] Moreover, he was suspicious that the Copernican position was the revival of the ancient views of Democritus and Epicurus,[37] that is, an atomism which could not be reconciled with Christianity.[38] For Democritus, all things came to be by the chance concatenation of atoms. Rigorously pursued, such a theory had two disastrous implications for Christianity. First, it provided no frame of meaning or reference in purposive terms. Second, on the basis that such combinations of atoms were valid for the entire universe, all distinctions

[34] E. Schlink, "Weisheit und Torheit," *Kerygma und Dogma*, I. Jahrgang (1955), pp. 7-8.
[35] *Corpus Reformatorum* 13, 292. Hereafter cited as CR.
[36] CR 13, 216.
[37] E. Hirsch, *Geschichte der neuern evangelischen Theologie* (Gütersloh, 1949), I, p. 117.
[38] See Thomas S. Kuhn, *The Copernican Revolution* (Cambridge: Harvard University Press, 1957), p. 237. It is interesting that Kuhn unwittingly confirms that the Copernican philosophical outlook was in opposition to the Christian drama.

disappeared. The universe was alike throughout. It is no wonder, therefore, that to Melanchthon and others the notion that the earth was like other planets immediately suggested the revival of atomism. It was as if a classical revival could only take place safely in terms of those sources which had already been Christianized and that the rest must be rejected now, as they had been previously. Aristotle had been made compatible; the rest had generally remained alien.

Hence, Melanchthon's problem was not so much scientific or Biblical as it was philosophical. Although eclectic in many ways, Melanchthon stood within one philosophical tradition, and from this he would not be moved. Given that assumption, his attitude toward Copernicus was remarkably level-headed and even-tempered. There are several favourable references to Copernicus in Melanchthon's writing, including his correspondence.[39] But there are also some negative allusions.[40] In his work on physics, the *Initia Doctrinae Physicae*, Melanchthon simply stated that the Ptolemaic system would be followed in the exposition of astronomical matters.[41] In the commemorative address on Cruciger in 1549, an address which is ascribed to Melanchthon and with which he undoubtedly had something to do, there was a very positive reference to Copernicus.[42] And while he did not subscribe to the Copernican views of the mathematician Rheticus, he was friendly toward him and undoubtedly exercised a positive rather than a negative influence in Rheticus' assumption of a new position at Leipzig.

More controversial than the views of Luther, Melanchthon, and Calvin was the preface to Copernicus' book, *De Revolutionibus Orbium Caelestium*. This was written by Andreas Osiander, a Lutheran theologian. The context for this problem includes the activity of Rheticus, who in 1536 was a young professor of mathematics at Wittenberg. Interested in the work of Copernicus, of whom he had heard so much, the Protestant Rheticus went to Roman Catholic territory and to the Roman Catholic Copernicus in order to learn first-

[39] CR 11, 839; 13, 241 and 244.
[40] CR 13, 216-17 and CR 4, 679.
[41] CR 13, 292.
[42] CR 11, 839.

hand of the latter's theories. He stayed two years, wrote an account of Copernicus's view, and sent it to his friend from student days, John Schöner. This was then published as the *Narratio Prima*. The reception of this material was a factor in Copernicus's final decision to follow the advice of his friends and publish his manuscript. Copernicus had previously published a brief sketch of his own views, entitled the *Commentariolus*.

Rheticus was commissioned to see the major work of Copernicus through the press. When he left Wittenberg to take up a teaching position at Leipzig, he turned over the completion of the publishing task to Osiander. When the book appeared, it carried not only an introduction by Copernicus, but also an unsigned preface which preceded the introduction. This preface read as follows:

Since the newness of the hypotheses of this work—which sets the earth in motion and puts an immovable sun at the centre of the universe—has already received a great deal of publicity, I have no doubt that certain of the savants have taken grave offence and think it wrong to raise any disturbance among liberal disciplines which have had the right set-up for a long time now. If, however, they are willing to weigh the matter scrupulously, they will find that the author of this work has done nothing which merits blame. For it is the job of the astronomer to use painstaking and skilled observation in gathering together the history of the celestial movements, and then—since he cannot by any line of reasoning reach the true causes of these movements—to think up or construct whatever causes or hypotheses he pleases such that, by the assumption of these causes, those same movements can be calculated from the principles of geometry for the past and for the future, too. This artist is markedly outstanding in both of these respects; for it is not necessary that these hypotheses should be true, or even probable; but it is enough if they provide a calculus which fits the observations . . . And if it constructs and thinks up causes—and it has certainly thought up a good many—nevertheless it does not think them up in order to persuade anyone of their truth but only in order that they may provide a correct basis for calculation. But since for one and the same movement varying hypotheses are proposed from time to time, as eccentricity or epicycle for the movement of the sun, the astronomer much prefers to take the one which is easiest to grasp. Maybe the philosopher demands probability instead; but neither of them will grasp anything certain or hand it on, unless it has been divinely revealed to him. Therefore let us permit these new hypotheses to make a public appearance among old ones which are themselves no more probable, especially since they are wonderful and easy and bring with them a vast storehouse of learned observations. And as far as hypotheses go, let no one expect anything in the way of certainty from astronomy, since astronomy can offer us nothing certain, lest, if anyone take as true that which has been constructed for another use, he go away from this discipline a bigger fool than when he came to it.[43]

It was not unusual for prefaces to be unsigned in that day. It is a far greater mystery how the phraseology of this preface could be accepted as the work of Copernicus himself, and then only later be discovered by Kepler to be the malicious work of Osiander.[44] Most astronomers were undoubtedly not fooled into believing that the preface was by Copernicus.[45] The issue, in any case, rests upon a double question. First, had Osiander's preface violated the fundamental premise of Copernicus, namely, that his theory was indeed true? Second, was it in fact written by Osiander knowing how Copernicus felt? The correspondence by the principals on the question of the preface is not complete; but it is clear that there was a difference of opinion about the way in which the book should be introduced to the public. There was an old tradition which permitted the propounding of fairly unorthodox theories, provided they were given as hypotheses which might or might not be true, and which could be set forth for the sake of testing their validity. The issue is not as simple as Prowe, the great nineteenth century interpreter of Copernicus, has suggested, namely, that Copernicus never used the term hypothesis. While the title, *Nicholas Copernicus, Sketch of his Hypotheses for the Heavenly Motions,*

[43] Copernicus, op. cit., p. 505-6
[44] J. Kepler, *Opera*, (ed. Frisch), III, 136. The source is an incomplete and unpublished article by Kepler, which was brought to light again in the nineteenth century.
[45] Kuhn, op. cit., p. 187.

43

may not be from Copernicus, the argument cannot be clinched, as Rosen has shown, by Prowe's statement.[46] The facts are that Rheticus did use the term hypothesis in his own account, that it appeared in the major work of Copernicus, and that Kepler himself used it in referring to the entire matter.[47]

Both Copernicus and Osiander were concerned about the best way of launching the *Revolution of the Celestial Spheres*. In his own opening statement to the book, Copernicus mentioned that two learned men, Cardinal Schönberg and Bishop Giese, had encouraged him to lay aside his fear and publish his mathematical discoveries. He also stated that surely his Holiness, the Pope, would want to know how he came " to imagine any motion of the earth." This, he continued, stemmed from the disagreement among the mathematicians themselves and from the rereading of the philosophers in order to determine if any other conjectures of the motions of the spheres had been suggested. We have already quoted the passage in which he related how he learned from Cicero that Nicetas thought the earth moved, that Plutarch had mentioned that some had held that opinion, and then that some of the Pythagoreans assigned a motion to the earth. He then added:

> Therefore I also, having found occasion, began to meditate upon the mobility of the Earth. And although the opinion seemed absurd, nevertheless because I knew that others before me had been granted the liberty of constructing whatever circles they pleased in order to demonstrate astral phenomena, I thought that I too would be readily permitted to test whether or not, by the laying down that the Earth had some movement, demonstrations less shaky than those of my predecessors could be found for the revolutions of the celestial spheres.[48]

Then he continued with the results, which we also previously quoted in another context:

> And so, having laid down the movements which I attribute to the

[46] E. Rosen, *Three Copernican Treatises* (New York: Columbia University Press, 1939). pp. 29-31.
[47] Ibid. pp. 22-26.
[48] Copernicus, op. cit., p. 508.

Earth farther on in the work, I finally discovered by the help of long and numerous observations that if the movements of the other wandering stars are correlated with the circular movement of the Earth, and if the movements are computed in accordance with the revolution of each planet, not only do all their phenomena follow from that but also this correlation binds together so closely the order and magnitudes of all the planets and of their spheres or orbital circles and the heavens themselves that nothing can be shifted around in any part of them without disrupting the remaining parts and the universe as a whole.[49]

From these passages it is clear that Copernicus thought his conjectures or hypotheses best explained the phenomena, particularly in their mathematical form. It was not a *mere* hypothesis; it was a hypothesis which he believed squared more adequately with the materials at hand. Copernicus believed in the essential correctness of his hypothesis.

There are two other items in the preface which indicate that Copernicus as well as Osiander wanted to find a way around opposition. The first is indirect. Although Copernicus made reference to other learned men, it is to be noted that the Protestant Rheticus who had helped Copernicus in publication matters on the basis of his mathematical competence, was not mentioned by name. That would probably have been indiscreet. The second is an attempt to sidetrack the criticism of those who appealed to Scriptural texts in opposition to new scientific statements. Copernicus affirmed that to use Scripture in this way was to distort it. Further, those who cited Scripture were usually ignorant of mathematics and had no business making scientific judgments. He then recalled that many of the Church Fathers, with reference to similar matters, had made foolish mistakes in the citation of Scripture.

Osiander and Copernicus differed on the way in which the anticipated opposition was to be met. Osiander preferred to take the traditional path of meeting the opposition of the Aristotelians by frankly setting the new view forth in the old sense as a hypothesis for which

[49] Ibid., p. 508.

45

no truth claims were necessarily made. In that way he believed that the rage of the peripatetics could be deflected.[50]

Osiander's older view of hypothesis was grounded in his theological understanding. It may be appropriate to recall the relevant section from the preface which he wrote:

But since for one and the same movement varying hypotheses are proposed from time to time . . . the astronomer much prefers to take the one which is easiest to grasp. Maybe the philosopher demands probability instead; but neither of them will grasp anything certain or hand it on, unless it has been divinely revealed to him.[51]

By definition, astronomy as such was not the domain of truth and there was even an echo that philosophy was nearer the truth than astronomy. Theology alone was the arena of truth. Astronomers and philosophers could discover certainty only when their findings participated in revelation. This was a dangerous and pretentious view. But it certainly did not mean that Osiander contended that the Bible, rather than astronomy, was true in astronomical matters. Osiander's views dictated a particular conception of the discipline of astronomy, but it did not prescribe any particular theory. The difference between Copernicus and Osiander with reference to the meaning of hypothesis, as Bornkamm has suggested, is that between a more realistic and a more critical philosophy.[52]

In the controversy over Osiander's preface, both sides made exaggerated claims. Those who stood against Osiander did not sufficiently appreciate his conception of the relations of the disciplines and his particular views on astronomy. On the other hand, it is doubtful that Copernicus was as doctrinaire in his claims for the truth of his hypothesis as were his successors. The latter had the advantage of

---

[50] A few interpreters have doubted that Osiander had a genuine interest in science and have gone so far as to speak of a plot to discredit Copernicus on the part of Melanchthon and Osiander. For a discussion and refutation of this issue, see H. Bornkamm, op. cit., p. 175. Osiander's interest in astronomy was undoubtedly associated with astrological concerns and his interest in the end of the world. He studied the Jewish Kabbala and the Talmud with this interest. An interest in alchemy was apparently more related to medical problems than to astrology. For an account of Osiander's relation to astrology and alchemy, see E. Hirsch, *Die Theologie des Andreas Osiander und ihre geschichtlichen Voraussetzungen* (Göttingen, 1919), p. 120 ff.
[51] Copernicus, op. cit., p. 506.   [52] Bornkamm, op. cit., p. 176.

additional evidence and were inclined to read Copernicus in the light of it. To read Copernicus in the year 1600 is quite different from reading him in 1543.

But even if one grants his theoretical views, no defence of Osiander's views will completely vindicate him. Osiander was convinced of the rightfulness of the inclusion of his own preface in the book. Certainly he had kept both Rheticus and Copernicus informed of his views and pleaded with them concerning the way in which the book should be introduced to the public. Osiander's guilt was not deception, since an unsigned preface in that day did not have the moral condemnation attached to it that it did later. His guilt was that of a man who insisted on having his conception of the work appear also for the good of the cause. And men with a cause have great capacities for rationalization.

It is a matter of conjecture whether or not Osiander's preface accomplished its purpose. It is also a matter of conjecture that the preface hastened the death of Copernicus. Copernicus was already on his deathbed at the time of publication of the volume. The charge that the preface was responsible for the book being put on the Roman Catholic Index in 1616, as was indicated by the older interpreters, is as hard to understand as it is unconvincing.[53] The argument runs as follows: Without the preface, the views of Copernicus could not have been put forward as a hypothesis. If the views would have had to be faced as a matter of truth, it would have been too embarrassing to put the book on the Index. To be sure, the preface could give the Roman Catholics a way out. In 1620 the suggestion was made that Copernicus's views be used by Catholics in the sense of what we now call " mere hypothesis," though the latter term was not specifically used.[54] But it seems to me to be a forced interpretation to argue that whatsoever is hypothesis is a fit subject for the Index, but that which claims to be truth is not.

We have previously stated that Rheticus asked Osiander to undertake the completion of publication of the book when he, Rheticus, left Wittenberg for the University of Leipzig. But Rheticus occasion-

[53] Ibid., p. 178.　　　　　[54] Ibid., p. 178.

ally travelled to Nuremberg in connection with publication matters. Melanchthon wrote several letters of introduction to his friends in Nuremberg in behalf of Rheticus. All these letters praised Rheticus. One of them did express reservations concerning Rheticus's Copernican views. But it also indicated that Rheticus was missed in Wittenberg. Furthermore, such positive correspondence continued as late as 1550.[55] The notion, repeated in book after book, that Rheticus left Wittenberg under pressure because of his Copernican views does not have genuine support.[56] It is doubtful that Rheticus would have been appointed dean of the Arts Faculty in Wittenberg in 1542, just prior to his departure, had Copernicanism been an issue. It was known that Rheticus held such views even then. Rheticus did eventually give his full time to the development of mathematical tables rather than directly to the Copernican problem. But he was a mathematician by vocation, not an astronomer. It should further be recalled that Reinhold, a convinced Copernican, continued to teach in Wittenberg, and that Melanchthon assisted him in the publication of a volume of a definitely Copernican nature. Further, Melanchthon praised Reinhold long after the latter's death.[57] And while Reinhold was expected to teach the Ptolemaic system as part of his curricular responsibility, there is no indication that he had to keep quiet about his Copernican views.

A number of definite conclusions emerge from our discussions of the period between 1539 to 1554. The theologians were positive about the role of the sciences generally and of astronomy particularly. The theological approach of Luther and Calvin provided a view of Scripture and science which could have been open to Copernicus. In the instance of Melanchthon, the issue was complicated by his conscious adherence to the Aristotelian tradition. But it must always be remembered that there was no compelling reason for accepting Copernicus in this period. Most scientists were unconvinced, however much

[55] CR 7, 601. For other letters, see CR 4, 810; 839; 847; 815. See also W. Elert, *Morphologie des Luthertums*, I. 370.
[56] Repeated for instance, by Dorothy Stimson, *The Gradual Acceptance of the Copernican Theory of the Universe* (New York, 1917), p. 31; Grant McColley, *The Defense of Galileo*, p. xv. The theory of general opposition is repeated as recently as 1957, by Kuhn, op. cit., p. 195-96.
[57] Elert, op. cit., I, p. 373-74.

Copernicus himself believed in the truth of his work. In retrospect, it is easy to see that the theological opponents of Copernicus were wrong and one might wish they had kept quiet. In point of fact, however, the amount of opposition in this period is slight and there were Protestants in favour of Copernicus. The dispute concerning Osiander cannot change that. It is wrong to read the early, sporadic opposition as a developed organized pattern, as even reputable historians have done.[58]

[58] Even Herbert Butterfield, who otherwise is such an excellent historian, repeats the old unsusbtantiated phrases. Butterfield, op. cit., p. 42.

II

The Formation of a Protestant Scholasticism

In spite of sporadic negative comments concerning Copernicus, the theological context was not as such inimical to the new science until approximately 1560. But the manner in which the situation developed made openness from the side of the theologians increasingly difficult. Three related factors were responsible for this. First, a post-reformation Scholasticism developed, the philosophical assumptions of which were antagonistic to the philosophy of the new science. Second, a gradual transition in Biblical understanding took place. While the reformers had not denied an inerrant Biblical text, they had neither interpreted nor defended the Bible in terms of it. But there soon developed a defence of the Bible on the basis of its literal accuracy. Such a defence included the claim to inerrancy with respect to astronomy as well as theology. Third, both the religious and philosophical assumptions of many of the scientists appeared contrary to Christian theology, and the protestations of the scientists to the contrary only seemed to confirm this.

In this chapter and the next, it will be our task to develop and evaluate these three factors. Since the various elements interact in decisive ways, it will not be possible to take them in turn, even though they are roughly chronological. In developing any one factor, it will be necessary to keep the others in mind.

A: PROTESTANT INTERPRETATION OF ARISTOTLE

Reference has already been made to the increasing influence of philosophical conceptions in the theological work of Melanchthon. The successive editions of Melanchthon's *Loci* disclose an increasing concern with philosophy. We have also indicated Melanchthon's influence on the educational curriculum. Both factors show that Melanchthon's preoccupation with philosophical matters far exceeded that of either Luther or Calvin. Nevertheless, the subsequent theological interest in philosophy cannot be explained only in terms of Melanchthon. Neither the nature nor extent of this development can be explained that simply. But it is true that concentration on Aristotle in the subsequent period owes much to the place which it held in the esteem of Melanchthon.

For Melanchthon and his sympathizers, this early interest in Aristotle was associated with the humanist tradition. While humanists were generally more interested in Plato, Neo-Platonism, and related traditions of the ancient world, this concern was by no means universal. However, more to the point for our immediate purpose is the fact that the humanist influence coloured the early Protestant School philosophy, that is, the philosophy which was actually taught in the educational curriculum. This meant that logic and rhetoric were more important than metaphysics, and that there was as yet no great concern with the entire Aristotelian corpus.

Humanism also influenced theological thought in another initially decisive sense, though it was not directly discernible with reference to subject matter. This had to do with methodology, with the subtle influence of form upon content. The early humanist association with the kind of Aristotelianism exemplified in Melanchthon started a tradition in which the stress fell upon the nature of human expression, upon right statement and interpretation. Logic and rhetoric developed in this direction; they had metaphysical overtones, even if metaphysics had not yet consciously entered into the picture.

The extension of the notion of proper and right formulation as the key to truth received a genuine impetus in the controversies which soon developed within Protestantism. The Christological issue within Lutheranism, the predestinarian problem within the Reformed tradition, and the problem between the two Confessions of Christ's presence in the Lord's Supper, all had the consequence of intensifying this tendency to express truth through precise definition and the drawing of fine distinctions. There was a strong feeling that such procedures would solve the issues, and hence philosophy, which was the ground of genuine distinctions, acquired fresh importance. But in retrospect, it is clear that the definition of terms, so essential in controversy, actually deepened the chasm between the disputants. Even when their theological instincts were correct, the terms used to make definitions and distinctions carried hidden metaphysical assumptions that made solution of their problems virtually impossible. For instance, the debate concerning the nature of man in the light of the Fall could not really be answered in terms of a debate over the terms " substance " and " accident."

The developing Protestant interest in philosophy grew directly out of its own problems. It did not first arise in the later debates with Roman Catholicism.[1] Nor was there an independent interest in philosophy. In order to use philosophy in its own domain, the Protestants, of course, had to look to definite philosophical antecedents. Here the sources are not difficult to find, even if the details of the picture are not altogether clear. Three men were particularly important: Zabarella, Schegk, and Scaliger. They provided many of the philosophical distinctions utilized in the theological debates, and they were praised by subsequent writers of a philosophical and metaphysical interest. Zabarella was given the credit of having put logic back on a firm foundation. Scaliger developed Scholastic philosophical distinctions

[1] The old theory was that it first grew out of the need to meet Rome on its own terms. This theory was endlessly repeated: Elswich, 1720; Brucker, 1743; Gass, 1854; Gudhaven, 1850; Pünjer, 1880. That the philosophical development was first an internal need in the Protestant development was first pointed out by E. Troeltsch, *Vernunft und Offenbarung bei Johann Gerhard und Melanchthon* (Göttingen, 1891). For more extensive discussions of the issue, see E. Weber, *Die philosophische Scholastik des deutschen Protestantismus im Zeitalter der Orthodoxie* (Leipzig, 1907), p. 7 ff., and Peter Petersen, *Geschichte der aristotelischen Philosophie im protestantischen Deutschland* (Leipzig, 1921), pp. 278-79.

used by Lutherans in debates concerning the supernatural body of Christ.[2] Schegk wrote a book on the two natures of Christ in which he developed and employed Scholastic distinctions.[3]

These men introduced a type of Aristotelian philosophy into central Europe which was more extensive than that found in Melanchthon. First, the type of Italian Aristotelianism represented in these men was less associated with the humanist tradition, and it had maintained a very positive relation to the churches. Second, these men were concerned with returning to the philosophical sources. Schegk was a pioneer in this enterprise. They were impatient with the text books introduced into the educational system by Melanchthon. Such books, they maintained, were not the true Aristotle, even in as far as they touched upon him. They were confined too much to logic. A true knowledge of Aristotle demanded a growing interest in Aristotle, the metaphysician, the philosopher, who had exhibited the unity of all the sciences. The Italian philosophical tradition had even developed a metaphysical conception of nature which played a subsequent rôle in theology.

Thus, the philosophical task was seriously pursued by Protestants. Nor did the theologians simply borrow from the philosophers of the time. Theologians themselves carried on the philosophical enterprise. Many of the professors who lectured on philosophy also lectured on theology, or moved freely from one to the other as they switched within or between universities. The theologians were particularly interested in the new stress on metaphysics which came out of the Italian scene. By the last decade of the sixteenth century, there was considerable lecturing and publishing in metaphysics. Taurellus continued the Italian peripatetic tradition. Solomon Gessner had Versor's *Quaestiones* of 1480 republished. R. Goclenius had a book published on Aristotle's metaphysics. D. Cramer, C. Martini, J. A. Osiander, and D. Rungius were among those who lectured on metaphysics during this period.

It was this background which made possible the fully developed

---

[2] *Exercitationes* . . . (Frankfurt, 1592).
[3] *De una persona et duabuis naturis Christi* (Frankfurt, 1565).

Protestant scholastic systems which one finds already in the first decade of the seventeenth century. Among such Protestant metaphysical works are the following: J. Martini, *Exercitationes metaphysicae*, Wittenberg; C. Timpler, *Metaphysicae systema methodicum*, Marburg; C. Martini, *Metaphysicae commentatio*, Strasbourg (consisting of the previously mentioned lectures); C. Bartholinus, *Enchiridion metaphysicum*, Basel; and H. Alsted, *Metaphysica tribus libris tractata*.[4] Within Protestantism itself, a tremendous philosophical development had taken place in three stages. First, there had been the more humanistic interpretation of Aristotle in Melanchthon and his followers. Second, there had developed a greater stress on the sources and consequently on the genuine Aristotle. Third, the metaphysics of Aristotle, rather than his logic and rhetoric, had become central. In many ways, Melanchthon himself exhibited this development.

In the beginning of the seventeenth century the metaphysical development in Protestantism was strengthened by a vigorous intellectual encounter with Roman Catholicism. The writings of such men as Bellarmine and Suarez immediately come to mind. Much of the material is polemical in the best sense of the term. That is to say, the debate was conducted out of a mutual concern and a common conviction. The concern was for the unity of the Church and the conviction was that matters of truth could be settled through logical and metaphysical debate.

The very fact that the philosophical side should loom so prominently within the Confessions, between the Protestant Confessions, and in the debate with Rome, needs further clarification. It is not sufficiently explained in the internal development of a philosophical interest along the lines we have developed. Although Protestants insisted upon Scripture for the norm of their thinking, they continued an ancient tradition of the Church in which philosophy was employed as a weapon against heresy. Heresy, it was believed, resulted from an inadequate understanding of philosophy, or the employment of a poor philosophy in theological debate. Heresy was the consequence of an erroneous understanding of Biblical faith, requiring the correc-

---

[4] The latter book was already in its third edition in 1616. See Weber, op. cit., p. 9.

tion provided by proper philosophical analysis. The Lutheran Chemnitz saw the problems associated with the conception of the Trinity in this way. Since heretics had distorted the Biblical passages with Trinitarian meanings, the fathers of the Church had to explicate them in terms taken from Greek and Latin. Chemnitz wrote:

> . . . the Church departed from the simple usage of Scriptural words, not from any wanton affectation of novelty, but, as Augustine elegantly and truly says, that, by the necessity of speaking, these terms were acquired from the Greeks and Latins, because of the errors and snares of heretics . . . The heretics who certainly did not believe aright concerning these articles of faith, spake in the very same words in which the Church spake, and, by this deception, instilled their poison into many unwary ones, who feared no evil, because they heard the same words that are recorded in Scripture, and are proclaimed in the Church. What was the Church to do under these circumstances? It is very certain that it ought to have done this, viz., to defend against heretics that faith concerning the article of the Trinity which the Holy Ghost revealed in the Scriptures. But this could not be done in the words of Scripture, because of the petulance of heretics, who cunningly evaded all the words of Scripture, so that they could not be convicted and held fast, and who meanwhile led captive, by this artifice, the minds of the simple. *Therefore it was necessary to seek for such terms as might express, in some other manner, the facts delivered, concerning this article, in Scripture; so that heretics might not be able,* by a deceitful interpretation, to elude them.[5]

And Chemnitz does not leave us in doubt about his point. Just as heretics had been repulsed in the early Church through precise philosophical language, so too, Protestantism must undertake the same task. In similar fashion Schegk maintained that only metaphysics, that science which was the basis of all genuine distinctions, could be the bulwark and weapon against heresy. Schegk particularly believed that the absence of good metaphysics was the root of the rejection of the

---

[5] Chemnitz, Loc. Th. I, 36, quoted in translation of Heinrich Schmid, *The Doctrinal Theology of the Evangelical Lutheran Church* (2d Eng. ed., Philadelphia, 1889), pp. 147-48.

Trinity in his own time.[6] Many theologians saw the Socinian problem in this light. It was not that the Socinians were non-believers in the sense in which we use the term.[7] Their doubts concerning a proper Trinitarian view were not in the first instance seen as a defect of faith; it was believed rather that an inadequate philosophical concern had led them to reject the Trinitarian formulation. Historically, it was considerably later that the denial of the Trinity was interpreted as a change in faith itself. At the end of the seventeenth century, Francis Turretin still contended against Socinians by making what he thought were the proper philosophical distinctions. In the second decade of the seventeenth century, Meisner referred to the Anabaptists in a similar setting. But he believed that the Roman Catholics were primarily guilty of self-glorification, and were only indirectly guilty of the misuse of Philosophy.[8] But the major thrust against the Roman Catholics had also begun to be waged in philosophical terms in the seventeenth century. While the charge against the Socinians and the Anabaptists was that their philosophy was inferior or that they ignored philosophy altogether, the battle with Rome centred in the question of the proper interpretation of Aristotle. But with Rome, the question of the interpretation of Aristotle was not that of inferior and superior; some of the Roman Catholics spoke with high esteem of the Protestant metaphysicians, and vice versa.

But there were fundamental differences between Protestant and Roman Catholic Scholasticism. The former was not simply a return to the older Scholasticism. The Reformation and Renaissance had intervened, and in principle, the Protestant Scholastics were committed to the Reformation. They believed that their philosophical enterprise explicated and defended the Reformation. But the Reformation was responsible for two fundamental differences from Roman Catholic Scholasticism.[9] First, the central notion of justification by

[6] See E. Weber, *Die philosophische Scholastik des deutschen Protestantismus im Zeitalter der Orthodoxie* (Leipzig, 1907), pp. 30-31.
[7] While the term atheist is used in this period, it does not mean the denial of God but the rejection of the true Christian understanding of God.
[8] Weber, op. cit., p. 12-13.
[9] This is true even though the citations on certain problems in the doctrine of God ran ten to one from the Medieval rather than from either Luther or Calvin. While Luther

faith continued to give a distinctive character to Protestantism. While metaphysical concepts were developed by the Protestant Scholastics, justification by faith could not completely be put into metaphysical terms. Here the experiential side of the Reformation was too strong. But it was exactly this which mystified the Roman Catholic opponents, for whom faith only made sense if it could be placed in a context of causation.[10] In order to deal with justification, the Protestant Meisner, for example, had to transcend the traditional conceptions of causality. On this question it was still evident that the Protestants held to the centrality of faith, Biblically grounded, and that metaphysics had to play a subservient role.

The second major difference between the Protestants and the Roman Catholic Scholastics had to do with the relation between metaphysics and Biblical faith. The Protestants insisted that metaphysics be subordinated to Biblical understanding. Such subordination did not permit an independent metaphysics. There could be no independent conception of reason standing alongside revelation. However lengthy the sections on the natural knowledge of God among the Protestant Scholastics' writings, such sections did not stand in their own right as they had tended to in the Roman Catholic tradition. Such material demanded faith or the revelation matrix as its logical centre and completion. At best, natural knowledge had a relative independence; it existed rightfully only to serve the faith.

For the Protestant Scholastics, metaphysics had to provide the unity of all the sciences. But it had to do this in the light of a Biblical understanding superior to it and determining it. This was, of course, a very difficult balance to maintain. For Zabarella, metaphysics was already the " master and lord of all the sciences." But he still meant that the unity of all knowledge had to be maintained in the light of faith. While only metaphysics could maintain this unity, it could not contradict the first principles of Scripture. Hence, most of the Protes-

---

was cited extensively in the early period by Lutherans, the general citations were certainly from other authors. The same was true in the Reformed tradition. Calvin was cited more by English writers than in the Reformed tradition on the Continent. Both Luther and Calvin enjoy more prestige to-day than then.
[10] For example, Bellarmine.

tant Scholastics rejected the Medieval notion of double truth. If truth was indeed one, then what was true in philosophy could not possibly be false in theology, or vice versa. More precisely, those who denied the notion of double truth defended the notion that the truth of theology dictated the truth of philosophy. If philosophy contradicted theology, philosophy had to be given up. Melanchthon had already denied the notion of double truth. Taurellus was against it and Martinius referred to the notion as a false spiritualism which does not think. Meisner, who also rejected it, went so far as to say that the time needed in the study of theology could be cut by a third through a thorough grounding in good philosophy.

The unity of the sciences, which Melanchthon had believed so essential, was fully expressed among the Protestant Scholastics. They not only set themselves the task of writing on all phases of philosophy; they covered the entire range of knowledge. Frequently such writings were published in the form of Encyclopedias which included metaphysics, logic, geology, astronomy, in fact, all the sciences. The Encyclopedia by Alsted is a good illustration. But Alsted was also a good example of what happened in the Protestant development. At the very time that Galileo was making his discoveries, Alsted developed a conception of theology and its relation to metaphysics in which Aristotle was enshrined in the very citadel of theology. The net result was that the Aristotelian-Ptolemaic world picture, buttressed by a profusion of Biblical passages, could not be denied without challenging the Christian position itself.

The inescapable question in confronting Protestant Scholasticism is whether metaphysics was really subservient to Biblical understanding, or whether metaphysics actually determined the character of Biblical comprehension. In intention, metaphysics was subservient to theology in the exposition and meaning of a Biblical text. Certainly this operated in the rejection of philosophical movements which did not agree with the Biblical text. But on a deeper level the question remains whether the Biblical actually determined the metaphysical. With respect to obvious content, one could undoubtedly answer in the affirmative. But with reference to the *form* of Biblical understanding, a different answer must be given. The Bible was now understood quite differently than it had been in the case of Luther and Calvin. We noted that for them the conjunction of Spirit and Word was the key to Biblical interpretation. We also noted that Melanchthon's emphasis, with its overtones of humanism and Aristotelian logic, contributed to the tendency to regard the Bible as objective information. It was the latter tendency which now became accentuated and decisive. It was encouraged through the internal Protestant debates and through the polemical battle with Rome. More and more a text became important as information—philosophical, or factual, or both. The text of the Bible, a theological interpretation, and an item of scientific knowledge were alike construed as metaphysical knowledge. The interpretation of the three was not essentially different. This stress upon the unity of knowledge increasingly passed over into a formal identity of all knowledge. All distinctions in different modes of knowing were blurred.

When the Bible was also viewed as a book of knowledge, a drastic shift had taken place in the way of reading and interpreting Scripture. For Luther and Calvin, the conjunction of Word and Spirit made the Scripture normative through the way in which it created and nourished faith. It was precisely what was beyond the level of information which made the searching of Scripture different from the concern with other literature. The accuracy of the Bible in all matters was still accepted: but it was not a matter of direct concern. But when the Bible was thought of as a book of metaphysical knowledge, concentration upon what it directly said assumed a greater role. Now the accuracy or infallibility of the text was important. The efficacy of Scripture rested no more upon the work of the Spirit, but upon the identification of the text and the Spirit through a conception of the Bible as verbally inspired and inerrant. At that juncture, the defence of the Biblical message rested upon its transformation into and identification with the divine information given in a book, the very words of which were the Word of God. Now the Bible was a book of delivered truth. Theology was the proper and orderly statement of this truth. Truth was identical with propositional statement.

The acceptance of the Bible as the inerrant deposit of the Word of God was called the first or Scriptural principle. Theologians tirelessly repeated that he who doubted this principle was not worthy of being a theologian. But such a literalistic attitude had disastrous consequences for Biblical understanding. Except in such instances when a tradition was so strong and clear that it could not be circumvented, as in the term "sitting at the right hand of God," the result was a literalistic and unimaginative adherence to the text. The theory of accommodation, so eloquently propounded by Calvin, was rejected by increasing numbers.[11] It was felt that this principle threatened the unity of all knowledge by admitting a split between philosophical and Biblical truth. The notion of accommodation, it was argued, gave credence to such a division. Instead, they believed that the root of the difficulty lay in rational inquiry, in dependence of a Biblical understanding. But in retrospect, we can see that they were victimized by the very thing they feared. A particular conception of reason in fact determined Scriptural understanding on the part of those who insisted most that reason must be subservient to Scripture. Scripture was no longer interpreted in terms of its own logic; it was interpreted through the metaphysics of Aristotle.

A theological and philosophical alliance demanded a uniform conception of knowledge of the world or nature and of Scripture. It was the task of logic and metaphysics to make the necessary adjustments. This is well illustrated in the commentaries on Genesis throughout the sixteenth and early part of the seventeenth centuries. The book of God's works (nature) and of his Word (Scripture) contained identical knowledge of the world. Genesis, too, was science and therefore knowledge of nature. While it was conceded that Moses did not elaborate scientific concepts, his statements, nevertheless, were considered scientifically true; further, the seeds for all future scientific discoveries were contained in the writings of Moses.[12] Zanchius even saw a parallelism in the order of Genesis and the *Physics* of Aristotle.

[11] L. Danaeus, *The Wonderful Workmanship of the World* (London, 1578), p. 9.
[12] Arnold Williams, *The Common Expositor* (Chapel Hill: The University of North Carolina Press, 1948), p. 176.

In the light of his studies of the commentaries on Genesis through this period, Williams has written:

. . . With all the variations and contradictions among and within the commentaries, it still remains true that the exegetes of the sixteenth and seventeenth centuries incorporated within their work a larger amount of what they took to be science than any exegetes before or since their day. They took Genesis far more as a literal, rather than as a merely religious or even literary account than have commentators since their time.[13]

The traditional pattern was followed in the theological exposition of astronomical matters. The philosophical notions of the incorruptible heavens, the sublunar corruptible area, circular motion and spherical shape as symbols of perfection, are assumed throughout the theological writings. Even when difficulties in the Aristotelian-Ptolemaic scheme resulted in accepting the mathematical tables of the Copernican position for calculating the size and distance of planets, the Copernican view was not accepted.[14] No basic change in outlook was acceptable.

For such thinkers, nature could not rightly be explored apart from what they considered the normative character of the Bible to be. If anything discovered in the investigation of nature contradicted the Bible, such discoveries needed to be corrected by the Bible.[15] Thus, disagreement between science and the Bible meant that a mistake had been made in the interpretation of nature.[16] Such mistakes were equivalent to atheism, that is, a distortion of a full Christian understanding. The investigation of nature, when rightly pursued, had a Christian context and led inevitably to the God of the Bible. Unless the understanding of nature was bound to the Bible, they believed, it was given a false independence. Therefore, the natural and the revealed could not be separated. There was considerable resistance even to a formal distinction between them. The relative independence given to the natural order by Roman Catholic thinkers was resisted by most

[13] Ibid., p. 174.
[14] Ibid., pp. 184-85, 188.
[15] Danaeus, op. cit., pp. 6-7.
[16] Ibid., p. 11-15.

Protestants in this period. Nature, for Protestants, was to be investigated, but always with reference to what it said about nature and history.

Until well into the early decades of the seventeenth century, the Lutheran and Reformed traditions on the continent held the views here delineated. A minor exception resulted from the influence of Ramism. Peter Ramus believed that the distinctions of Aristotelian logic were sterile and of no use whatsoever. Aristotle, he said, had introduced a series of fables, although it must be added that his work was not as distinct from Aristotle as he believed. Nevertheless, the Ramist logic was more akin to the tradition of rhetoric and of practical concerns. It was definitely antimetaphysical. The Ramist logic did make an impact upon sections of the Reformed tradition. In an early period, universities of German Lutheranism also had representatives of the Ramist position. But as the interest in Aristotle's metaphysics increased, the teaching of Ramist logic was forbidden in one Lutheran university after another.[17]

With some exceptions, the theological situation in the Netherlands was similar to that of the rest of the Continent. Among theologians, the Aristotelian influence continued to be strong until the third and fourth decades of the seventeenth century. In the English scene, the Aristotelian hold was also firm. But it was broken somewhat earlier than on the Continent. Nevertheless, originally the English shared the belief in the metaphysical unity of nature and of Scripture. They, too, made the problem of knowledge central.

The development of the Protestant Scholasticism we have delineated in this section occurred in the period in which no new evidence for the Copernican position was available. But the very internal development of an essentially Aristotelian metaphysical approach within Protestantism made acceptance of the Copernican position virtually impossible. This was a new development. Unlike Luther and Calvin, these writers could not have adapted to the Copernican position without abandoning their views of philosophy, Bible and theology. The Reformers had not gone beyond the decisive religious break-through.

[17] For example, Leipzig, 1591; Helmstedt, 1597; Wittenberg, 1603.

Understandably they had not spelled out the implication of their newly won theological understanding for other areas of thought. Luther, for instance, spoke disparagingly of Aristotle and of philosophy; but he did not bother to suggest even the minimal lines for a new philosophical view of the world. He unwittingly accepted many of the older views, but they did not consciously enter into his theological understanding.

We noted how the philosophical interest entered at first formally, and then substantively, into the very structure of theological thought after Luther. But it was a subtle development in which metaphysical principles influenced the substance of thought by forcing its content into definite moulds of knowledge. Troeltsch, Weber, and Althaus have documented this subtle influence.[18] The development is most ironic. A metaphysical interest was entered into in order to guarantee the logic of faith. But faith was instead formed and overcome by the metaphysic which was supposed to defend it.

One further characteristic of the entire period needs to be mentioned if we are to understand some of the ensuing debates and the arguments advanced in their support. Protestants followed the normal practice of the period in citing the ancient authors as if any citation was itself the resolution of the issue. This is hard for us to understand; but without its significance, this period is unintelligible. The re-discovery of classical knowledge formed the Renaissance mind, and it made the Renaissance men suspicious of the accepted authority of the Church in all matters. But it did not mean that they rejected the authority of antiquity. Many matters formerly accepted on the ancient authority of the Church were now resolved by appeal to ancient philosophers, especially Aristotle and Plato. Only those who were not directly under the spell of the Aristotelian and Platonic revivals became acutely conscious of the problem posed by the conflict of authorities in ancient, classical sources. Copernicus was one of these; he saw the issue with great clarity. Many others, including theologians, cited Aristotle and the Bible on matters pertaining to the

18 E. Troeltsch, *Vernunft und Offenbarung bei Johann Gerhard und Melanchthon* (Göttingen, 1891); Weber, op. cit.; P. Althaus, *Die Prinzipien der deutschen reformierten Dogmatik im Zeitalter der aristotelischen Scholastik* (Leipzig, 1914).

natural world as self-evident authorities. Such citing of ancient meta-physical authorities was more convincing in this period than any appeal to observation. It was a metaphysical age, in which the citation of authority, not the openness of investigation, was the criterion of truth. The prevailing question was not how to secure freedom from authority, but which authority ought to be regarded as decisive. This was true even for the new scientists.

B: ISSUES AND MEN (1560-1610)

1. *Recurring Problems.* Having elaborated the broad outlines of the new Protestant Scholasticism, we turn now to the exposition of a series of areas in the light of this basic approach. The particular areas selected include those which later became controversial in the light of the further development of science. As we undertake this, we need to remind ourselves that while the interpretation of Scripture became increasingly literalistic, this development was not equally significant for all areas of exegesis.

Literalism manifested itself mostly in controversy, whereas non-controversial areas were left freer, or had already given way under the weight of undeniable evidence. Certainly literalistic categories did not extend to the doctrine of God so much as to conceptions of the world. While the debates concerning the Lord's presence in the Supper implied conceptions of space, such conceptions were neither promi-nent nor were they always literally conceived. Both Lutheran and Calvinist traditions manifested considerable sophistication in these areas. The expression, " the right hand of God," as we noted previ-ously, was not understood as a literal place. Anthropomorphic terms were understood in a non-literal way. The Lutheran tradition main-tained that the right hand of God was an expression of the equal divinity, majesty, and power of Christ. The Reformed tradition affirmed the same, but in respect to the body of Christ, their tradition insisted on spatial connotations.[19] But they refused to elaborate on the meaning of the spatial. Their concern was to protect the humanity

[19] For example, G. Bucanus, *Institutions of Christian Religion* (1606), pp. 281-82; Z. Ursinus, *The Summe of Christian Religion* (Oxford, 1595), pp. 594-95; H. Zanchius, *His Confession of Christian Religion* (Cambridge, 1599), pp. 407-8.

of the risen Lord. Nor was there any speculation concerning the nature or precise place of heaven and hell. Heaven was thought to be beyond the traditional spheres; the idea of hell being located in the centre of the earth was no longer widely held. Instead of worrying about the location of hell, one was counselled to worry about how one might escape it.

Considerable latitude was maintained on the question of the number of spheres. The astronomers, maintained Hyperius, were themselves not in agreement, nor did the Scripture mention any number of spheres. At the same time, Hyperius maintained that the earth was the centre of the universe, that the earth did not move, and that the sun did.[20] Danaeus likewise maintained the centrality of the earth, but he, like Bucanus, admitted the fact of life on the antipodes.[21] In fact, it was no longer possible to deny the existence of life on the antipodes and acceptance of that was made easier by the fact that Moses had happily said nothing about it. The possibility of more than one inhabited world was rejected. Danaeus, for example, stated that if there were life on other planets, we would have been told about it in Scripture. Beza's students also rejected the idea, and hastened to add, that they did so not because of Aristotle but because of Scripture.[22] At the same time, the students of Beza argued for the centrality of the earth on Aristotelian grounds, namely, that the earth was made up of the lowliest of the elements. Copernicus was also rejected by name.[23] Hyperius specifically felt called upon to reject the mathematical harmonies of the Pythagoreans, and stated that he was willing to refute them from Aristotle.[24] This latter became a central concern as the new science unfolded.

Natural philosophy was encouraged, provided its limits were recognized. Danaeus suggested that the Apostle Paul condemned the wisdom of the world, not the wisdom concerning the world. He repeated Augustine's warnings against undue speculation and declared

[20] A. Hyperius, *Two Common Places* (London, 1581), p. 17.
[21] Danaeus, op. cit., p. 65; Bucanus, op. cit., pp. 54-55.
[22] Danaeus, op. cit., p. 27; *Proposition and Principles of Divinity* (1595), p. 43. This work was written by a variety of authors in the tradition of Beza.
[23] *Propositions and Principles of Divinity*, pp. 52-53.
[24] Hyperius, op. cit., p. 20.

that there were those in his own day who were so concerned with the book of nature that they ignored the central concern of salvation.[25] This warning was frequently encountered in the literature. While men were counselled to check the limits of curiosity, the intent was not to present an obstacle to science; it was rather to remind men that the observation of nature could detract from the concerns of salvation. They were afraid, as we shall see, that the drama of the Bible would be read on the basis of the book of nature. In fact, they contended for the exact opposite. Time and again it was affirmed that there was more truth concerning nature in Scripture than among the naturalists, although the latter were not to be despised.[26] In England, over-curiosity with respect to nature was opposed because it appeared as a presumptuous attempt to pry into the mysteries which belonged to God alone. The English had a proper fear of the assumption that categories appropriate to nature were also appropriate for the understanding of God.[27]

Scripture was authoritative; but it could not always be said to be clear. There was much dispute about the question of clarity and obscurity in Scripture. Luther and Erasmus had already exchanged vigorous statements on the question of the clarity and the obscurity of Scripture, and Calvin had extensively discussed this question. The usually accepted position was that the crucial passages of Scripture, those dealing with the message of salvation, were sufficiently clear.[28] Bucanus declared the Scriptures to be a lantern of salvation, but freely admitted that there were mysteries in the Bible for the faithful as well as for those who looked at it from without. He found that obscurity was a guard against undue pride of intellect, a spur to the diligent study of the Bible and to concentration on the Word alone. Zanchius believed that the common and vulgar language of Scripture particularly testified to clarity in matters of salvation. The students of Beza declared there was sufficient clarity in Scripture, while its obscurity

[25] Danaeus, op. cit., pp. 4-5.
[26] Propositions and Principles of Divinity, p. 42 ff.
[27] P. Kocher, Science and Religion in Elizabethan England (San Marino, Calfornia, 1953), p. 64.
[28] For example, Bucanus, op. cit., p. 45; Zanchius, The Whole Body of Christian Religion (London, 1659), pp. 11-12; Propositions and Principles of Divinity, pp. 234-35.

was responsible for the variety in Biblical interpretation. Common to all interpreters was the notion that the more obscure passages of Scripture were to be interpreted in the light of the more clear. Technically, this procedure was known as the analogy of faith, namely, the interpretation of various unclear sections of the Bible in terms of the message of the Bible understood in and through faith.

The obscurity of Scripture was a problem to all. For those who were not genuinely sympathetic with the Christian understanding, the obscurity of Scripture was both a natural hurdle and a convenient excuse. But within the Christian camp, it was not a comfortable fact either. Those who believed in the clarity of logic and metaphysics could not tolerate obscurity. For them, a mystery at least had to be explicated if not explained, and there was no awareness that explication frequently distorted the truth veiled beneath obscure expressions. Nevertheless, there was a limited comfort to be had from the fact that nature also could be said to be clear and obscure. There was a correlation between the books of nature and of Scripture. In various degrees, both were clear and obscure.[29] It was easier to state the balance between the books of nature and of Scripture than to maintain it in any individual instance. Initially, the hope had been that the metaphysics of Aristotle would clarify the obscurities of Scripture more readily than it could the obscurities of nature. But instead, nature became clearer while the obscurities in Scripture remained. Nevertheless, the analogy was insisted upon, and as late as the eighteenth century, it was propounded by Bishop Butler in his *Analogy of Religion*.

The clarity of nature involved its orderliness, and from the philosophical side this was expressed through the concept of causation. Most of the theologians had recourse to the distinction between secondary and final causation. They readily accepted secondary causation, the notion that things are caused or conditioned in a sequential sense, so long as it was admitted that God worked through such causes. They did not hesitate to employ the usual Scholastic terms,

[29] The Englishman, Walter Charleton, was fond of this correlation.

such as necessity, contingency, mutability, etc. Such terms described aspects of the operation of nature but not in such a way as to exclude God's relation to them. Secondary causes were compared to the tools of a carpenter. They are real, but their functioning depends on power not inherent in them. Secondary causes are not to be despised. They are among the visible things of God's creation. But they cannot be understood in terms of themselves.[30] In fact, to understand secondary causes without reference to their principal or first causes, that is, in a Christian context, was considered heathenism.[31] God sustained secondary causes without changing their secondary nature.[32] Their dignity, in fact, existed in that God governed both the world and the Church through them.[33]

While it was affirmed that God worked in the world primarily through secondary causes, the point was also made that, at times, God suspended them or worked apart from them. But such an attitude should not be misunderstood. In this period, there was a new respect for the order of nature. But this order was not considered to be so inflexible as to admit no exceptions. Hence, theologians did not sense any contradiction in God's working through and apart from secondary causation even when the same occurrences were under consideration. For instance, Bucanus repeated the notion that according to one way of thinking, the bones of Christ could be broken, and to another they could not. More directly with reference to astronomy, he declared that " the sun ordinarily and necessarily moveth, but yet it standeth still at Joshua's sight."[34] It would not have occurred to these writers that God was bound to an order of nature. The orderliness of nature had not yet become oppressive.

It was assumed that God worked through ordered means and apart from them. However, God's activity apart from the regular course of things was considered a safeguard against those who stressed only

[30] A. Hyperius, *A Special Treatise of God's Providence and of Comforts against all kinds of Crosses* (London, 1588), no pagination.
[31] Danaeus, op. cit., pp. 12-13.
[32] Ursinus, op. cit., pp. 145-46.
[33] H. Zanchius, *His Confession of Christian Religion* (Cambridge, 1599), p. 27; *The Whole Body of Christian Religion* (London, 1659), p. 38.
[34] Bucanus, op. cit., p. 147.

secondary causes. Undue stress on secondary causes would prove debilitating to piety. As Bucanus reminded his contemporaries, in adversity one lifts up one's eyes unto God, the first cause of all things, not to secondary causes.[35] While these theologians tended to be open to the relative independence of order and causation, they nevertheless wanted it to be clear that God was the active foundation of causation and order and that nothing happened outside His active will. Further, as the Lord of Creation, God was considered free of all causation.[36] In this manner the theological grounds were laid for the subsequent opposition to the attempt to abolish final causes from the field of science.

God's direct and directing relation to nature was also expressed in the concept of purpose. The earth, it was frequently declared, was created both for man's use and for God's glory. Nothing was without purpose, and the purposes were elaborated in endless detail. Purposes must be spelled out. Failure to do so was tantamount to ignoring the Creator, much in the same way as when secondary causes were disassociated from the First Cause.

To be sure, a rigorous adherence to the elaboration of purpose always encountered difficulty with calamities and the apparently worthless and harmful things in nature, such as snakes and insects. Calamities were always interpreted as signs from God, much in the same way as were comets and meteors. But such signs were ambiguous and demanded interpretation in a structure of purposes. This was true also with respect to such things as snakes. They belonged to some higher purpose of which man was not aware. Sometimes it was simply stated that snakes were necessary for balance within the animal kingdom. It was apparently not asked whether the need for such balance did not call the wisdom of creation into question.

Much of the elaboration of purpose is most tedious. Long before such an eighteenth-century figure as Christian Wolff, Hyperius declared that the day was made for labour, the night for rest, the sun to

---

[35] Bucanus, op. cit., pp. 153-54 (incorrectly numbered 150).
[36] William Perkins in England (1595) said virtually the same, maintaining that God ordinarily worked through secondary causes but also apart from such means. The latter He did in accord with what seemed good to Him, such as the sun standing still. See Paul H. Kocher, *Science and Religion in Elizabethan England* (San Marino, California, 1953), p. 108.

warm and dry, the moon for gentle cold and moisture.[37] Bucanus recounted that the sun, moon, and the stars were made as receptacles which retained and diffused the light created on the first day. Further, they were natural signs of such matters as rain, wind, and heat; but through such events, one also encountered signs of the anger and mercy of God.[38] Thus the same event could have a natural and a supernatural meaning. In subsequent periods, natural purposes were not so readily discerned. Then some had recourse to the suggestion that while everything which happened did not have a natural purpose, it ought to be understood with reference to its supernatural meaning.

The severest blow to the concepts of design and purpose occurred in an area which had heretofore been exceptionally helpful, namely, astronomy. The events in this realm had possessed sufficient regularity to convey purpose; while their irregularities were both sufficiently dramatic and infrequent to testify to the miraculous working of God. But when new stars began to appear in successive waves in 1572 and in ensuing years, new questions were raised which could no longer be answered in the traditional pattern. As long as new stars appeared in the sublunar world, acceptable explanations were at hand. But when it became apparent that the comets appeared in the allegedly incorruptible heavens, two difficult alternatives remained: either to deny the incorruptibility of the heavens, or to affirm their appearances as a special miracle of God. The first was obviously unacceptable; the latter was difficult because appearances of comets had now become too frequent to qualify as miracles. Such great miracles as the star of Bethlehem, the eclipse at the time of the crucifixion, the sun standing still, had indeed been rare. Hence, the initial answer to the new star of 1572 had been that its appearance was also a special miracle wrought by God. Even those with a genuine interest in the new science, like the Englishman Digges, or even Tycho Brahe, so interpreted it. But that answer was no longer satisfactory when the appearances became more frequent, and especially, when later, they could also be pre-

[37] Hyperius, *Two Common Places*, p. 4. Already Luther and Calvin made similar suggestions, though not in a conspicuous way. See *Luther's Works*, I, p. 42. Calvin, *Institutes*, III, x, ii.
[38] Bucanus, op. cit., pp. 56-57

dicted. When that occurred, both the notion of the incorruptibility of the heavens and the traditional explanation of special miracles had to go.

2. *Copernican currents.* Throughout this period the views of Copernicus gained little acceptance. But it would be wrong to say that there was active opposition. Most theologians elaborated their own views of the world along the traditionally accepted lines of Aristotle. Only rarely did someone speak out against Copernicus. The usual notion that astronomers of a Copernican bent were suppressed right and left is not true for this period. By the second decade of the seventeenth century, there were in fact Copernican mathematicians in most intellectual centres. While such mathematicians were not always Copernican, the full Copernican view was frequently represented. It is true that when men of this type were active in the university circles, the Protestant theologians were anxious, fearful, and sometimes hostile.

On the Continent, Caesalpin, an early metaphysician, maintained that the earth moved. In this he was opposed by Taurellus. Nevertheless, the metaphysical writings of Caesalpin were used among the Protestant Scholastics. It must be said that while Caesalpin believed in the movement of the earth, he did so on metaphysical grounds and opposed the position elaborated by Copernicus. The credit for being the first genuine Copernican belongs to an English astronomer and mathematician, Thomas Digges. Like many of the early Copernicans, he kept silent about Scriptural passages which allegedly contradicted Copernicus. Silence frequently kept one out of trouble. But if Digges ignored the Scriptural problem, he did not remain silent about his own positive convictions. The Platonic-Pythagorean adoration of mathematics already present in Copernicus, was of crucial importance to him. Kocher wrote of Digges as follows:

> Digges brimmed with piety which overflowed spontaneously in his scientific writings on the 1572 nova and the Copernican universe. It was, however, a piety of a rather individual brand, not humble, not directly concerned with salvation. It was a worship of God the

supreme mathematician, whose high mysteries could be properly celebrated only by the mathematical initiate . . . He adjured his readers to rise ' above the common sort,' to throw off the beast in them that clung to the lowly earth, and soar, as God intended man to soar, into the secrets of the highest heavens.[39]

The first defence of Copernicanism in the English language was by Robert Recorde, though he was not as thorough-going a Copernican as Digges. Already in 1551, Recorde set the various planetary systems beside each other and defended the possibility of the Copernican view. He saw no genuine contradiction between it and the Biblical view.

His implication, if not his express statement . . . is that the findings of science are not inconsistent with but supplementary to the Bible as rightly interpreted, and that if any apparent contradiction arises it is because the Bible has not been correctly understood. Clearly he started from science and expected Holy Writ to conform to it, not vice versa.[40]

But Copernicanism was also vigorously opposed, and increasingly so on Biblical grounds. Du Bartas, in *The Divine Weeks* of 1578, represented a conservative defence of the Biblical faith. Helisaeus Roeslin (1597) rejected Copernicanism on the grounds that it was contrary to experience, physics, and the Sacred Scripture. In England, Thomas Blundeville (*Exercises*, 1597) and Thomas Hill (*The Schoole of Skil*, 1599) opposed the Copernican view both on grounds of scientific argument and Scriptural content. The problem of Scripture intruded more and more, while many a Copernican would have preferred to ignore it.

Gilbert, in *De Magnete*, accepted the diurnal rotation of the earth but not the full Copernican position. He, too, ignored the Biblical problem, though his book was written as late as 1600. He did reject the traditional interpretation of Psalm 74, however. Edward Wright's address, which was added to the beginning of the *De Magnete*, attempted to meet the Biblical problem through the old notion of accommodation, namely, that God accommodated his way of speaking to the notions and capacities of ordinary discourse and observation.

[39] Kocher, op. cit., p. 171.   [40] Ibid., p. 192.

Nor do the passages quoted from Holy Writ appear to contradict very strongly the doctrine of the earth's mobility. It does not seem to have been the intention of Moses or the prophets to promulgate nice mathematical or physical distinctions: they rather adapt themselves to the understanding of the common people and to the current fashion of speech, as nurses do in dealing with babes; they do not attend to unessential minutiae.[41]

According to McColley, this was the first time that the theory of accommodation was used with reference to the motion of the earth.[42] As another way of reconciling the Copernican and the Biblical passages, we quote here the following from the *Commentary on Job*, by Didacus à Stunica, 1584:

. . . And yet the reasons of these things are most plainly explained and demonstrated by Copernicus from the Motion of the Earth, with which he showeth that all the other Phenomena of the Universe do more aptly accord. Which opinion of his is not in the least contradicted by what Solomon saith in Ecclesiastes: (Chap. 1, v. 4) " But the Earth abideth for ever." For that text signifieth no more but this, That although the succession of Ages, and generations of Men on Earth, be various; yet the Earth itself is still one and the same, and continueth without any sensible alteration; For the words run thus: " One generation passeth away, and another Generation cometh; but the Earth abideth for ever." So that it hath no coherence with its Context, (as philosophers show) if it be expounded to speak of the Earth's immobility, And although in this Chapter Ecclesiastes, and in many others, Holy Writ ascribes Motion to the Sun, which Copernicus will have to stand fixed in the Centre of the Universe; yet it makes nothing against his Position. For the Motion that belongs to the Earth, is by way of speech assigned to the Sun, even by Copernicus himself, and those who are his followers so that the Revolution of the Earth is often by them phrased, The Revolution of the Sun. To conclude, No place can be produced out of Holy Scripture which so clearly speaks of the Earth's Im-

---

[41] Quoted by Kocher, op. cit., p. 194.
[42] Grant McColley, *The Defense of Galileo of Campanella*, p. xxv.

mobility, as this doth its Mobility. Therefore this Text, of which we have spoken, is easily reconciled to this Opinion. And to set forth the Wonderful power and Wisdom of God, who can indue and actuate the Frame of the Whole Earth (it being of a monstrous weight by Nature) with Motion, this our Divine pen-man addeth; " And the pillars thereof tremble ": As if he would teach us, from the Doctrine laid down, that it is moved from its Foundations.[43]

We conclude that there was as yet no uniform response to the Copernican view in this period. Kocher's judgment concerning the English scene is also true for the Continent:

For, so far as I can discover, these reactions, at least in England before 1610, were by individuals rather than by creeds. In other words, there was nothing in the dogmas of Catholicism, Anglicanism, or Puritanism which made any one of them more or less favourable to science in general than any of the others, Doctrinally, all were equally vulnerable or invulnerable to the insinuations of science; all could equally be served by it.[44]

Until the time of Galileo, the responses were individual, rather than along definite party lines. But a philosophical basis for opposition to the new science had unwittingly been developed.

[43] Salusbury, *Mathematical Collections* (London, 1661), pp. 469-70.
[44] Kocher, op. cit., p. 4.

III

The Diverging Traditions of Science and Theology

A: THE NEW SCIENCE AT THE TURN OF THE CENTURY

1. *Toward the substantiation of the Copernican view.* During the last three decades of the sixteenth century, the dominant authority in astronomy was Tycho Brahe. Even after Brahe's death soon after the turn of the century, his system remained the hope of all those who for one reason or another could not accept the theories of Kepler or Galileo. Brahe was mentioned in the last chapter in connection with the new star which appeared in 1572. He further observed comets in the region beyond the moon on six occasions in the latter decades of the century. He also noted that the planets moved through the boundaries of the supposed spheres which enclosed them. Hence, he rejected the notion of the crystalline spheres. But such a modification of the old Aristotelian picture did not lead Brahe to accept the Copernican view. Aristotelian thought had a firm hold on him and he was not enamoured of the mathematical harmonies held by those trained in the Neo-Platonic and Pythagorean traditions. Philosophically, he stood in a tradition which was antagonistic to the Copernican position.[1]

[1] He is frequently called a conservative; but this only makes sense if one previously decides that those who accepted the Pythagorean background over against a dominant Aristotelianism were not conservative. This is a reading back into history which unnecessarily prejudices the issues.

Much could be said for Brahe. He was a painstaking observer who kept a record of his observations. He was exceedingly accurate even with the naked eye and he developed various astronomical instruments. His detailed observations were inherited by Kepler and incorporated into the latter's Copernican outlook. The earth remained in a central and unmoved position, according to Brahe. The sun and the moon moved around the earth, but the other planets moved about the sun. It was a very satisfactory system. It did not challenge the traditional views, but could utilize the mathematical discoveries associated with Copernicus.

The remarkable and historically significant feature of the Tychonic system is its adequacy as a compromise solution of the problems raised by the DE REVOLUTIONIBUS. Since the earth is stationary and at the centre, all the main arguments against Copernicus' proposal vanish. Scripture, the laws of motion, and the absence of stellar parallax, all are reconciled by Brahe's proposal, and this reconciliation is effected without sacrificing any of Copernicus' major mathematical harmonies. The Tychonic system is, in fact, precisely equivalent mathematically to Copernicus' system . . . It retained the mathematical advantages of Copernicus' system without the physical, cosmological, and theological drawbacks.[2]

The obvious advantages in this view are apparent. Certainly, one need not conclude, as some interpreters have, that Brahe developed it out of a fear of upsetting the traditional views. Given both his philosophical heritage and the lack of further proof of the Copernican outlook, Brahe could hardly have come to different conclusions. His rejection of the crystalline spheres did not demand that he become a Copernican. But history was not on Brahe's side and as a result, his position did not receive the sympathetic interpretation it deserved. The problem of properly appreciating Brahe has been further complicated by those who absolutized his position while refusing to accept the new proofs for the Copernican view.

It was Johannes Kepler who carried the observations of Brahe into the Copernican camp. At an early age he was converted to the Coper-

[2] Kuhn, op. cit., pp. 202, 205.

76

nican system by his teacher, Maestlin, at Tübingen. Philosophically, Kepler became a convinced Neo-Platonist and Pythagorean, thereby being relieved of the problems facing the Aristotelians. He was a brilliant mathematician and became obsessed with the harmonies of mathematical proportions.[3] Hence, Kepler brought extensive philosophical convictions to his scientific work. But he had an equal respect for concrete and detailed observations. This was a working principle which he undoubtedly inherited through his associations with Brahe.

On the basis of an acute mathematical interest, concrete observations, and indefatigable labour, Kepler succeeded in bringing mathematical proof to the basic position of Copernicus. Moreover, he made Copernicus into a more consistent Copernican by eliminating remaining Aristotelian notions concerning the earth. For Kepler, the radical centre of *all* orbits was the sun, not the earth, as was still the case for Copernicus in many instances. By combining detailed observations and innumerable hypotheses, Kepler solved the age-old problem of how to plot and understand the orbit of Mars by making the assumption of an elliptical path. Such ellipitical patterns, he discovered, applied to other planets as well. He was also able to solve the problem of the lack of a uniform speed for the planets by relating elliptical patterns to the proximity of the planets to the sun. In short, he provided a greatly simplified and unified picture of the planetary system without being burdened by the unsolved problems in the systems of either Copernicus or Brahe. At long last, prediction and observation coincided.

For the first time a single uncompounded geometric curve and a single speed law are sufficient for predictions of planetary position, and for the first time the predictions are as accurate as the observations.[4]

Kepler, too, was proven wrong in detail; but he was right in his basic approach. His mathematical tables, published in 1627, would

---

[3] We shall return to this in our elaboration of his religious views.
[4] Kuhn, op. cit., p. 212.

have been enough to convert astronomers, if not others, to the basic Copernican view.

The more obvious evidence for the Copernican position came through his contemporary Galileo.[5] It is a simple fact that the telescope is more convincing and intelligible to most of us than mathematics. Galileo turned his newly made telescope to the heavens in 1610 and amazing confirmation was at hand for his Copernican views. New stars, in number best described in what we call astronomical proportions, appeared in the skies. The Milky Way was known now for the first time to be comprised of actual stars rather than vapours. Both the number and distance of the stars gave support to those who associated the Copernican views with the concept of the infinity of the cosmos. Of more immediate significance was the discovery of mountains and craters on the moon, and indeed, of spots on the sun. This meant that the heavens were no different than the earth. Whereas Copernicus had theoretically put the earth in the area of the heavens, Galileo now saw that the planets were of the same order as the earth. A major support for the notion of the incorruptibility and perfection of the heavens was now destroyed. Galileo noted too that Jupiter was a centre for the orbits of other bodies. Hence the earth could not be the centre around which all movement proceeded. The planet Venus was discovered to have phases, and these could not readily be fitted into the old scheme.

Still, there was no conclusive proof of the Copernican position. Galileo's telescopic discoveries could be fitted into the Ptolemaic system, provided one made enough adaptations. But the necessary adaptations were now so great that the overwhelming evidence, if one did not have other reasons for accepting the Ptolemaic outlook, was in favour of the Copernican position. Nevertheless, Brahe's position, even though Brahe was no longer living, retained great influence. But by the middle of the century, as contrasted for instance with 1630, most of the significant astronomers were Copernican. However, no totally

[5] Professor Kuhn evidently believes that the place of Galileo has been overestimated, particularly the place of the telescope. He calls its effect, not proof, but propaganda. (p. 224). This seems to me to overstate the point, particularly since he goes on to show the effective use of the telescope.

satisfactory theory was available. As a result, most of the competing theories were taught side by side in the Universities throughout the century. This was particularly true in the Protestant Universities where Copernicanism, in spite of scattered opposition, had not officially been banned. A fully satisfactory scientific view did not appear until late in the seventeenth century.

In the meantime, the widespread domination of Aristotle had been successfully challenged. Kepler and Galileo attacked the authority of Aristotle, and defended the place of observation and of mathematics. A great deal of Galileo's *Dialogue Concerning the Two Chief World Systems* consisted in the refutation of Aristotle's mistaken assumptions. It is to be noted that a considerable part of his difficulty with Church authorities was due to this fact.[6]

The most vigorous assault on the authority of Aristotle had been made by an Englishman, Francis Bacon, in the early part of the seventeenth century. Bacon stood against the heavy hand of antiquity as the arbiter of truth, and instead proposed an inductive, experimental method. We indicated previously that the very quotation of Aristotle was sufficient to settle a matter of debate. Such an attitude was hard to break. It rested deeply in the feeling of a people and persisted apart from all reflection. This was all the more reason why it needed to be dislodged. Bacon wanted the untrammeled right to pursue questions and this involved the rejection of Aristotelian imperialism. But this was a matter of general conviction. It was not related specifically to the views of the new science. While Bacon made positive allusions to Galileo, he did not accept the Copernican position. The brunt of his attack was upon the Aristotelian hold on English thought. The success of his attack is evident in the fact that the pervasive domination of Aristotle was broken in England before his authority was successfully challenged on the Continent.

2. *Philosophical and religious assumptions in the New Science.* From the time of Kepler and Galileo, a pattern of opposition to the new

[6] The condemnation of Galileo lies outside the scope of this inquiry. For a full, balanced, and scholarly account, see de Santillana, Giorgio, *The Crime of Galileo* (Chicago: The University of Chicago Press, 1955).

science developed in Protestant circles. We have already made reference to the obvious reasons: the philosophical domination of Aristotelian thought and the development of an inerrant view of Scripture. But to these must be added the fact that there were philosophical and theological assumptions in the new science which were quite unacceptable to the Protestant theologians. These we must now examine. But in so doing, we must bear in mind that in this period such philosophical assumptions could be not disassociated from the scientific discoveries.

While the authority of Aristotle was already attacked by Copernicus, and specifically challenged by Kepler and Galileo, the grounds of the opposition rested not in an inductive, experimental science, but in a different philosophical or metaphysical position. The experiments and observations entering into the work of Copernicus, Kepler, and Galileo, substantiated a previously held position. Such experiments did not prescribe a new position. In fact, the experiments and observations could be reconciled with a variety of philosophical views. That is why one needs to distinguish between the substantiation of positions and the determination of views. For Copernicus, Kepler, and Galileo, experiment still confirmed a position which rested upon other than scientific assumptions. In the period subsequent to Galileo, experiments and observation began to determine the views of science quite apart from a particular philosophical tradition. When that moment arrived, as it dramatically did in Newton, the new science itself became a philosophy which could stand over against the philosophies once integrally associated with the new science. But that is still ahead of us. We must return to the period of Kepler and Galileo.

We have made repeated reference to the Neo-Platonic Pythagorean background of the new science, particularly to the interest in mathematical exactitude and proportion. For Copernicus, such mathematical interest was still associated with a good deal of Aristotle. Even the opponents of Aristotle were in debt to him, and the Aristotelian domination was broken as much through its transformation as through outright opposition. But for Copernicus and his followers, the mathematical interest derived from the Pythagorean tradition was paramount. A mathematical philosophy provided a view of the nature of things and a way of knowing reality. Reality and knowledge had a direct and proportionate relation to each other in this way of thinking. In addition, the mathematical understanding had two distinct advantages. In the first place, if the mystery of number was the essence of things, there was no need to ask additional questions pertaining to purpose or meaning. To see things in their geometrical, mathematical form was to have found their reason; no further questions were relevant. The world was mathematical through and through and one could think God's thought after him. Plato's statement to the effect that God ever geometrizes was frequently recalled in this period. In the second place, it was through such a mathematical understanding that the new science became a philosophy in its own right. For example, through the successful use of mathematics in astronomy, scientists could provide a clue to the nature of things that could receive a greater experimental verification than that provided by either Aristotle or the theologians. All believed that the functioning and nature of things coincided. The theologians had elaborated this through the concept of purpose, which we discussed in the previous chapter. But such purposes had to be elaborated, and as we noted, this was not always easy. But the world which the scientists touched seemed naturally to fall into mathematical form. Perhaps God's creation was a marvellous mathematical scheme, the understanding of which would prompt us to sing His praises. In any case, such a possibility was a far cry from what the theologians or Aristotelians had to say. For Aristotle, we may recall, mathematics was but one of the categories and even then, not the most important.

The mathematical understanding of reality was most vigorously expressed in Kepler. He abandoned all abstract conceptions which did not directly correspond to the mathematical functioning of things. Mathematics disclosed the unity in and through the apparent chaos. It uncovered the actual structure and order of things. It provided a single quantitative and mechanical picture, thus clearly delineating the structure of God's creation. Kepler wrote:

May God make it come to pass that my delightful speculation (the

MYSTERIUM COSMOGRAPHICUM) have everywhere among reasonable men fully the effect which I strove to obtain in the publication, namely, that the belief in the creation of the world be fortified through this external support, that thought of the creator be recognized in its nature, and that his inexhaustible wisdom shine forth daily more brightly. Then man will at least measure the power of his mind on the true scale, and will realize that God, who founded everything in the world according to the norm of quantity, also has endowed man with a mind which can comprehend these norms. For as the eye for colour, the ear for musical sounds, so is the mind of man created for the perception not of any arbitrary entities, but rather of quantities; the mind comprehends a thing the more correctly the closer the thing approaches toward pure quantity as its origin.[7]

In this, as in many other passages, it is apparent that Kepler combined a quantitative mathematical conception of things with an intense religious concern. His original vocational interest was in the field of theology and from an extant letter, we know that he was restless until he discovered that he could celebrate God in his astronomical work.[8]

There are aspects of this celebration of God which we must examine. Certainly we should not make too much of the adulation of the sun which comes from an early Tübingen disputation of 1593.[9] Professor Burtt is right in calling this material sun-worship, for everything ascribed to the sun would more appropriately be ascribed to God. But it comes from his youth, and Kepler, like Boehme, may have been more sophisticated than the words imply.

In any case, there were reasons why the sun should figure so dominantly in his thinking. First, the sun was prominent in the classical, philosophical heritage associated with Pythagoreanism. Second, Kepler was the first astronomer for whom the sun was the precise centre of the universe and who interpreted all the movements of the planets

[7] Quoted from G. Holton, "Johannes Kepler's Universe: Its Physics and Metaphysics," *American Journal of Physics*, XXIV, No. 5, (May, 1956), 349-50, Letter to Maestlin, April 19, 1597. For the interpretation of the unity of various elements in Kepler, I am particularly indebted to Professor Holton.
[8] Letter to Maestlin, October 3, 1595.
[9] *Opera*, VIII, 266 ff. The passage is quoted by Burtt, op. cit., p. 48.

in terms of it. Copernicus had not been able to achieve that. Third, the sun provided a plausible explanation of the problem of motion. If the *source* and *centre* of all motion was identical, as it would be in the case of the sun, one had a view which combined symmetrical proportions, simplicity of explanation, and motive power for the universe. Fourth, the sun appeared as the appropriate dwelling place of the deity. God, too, was at the centre of a universe which He had made, including his own abode, the sun. In one sense, the attempt to place the deity in the sun was a way of bringing God back into a universe from which the abolition of the older spheres had virtually banished him. Kepler was the architect of a system in which place and function, reality and spatial categories, again coincided. This was certainly more so than in the case of either Copernicus or Galileo. In describing this Gerald Holton has written:

The sun at its fixed and commanding position at the centre of the planetary system matches the picture which always rises behind Kepler's tables of tedious data—the picture of a centripetal universe, directed toward and guided by the *sun* in its manifold roles: as the *mathematical* centre in the description of celestial motions; as the central *physical* agency for assuring continued motion; and above all as the *metaphysical* centre, the temple of the Deity.[10]

From the standpoint of a classical theology, such views were not congenial, to put it mildly. But Kepler considered himself Lutheran and even touched on theological matters directly. He engaged in allegorical speculations in which the sun stood for the Father, the fixed stars for the Son, and the supposed ethereal medium through which the power of the sun operated to move the planets for the Spirit. It was fanciful speculation which had nothing to do with the genuine Trinitarian motif, not even the *vestigia trinitatis*.

[10] Holton, op. cit., pp. 347-48. Further relevant passages direct from Kepler on the " sun " are the following: " As regards movement: the sun is the first cause of the movement of the planets and the first mover of the universe, even by reason of its own body . . . Finally, as regards the harmony of the movements: the sun occupies that place in which alone the movements of the planets give the appearance of magnitudes harmonically proportioned." . . . " Wherefore most rightly is the sun held to be the heart of the world and the seat of reason and life, and the principal one among three primary members of the world; and these praises are true in the philosophical sense." *Epitome of Copernican Astronomy*, in *Great Books of the Western World*, Vol. XVI, pp. 855-56.

Kepler's theological views were so suspect that he was refused a professorship. This was not because of his scientific views,[11] as sometimes alleged, but because he could not accept the omnipresence of Christ or subscribe to the Formula of Concord. Hence, he was not accepted in Lutheran territory, and it was hardly to be expected that he would be acceptable in Non-Protestant territory. Hafenreffer, a Protestant theologian in Tübingen, suggested that Kepler keep his Biblical and scientific work separate.[12] But this sound advice would have gone counter to everything which Kepler believed.[13] He even tried to reconcile the Joshua passage with Copernican astronomy by suggesting that it was the earth which stood still, the sun only seeming to do so. But the point, suggested Kepler, was that the day was long enough.[14] Kepler was interested in the reconciliation of Scripture and natural events, and he was prepared to interpret the former in a flexible manner through the widely held notion of accommodation.[15] At the same time he was possessed by a conception of the unity of all knowledge understood in a mathematical manner. On that road, he believed it was possible to think God's thoughts after him.

Galileo made similar though less passionate statements on the place of mathematics. While we shall not repeat them here, we will give some attention to areas in which his thought is similar to and different from Kepler. For Galileo, mathematical thinking was akin to the mode of God's thinking. Admittedly one's thought lacked the completeness and richness of God's thought, but there was no question now but that one's thoughts *were* God's thoughts. The human mind had its nexus with the Divine at the point of mathematics. Galileo wrote:

> I say that as to the truth of the knowledge which is given by mathematical proofs, this is the same that Divine wisdom recognizes; but I shall concede to you indeed that the way in which God knows the

[11] This is the usual interpretation, apparently followed also by Butterfield, op. cit., p. 44.
[12] W. Elert, *Morphologie des Luthertums* (München, 1931), I, 376–77.
[13] Kepler, as Luther, must be seen in terms of the diversity of motifs which inform him, not through what he likes or dislikes, or what is modern or not modern. Neither suffered from such schizophrenia.
[14] "An Abstract of the Learned Treatise of Johannis Keplerus, the Emperor's Mathematician: entitled His Introduction upon Mars," in Salusbury, *Mathematical Collections* (London, 1661), pp. 462–63.
[15] Ibid., p. 467.

infinite propositions of which we know some few is exceedingly more excellent than ours. Our method proceeds with reasoning by steps from one conclusion to another, while His is one of simple intuition . . . I conclude from this that our understanding, as well in the manner as in the number of things understood, is infinitely surpassed by the Divine; but I do not thereby abase it so much as to consider it absolutely null. No, when I consider what marvellous things and how many of them men have understood, inquired into, and contrived, I recognize and understand only too clearly that the human mind is a work of God's, and one of the most excellent.[16]

Statements similar to those made by Kepler on the place of the sun are also found in Galileo. The sun was considered to be both motive power and an object of religious adoration. It was the " Great Minister of Nature, and in a certain sense the soul and heart of the world," infusing light and motion into it. The sun stood to the motive power of the planets, as the heart to the body. Even Dionysius the Areopagite was quoted in support of the significance of the sun.[17]

But there was one decisive difference between Kepler and Galileo. Whereas Kepler elaborated a mathematical vision of the universe, Galileo was conscious of mathematics as the key to an inexorable law of nature. While Kepler too, held to a mechanical conception of the operations of nature, he sensed that God stood in intimate relation to that process. Kepler, in spite of mechanical views, had a mystical temperament and Galileo, a more rational one. This is illustrated in their different analyses of causality. Both rejected the concept of final causality, namely, that things are to be understood with reference to their end or purpose. For both, the problem of ends or purposes did not belong to science; such problems represented a vestige of Aristotelianism. Nevertheless, for Kepler, the formal cause was the real cause; it represented a mathematical order which could be discovered to be the nature of things, including the nature of God. Harmony was its own rationale. No further questions needed to be asked. Through

[16] Galileo, *Dialogue Concerning the two Chief World Systems—Ptolemaic and Copernican*, trans. Stillman Drake (Berkeley: University of California Press, 1953), p. 103-4.
[17] Galileo, " Letter to the Grand Duchess Christina " in *Discoveries and Opinions of Galileo*, trans. Stillman Drake (New York: Doubleday Anchor, 1957), p. 213.

the knowledge of mathematical harmony one participated in the secrets of the universe and in the life of God. Such a mathematical understanding of the world was an act of adoration and worship which eclipsed the knowledge of God obtainable through the redemptive history of the Biblical tradition.

Galileo maintained that the world had a mathematical order. Such an order was known through rational reflection and religious affirmation. God was its efficient or Final Cause. But in contrast to Kepler, God was not directly perceived in and through the order. For Galileo, the process could be described apart from God, but the credit or by-line belonged to him. The seriousness of Galileo's own religious convictions were clear enough. But insofar as the description could proceed without a reference to the divine, the stage was set for removing God from any vital relation to the order of nature.

The stress on the quantitative, mechanical order in nature, so characteristic of both Kepler and Galileo, produced equally serious consequences for the understanding of man. Secondary qualities, which had defined nature with respect to its beauty and richness, were pushed to the periphery and virtually abolished. The stress fell upon what were known as primary qualities, those characteristics of nature which could be given an empirical basis. But such a mechanical conception of nature, ranging from the heavens to the surrounding order, had drastic implications. If man was a part of nature, he belonged to the mechanical order. And if he was defined in other terms, he apparently did not belong to nature. The latter alternative was almost too absurd.[18]

Descartes saw this problem on the philosophical level. While he was sympathetic to Galileo, he also saw the difficulties in a mechanical philosophy. For Descartes, it was the dignity of human reason which saved man in a mechanical world.[19]

[18] Burtt, op. cit., pp. 79-80.
[19] Much has been made of the influence of Descartes as the transmitter of the new science and of the basic split between subject and object. This influence is hard to trace and historians have even spoken of the view of Descartes as the very air which people breathed. In any case, his influence at this point began in the subsequent period, that is in the latter half of the 17th century. See for example, Martin Heidegger, *Holzwege* (Frankfurt am Main, 1950), p. 91 ff.

Blaise Pascal saw the problem even more acutely. While rejecting the Copernican position, he nevertheless faced the threat to man's position arising from his alleged proportion to nature and his nothingness before the infinity of space.[20] Human imagination taught Pascal that man was unique in nature. Man belonged to nature and transcended it, was superior to its minuteness and was threatened by its vastness. In short, man was dislodged from nature. But for Pascal, this argued for his uniqueness rather than for his insignificance. Thus the mechanical conception of the world was not accepted without some protests in both philosophy and science.

In the instance of Galileo, the problem was further complicated through the rebirth in this period of the atomism of Democritus. The atomist tradition flourished in the centres with which Galileo was associated, namely Paris and North Italy. The atomist position was already widely held at the turn of the seventeenth century, though it did not come to full bloom until after the middle of the century. But it is important to note that this philosophy was not adopted by Galileo and others in the light of their mechanical, mathematical discoveries; it had already become a powerful and independent philosophical position before it affected scientific understanding.[21] Atomism was of particular service to Galileo in eliminating needless aspects of Aristotelian thought with reference to terrestrial as opposed to celestial matters.

But the affirmation of small, self-contained, indivisible atoms also reinforced a theory of matter and motion which needed no reference, outside itself. Even if such a conception was held in a theological frame of meaning, it inevitably meant the development of a natural theology independent of revelation.[22] Still, in that context, atomism could have been accommodated. But when atomism was joined to a mechanical conception of the universe, serious philosophical and theological problems followed. The situation was further complicated by the fact that Galileo's theological views, just like his scientific outlook,

[20] Pascal accepted the challenge of Nicholas of Cusa and of Bruno with respect to infinity.
[21] See Anneliese Maier, *Die Mechanisierung des Weltbilds im 17. Jahrhundert*, Forschungen zur Geschichte der Philosophie und der Pädagogik (Leipzig, 1938), Heft 18, pp. 11, 12, 31.
[22] We have noted that the original theological impulse was quite the contrary.

were wedded to his philosophical ideas. This was still further aggravated by the fact that Galileo could not refrain from making pronouncements whenever his scientific work and the religious heritage encountered each other.

Galileo's attack on the authority of Scripture in determining scientific truth elicits our sympathy. He wrote:

> . . . I think that in discussions of physical problems we ought to begin not from the authority of scriptural passages, but from sense-experiences and necessary demonstrations; for the holy Bible and the phenomena of nature proceed alike from the divine Word, the former as the dictate of the Holy Ghost and the latter as the observant executrix of God's commands. It is necessary for the Bible, in order to be accommodated to the understanding of every man, to speak many things which appear to differ from the absolute truth so far as the bare meaning of the words is concerned. But Nature, on the other hand, is inexorable and immutable; she never transgresses the laws imposed upon her, or cares a whit whether her abstruse reasons and methods of operation are understandable to men. For that reason it appears that nothing physical which sense-experience sets before our eyes, or which necessary demonstrations prove to us, ought to be called in question (much less condemned) upon the testimony of biblical passages which may have some different meaning beneath their words. For the Bible is not chained in every expression to conditions as strict as those which govern all physical effects; nor is God any less excellently revealed in Nature's actions than in the sacred statements of the Bible.[23]

In the same section from which this passage is taken, Galileo further delineated his view of Scripture. Scripture was valid with reference to those truths which were above reason and which the Spirit made known. But it had no authority on other matters, such as astronomy. Moreover, the Bible hardly touched on astronomical matters. Where it did, it must be interpreted through the principle of accommodation.[24] Theology, as the interpreter of Scripture, was

[23] Galileo, op. cit., pp. 182-3.
[24] Ibid., pp. 181-82. Nevertheless, Galileo went to great length to try to show that the passage concerning the sun standing still actually corresponded to the Copernican system,

indeed the queen of the sciences. But that designation had reference to the dignity of its subject matter. It did not mean that theology could dictate the subject matter and results of other disciplines. Galileo was acutely aware that theologians had attempted this in areas where they had no competence.[25] Nor did Galileo believe that the arrogance of the theologians would be followed by the conceit of the astronomers. For astronomers, mysteries were increased as discoveries were made. Hence, the glory of God was served well by astronomy.[26]

The total context of Galileo's position, including that expressed in the preceding quotation, was less reassuring for the Christian mind. Two assumptions were sometimes explicit and certainly implicit. Both had to do with the distinction between the Book of Nature and the Book of Scripture. The first assumption was that the Book of Nature was no less significant for the Christian mind than the Book of Scripture. This, just as in the theory of the plurality of worlds, was a threat to Christian understanding. It put nature and Scripture on the same level. For Christians, the drama of salvation had always been central, and therefore more important than nature. If anything, nature ministered to the drama of salvation. But now nature had an independent status to which other truth must conform.

For since every truth is in agreement with all other truth, the truth of Holy Writ cannot be contrary to the solid reasons and experiences of human knowledge.[27]

On one level that is obviously true, but in its context, such a statement carried a hidden dogma.

The second assumption was that the Book of Nature was clearer and more precise than the Book of Scripture. Those who held this view certainly did not intend to depreciate the significance of Scripture. Nevertheless, a tradition was forged in which the increasing clarity discerned through nature was set against the prevailing un-

rather than to the Ptolemaic. Ibid., pp. 211-15. It is interesting that in spite of the attempt to exclude Scripture from the consideration of natural matters, both Kepler and Galileo tried to reconcile the sun passage with the new science. Their principles of interpretation should have left it as " vulgar accommodation."
[25] Ibid., pp. 191-95.
[26] Ibid., p. 196.
[27] Ibid., p. 186. Quoted favourably from Pererius.

clarity in Scripture, with the attendant hope that thereby the latter might be purged of its obscurity. In retrospect, it is clear that this could only be accomplished by a logic which no longer took its cue from the Biblical revelation but from a philosophy which determined the content from its own angle of vision. In Galileo, an independent natural basis for religion had begun to determine the Biblical understanding of revelation. Of this, Galileo was certainly unaware.

Some of the assumptions and implications became crystal clear in Campanella's *Defense of Galileo*, published in 1616. After citing the Bible and many Church Fathers concerning the positive place which nature occupied in matters of faith, he continued as follows:

Bernhard says in a further discourse, " I shall hear what the Lord declares to me: the world is the book of God, in which we should read continually." Nicephorus testifies Saint Anthony believed the same, and so did Chrysostom when he expounded the passage in Psalm 147, " God hath not done in like manner to every nation." No one can be pardoned who rejects the law that he search. Truly, " From all the earth went forth their sound." Corollary. Because the things which are more marvellous and excellent represent more completely their author God, and because their study confirms the divinity of the human soul, they are studied with the greater devotion. Among these things are the heavens and the stars, and the great systems of the world.[28]

Or a passage such as the following:

Therefore wisdom should be sought in the whole book of God, which is the world, where more wisdom always may be discovered. It is to this book and not to the little books of men that Scripture sends us.[29]

These passages were written against the domination of Aristotle and of Scripture. In spite of that context, these passages assume a role for the study of nature, including astronomy, which a Christian nourished by Scripture could not grant. Many of Galileo's concrete statements were true enough; but his total impact with regard to Scripture was

[28] *The Defense of Galileo of Thomas Campanella*, trans. and ed. with notes by Grant McColley, Smith College Studies in History, xxii (1937), p. 19.
[29] Ibid., p. 30.

in the direction of elevating nature to undue significance over against the redemptive history of the Biblical tradition. A rational and mechanical conception of the world had become the centre of nterest.

We indicated previously that Descartes set himself against the dehumanizing implications in the mechanical view of the world. But Descartes also encouraged these implications in that he extended the mechanical, mathematical conceptions and brought them to greater philosophical consistency. Those so minded could ignore the rest of his system and take just this part. Among those who took Descartes seriously and yet felt that the mechanical conception of the world led too easily to a materialistic interpretation was the Englishman, Henry More. In matters of physics, More accepted Descartes. But increasingly, he felt it necessary to interpret the mechanical order in other than merely mechanical terms. More, like Descartes, believed that the essence of reality included extension in time and space. But More insisted that spirit needed to be defined in a similar way, and that therefore a mechanical and spiritual order could be affirmed simultaneously. He expressed this identity in the designation "plastic nature."

Descartes' notion of extension also raised problems for the relation of God to the concept of space. Since the time of Galileo, time and space tended to be regarded as literal spatial systems as contrasted with previous views which were generally more symbolic than literal. This new view meant that God, if He were not to be removed again from the realm of nature, had to be conceived in spatial terms. Henry More was never clear how God and space were to be identified; but that they were, he affirmed. Occasionally, space was defined as the omnipresence of God. Henry More had genuine theological interests; but he did not succeed in working out a satisfactory relation of God to the world. The same was true of William Barrow, who also reflected on the co-existence of God and Space.

At this point, it may be helpful to summarize what we have said. Between the first and sixth decades of the seventeenth century, there was considerable evidence for the rejection of the Ptolemaic world picture. This marks a decided contrast to the situation which prevailed between the time of Copernicus and the first decade of the seventeenth century. Nevertheless, even in the decades extending well past the middle of the seventeenth century, there was no final proof of the Copernican view and the system of Brahe was widely held. During this period, Galileo was condemned, while in Protestant universities, Copernicanism was increasingly taught. But there were also philosophical and theological assumptions in the new science which could not easily be reconciled with central Christian concerns. Kepler represented mathematical, mystical convictions combined with a dash of Christian insight; and the Catholic Galileo revealed an incipient rationalism which, for all his protestations to the contrary, raised serious questions concerning the understanding of Christianity. Alongside such judgments, one must also state that the Protestant and Catholic traditions were not without blame for their own obscurantist and dogmatic claims.

For the Protestant mind, the problem was complicated by ancillary developments. We noted Melanchthon's interest in astrology, and also that the appearances of comets were considered to be signs from heaven. Beza had written a poem in which the appearance of a star was considered a sign of the end of the world. The Reformation period had been full of eschatological expectations. Protestant thinkers generally took the position that the stars bore some relation to human history and that the appearance of stars was a sign of God's activity. Such signs were generally interpreted as indicating God's displeasure. But predictions concerning the future were generally frowned upon by theologians.

Many of the scientists were also astrologers. It was one of the ways of making a livelihood. The Englishmen Recorde and Digges, and indeed both Brahe and Kepler, engaged in such prognostications. The close relation between astronomical thought and astrological matters is not to be ignored in seeking the theological basis for whatever suspicion of science there was. It was another instance in which the events of history were read through what was seen in nature. The stars held the secret of history and an ordered conception of nature expressed its character. Astrology and a mechanical conception of the world both focused attention on nature, over against history. Nature was no longer understood in Biblical terms. In the Bible what happened to man was reflected in nature; now nature externalized and mechanically understood, was considered to be the key for the proper interpretation of man and history.

Whatever the evidence against the Ptolemaic system and for the Copernican position, the issue of concern was still philosophical, not scientific. The theologians on the Continent still thought of Aristotle as a greater ally to the Christian cause than the new philosophy. On the whole, the new philosophy appeared alien to their concerns. Science eventually had to make its way in spite of the philosophy associated with it, even in the period after Aristotelianism had been rejected. The philosophy of the new science appeared too antagonistic to be taken up by the theologians.

The Protestant Aristotelian Scholasticism, the beginnings of which we sketched in the previous chapter, came to classical expression at the precise time when the new science received its first genuine confirmation in the work of Kepler and Galileo. This fact is of crucial significance if we are to understand the subsequent conflicts. The opposition between the new science and the Aristotelian theologians continued on the continent throughout the seventeenth century, though here and there new adaptations were made. While Aristotle's general hold on the university scene had abated by the end of the seventeenth century, the theologians still clung to him. The hold of Aristotle on English thinkers had been broken by the middle of the century, though there were pockets of resistance within the universities. Consequently, we shall next consider the continental theological scene as a unit throughout the seventeenth century, treating the English scene separately.

B: PROTESTANT SCHOLASTICISM EXTENDED
AND CHALLENGED

We have just stated that the Aristotelian hegemony in theology received classic Protestant formulation at the precise time when Kepler and Galileo had already made contributions to the further demolition of the Aristotelian-Ptolemaic world view. The Lutheran Gerhard and the Reformed Alsted are two such representative classical figures. Gerhard's aim was to expound the Biblical material with the aid of philosophy. Thus he stood in a heritage to which we have frequently alluded. The effect was that the Biblical material, insofar as it dealt with problems of the world, was definitely seen against the background of Aristotle. Thus Gerhard distinguished between the sublunar world, which included the world of man, and the celestial spheres. The latter included the orbs of the planets, the *primum mobile*, the crystalline spheres, and the empyrean heaven. All motion proceeded from the movement of the outer sphere. The traditional elements, including their appropriate heaviness, are contrasted with the subtlety of the heavens. Aristotle's one fundamental mistake was that he believed in the eternity of the world, a view which was Scripturally untenable. Gerhard goes so far as to say that Aristotle could not have been expected to know otherwise.[30]

Alsted argued in similar and detailed fashion in his *Encyclopedia*. The subtlety of the heavens, their circular motion, including their appropriate swiftness and constancy, all were reiterated in typical fashion.[31]   Much detail was given to distinguishing the various spheres, and of assigning to them their respective characteristics.[32] The immobility of the earth was affirmed on the basis of Scripture, reason and experience. The Scriptural evidence cited was Job 26:7, and Psalms 24 and 104. Under the argument from experience, Copernicus was mentioned by name, with the comment that his hypothesis was principally opposed to astronomy and geography.[33]

In the two decades following the middle of the seventeenth century, the Lutheran Calovius and the Reformed Voetius took a similar position. They quoted Scaliger extensively and referred to Aristotle as much as to Luther and Calvin. They employed Scholastic distinctions. Calovius, for example, distinguished the *causa efficiens*, the *causa im-*

---

[30] For references to the preceding, see E. Troeltsch, *Vernunft und Offenbarung bei Gerhard und Melanchthon* (Göttingen, 1891), p. 41 ff.
[31] *Alstedii Cursus Philosophici Encyclopaedia*, Herborn, pp. 18, 430-31.
[32] Ibid., pp. 981-1016.   [33] Ibid., p. 1354.

pulsiva, and the *causa instrumentalis*; or the *materia creationis*, the *forma creationis*, the *finis creationis*, the *tempus creationis*, and the *consequentia creationis*.[34]

Nevertheless, astronomical problems were more extensively discussed by Calovius and Voetius than by Gerhard and Alsted. They frequently made reference to Copernicus, Kepler, and Galileo. Reference was also made to the Pythagorean philosophy and to the new science generally. Calovius listed the arguments for and against the new science, together with a list of individuals who subscribed to each. His own defence of the older position, however, rested more upon Scriptural passages, particularly from Genesis and the Psalms, than upon philosophical assumptions.[35] Copernicus, he declared, was to have no more authority than the word of God on natural matters. Voetius, by contrast, was a full-fledged Scholastic theologian. Hence the philosophical arguments against the new astronomy loomed larger in his thought. But Voetius also defended the older astronomy on Biblical grounds.[36]

In the Protestant orthodox development of the seventeenth century, philosophical and Biblical motifs were intertwined. The theologians varied only in the degree to which one or the other aspect received greater stress. Certainly, in the first half of the seventeenth century and for the most part in the succeeding decades, stress fell upon philosophy as an aid to the proper explication and understanding of the Bible. Philosophy had no independent status and its concepts only unwittingly influenced theological content. The notion of double truth was usually resisted. Philosophical truth had to give way to Biblical truth, on the assumption that any deviation was either untrue, the result of a poor interpretation, or the product of a failure to make proper distinctions. Gerhard still distinguished between reason and that which was above reason. He apparently had no inkling that the latter might contradict the former. For example, he said that when

Theology teaches that Mary brought forth and yet remained a virgin, a truly sensible philosophy does not say this assertion is con-

[34] Abraham Calovius, *Systema locorum theologicorum*, Tomus tertius, pp. 889-901.
[35] Ibid., pp. 1036-49, particularly.
[36] *Voetii Selectae Disputationes Theologicae* (1648), pp. 608, 689-98.

trary to its conclusion, that it is impossible for a virgin to bear a child, because it knows that that conclusion must necessarily be received with this limitation, that for a virgin to *bring forth a child naturally* and yet remain a virgin, is impossible. Nor does Theology assert the contrary of this, for it says, *by supernatural and divine power it came to pass* that a virgin brought forth a child.[37] While such a distinction was still powerful in such concerns, it was no longer viable in astronomical matters. One could either abandon the belief that the Bible combined scientific truth, or affirm Biblical statements against the new science. Wherever philosophy was strictly employed as a helpmeet in interpreting a total deposit of truth in the Bible, the new science had to be rejected.

In the preceding chapter, we delineated the way in which the Bible had become a book of knowledge. This development reached its most extreme form at the very time when the new science was in a position to call it into question. In this sense, the view of the Bible as a book of knowledge reached its zenith along with the older, Aristotelian philosophy. The only change in Biblical understanding from that of the earlier Protestant orthodox statements was a greater insistence upon the *inspired*, infallible and inerrant text. Until shortly prior to the seventeenth century, revelation and inspiration of the Bible stood in an integral relation, with the latter definitely subsumed under the former. Now revelation and inspiration were severed. The consequence was that the inspiration of the Bible depended upon its dictation, upon the literal inerrancy of the text. The authority of the Bible rested on its having been dictated by God. That premise was not doubted in the debates on the nature of inspiration, as, for example, with reference to the problem of the vowel points of the Hebrew text, or whether God used or overrode the natural knowledge of the writers. While Luther and Calvin, as indicated previously, had moved from the authority of the Biblical word to the inerrancy of the text, now in this new situation, the reverse had taken place, Under the intense battle with Roman Catholicism over the authority of the

---

[37] Quoted by H. Schmid, *The Doctrinal Theology of the Evangelical Lutheran Church*, trans. Hay and Jacobs (Philadelphia, 1889), p. 44.

Bible, the Protestant orthodox defended the Bible as a recorded document of the very words of God Himself. The authority of the Bible did not rest in the context of the community of faith or of the Church. That would have been a concession to the enemy. The Bible, in good seventeenth-century form, was as such an unambiguous and absolute authority. The total Bible was the deposit of the actual words of God, even if given through the medium of human hands.[38] The Word of God was now the words of God.

Such a view of the Bible demanded its defence to the last iota of the text. Matters of geography and science belonged to the words of God as well as to all aspects of faith. For many, the theory of accommodation of Biblical passages to common ways of thinking would have been a hole in the dyke which would have grown to the point of destroying the dyke itself. Hence, a wooden literalism was embraced, since any other interpretation appeared as an acid that would eventually work the total corrosion of the authority of the Bible. Thus Calovius wrote:

No error, even in unimportant matters, no defect of memory, not to say untruth, can have any place in all the Sacred Scriptures.[39]

Voetius, in more sophisticated fashion, distinguished between the *authentia historica* and *authentia normalis* or *praecepti*. The latter had reference to the centre of the faith. But that made no difference inasmuch as the theory did not allow for any mistake even in details having no relation to faith.[40] Even Riisin, who was willing to concede flaws in the manuscripts, did not thereby concede that the pure text of Scripture could be scientifically wrong.[41]

Passages such as these can be quoted at random from seventeenth-century Lutheran and Reformed writers. Everything rested upon the accuracy of the deposit of knowledge in the Bible. Formally, it was a book of knowledge like other books of knowledge. Its

[38] For a sympathetic discussion of this viewpoint, see R. Preus, *The Inspiration of Scripture* (London: Oliver and Boyd, 1955).
[39] Quoted by Schmid, op. cit., p. 60, from *Systema Locorum Theologicorum*, Tom. I, p. 551.
[40] H. Heppe, *Reformed Dogmatics*, trans. G. T. Thomson, George Allen (London, 1950), pp. 26-27.
[41] Ibid., p. 28.

superiority rested upon its author, whose veracity was not to be doubted.

The impact of such a view of the Bible upon theological thought should not be underestimated. It brought a false view of theology into being which persisted even after adaptations were made on scientific matters. Theology, as the orderly development of Biblical content, had been transformed into an exercise in formulating propositional statements of truth. The only variation which emerged was the inability to decide which propositions had to be accepted. The Lutherans debated over which fundamental articles of faith it was necessary to accept. When it became apparent that new knowledge could no longer be ignored, the number of propositions was reduced. In fact, the history of the development from the most orthodox theologians to theologians of the Enlightenment is precisely the reduction in the number and nature of such propositional statements. This mode of Biblical interpretation continued long after the literal defences of the Bible collapsed. Here we are ahead of our story. But it does indicate the fateful consequences for theology which attended such an interpretation of the Bible. The question was no longer how the Spirit and the Biblical message coincided in the mystery whereby men become believers. And this had consequences for theology at every point.

One major theological consequence was the change that this involved for the relation between philosophical knowledge and the Bible. Whereas for Gerhard all natural knowledge of God had to give way if there was any contradiction in the Bible,[42] now two independent levels of knowledge developed in the Protestant theological field. Philosophy was no longer subservient to Biblical understanding. It no longer served only to lead to a Biblical truth. It now had an independent role. This had precisely been the position of Galileo and of the Roman Catholic, generally. In principle, the Roman Catholics could have been more open to the new science through the different levels of nature and Biblical revelation. But for other reasons, including also the clear adherence to Aristotle, this did not turn out to be the case. For an increasing number of Protestants, the affirmation of

[42] Schmid, op. cit., p. 47.

two levels appeared as an answer. One could give to philosophy and science all matters of the natural order, and to Scripture, all things relating to faith. This did not mean that there was to be no crossing of lines from one to the other. Musaeus, for instance, made concessions on details pertaining to nature in the Bible; but such details still possessed a supernatural meaning.[43] But the knowledge of science also had a theological meaning. It still was the *other* book of God, His other word alongside Scripture.

This position was elaborated by such Protestants as Hülselmann and Musaeus. It was not by accident that the Roman Catholics considered that these men were genuine Scholastic theologians. They quoted them and held them in esteem. Nevertheless, the notion of the two books, now distinct but each equally true in its own right, was full of danger. One could concentrate on either book, the natural or the revealed; but insofar as the latter was defined in terms of knowledge or propositional truth, it was determined by the former. The battle was increasingly between nature and Scripture. That is why some Protestants continued to oppose the notion of double truth, or of accommodation, or of the two books. Their instincts were correct, but their position was obscurantist.

In the preceding pages we indicated that Protestant Scholasticism between the years 1610-1660, while built upon the Scholastic thought of the previous decades, developed certain distinctive and inflexible characteristics. On individual problems, the views continued much as before and it would be superfluous to go through them. But it may be helpful to illustrate the continuity by indicating the views on causation and purpose.

In this period, God's relation to secondary causes was expressed through the concept of God's concurrence. This term became particularly important in the later Newtonian world. It was a means whereby secondary causes were accepted in their regular order but understood as grounded in God with reference to their existence and operation. J. H. Heidegger, for instance, wrote:

[43] B. Pünjer, *History of the Christian Philosophy of Religion from the Reformation to Kant,* trans. W. Hastie (Edinburgh, 1887), p. 165.

Concurrence or co-operation is the operation of God by which He co-operates directly with the second causes as depending upon Him alike in their essence as in their operation, so as to urge or move them to action and to operate along with them in a manner suitable to a first cause and adjusted to the nature of second causes.[44]

But beyond the level of secondary causation, Heidegger, as others, continued to affirm God's activity apart from all causation.

Government is direct, when God either does not use second causes or uses them above, beyond and counter to their nature . . . But he is not said ever to have done anything contrary to universal nature, i.e., the order of the whole universe, to which He bound Himself of His own free will. But he frequently operated without means, beyond and counter to them, to show that all things are by Him or his proximate and direct goodness.[45]

Similar passages are to be found in Keckermann, Alsted, Gerhard, Van Till, and others.

The concept of purpose was of course closely allied with the concept of causation. Purpose and causation had in common the notion that God's relation to every aspect of the world was direct and active. Moreover, it was considered necessary to spell out every purpose in detail. As one reads such detailed and tedious descriptions, one wonders if the concept of mechanism provided not only a way in which nature was depopulated of spirits but also a relief from the endless elaboration of purpose. But this problem will receive fuller treatment when we deal with the concept of design in a subsequent chapter. It is sufficient here to emphasize that a mechanical conception of the universe had much to be said for it when one was confronted either by a world of spirits or by an overly elaborated series of purposes.

Aristotelianism reigned supreme until the middle of the seventeenth century. But in the second part of the century, the situation was mixed. There was a group who held firmly to the orthodox Aristotelian outlook, defying all opposition. In 1665, Georgicus Agricola objected to the Copernican system on the basis that the earth could not be a star or we would all be in heaven! This was not untypical of their method

[44] *Quoted by* Heppe, op. cit., p. 258.   [45] Ibid., pp. 263-64.

of argument. The favourite philosophers of these theologians were, in addition to the venerated Scaliger, the nearer contemporaries, Christoph Scheibler, widely known as the Protestant Suarez, and Daniel Cramer, philosopher and preacher. The last-ditch Aristotelians included Thomas Wagner (1677); Johannes Weiss (1630-83); John Christian Lange (1664-1723); Valentin Alberti (1635-97); Kaspar Posner (1626-1700); and Georg Paschius (1661-1707).[46]

There was some opposition to Aristotelianism before the middle of the century. But it was not until after the middle of the century that such opposition proved to be effective. William Ames (1651) had called metaphysics the work of the devil. Johann Arndt, still earlier in the century, had simply ignored the philosophical problem in his exposition of *True Christianity*. From the philosophical side, the Aristotelian domination was challenged through the work of Descartes. Descartes had his impact on theology primarily in the Netherlands. There his thought was frequently amalgamated with Aristotle's, with the result that the Cartesian position could equally well be held along with or in opposition to the Copernican system. Moreover, Cartesianism was theologically no less intellectual or rationalist than Aristotelianism.[47]

One of the most prominent of the Cartesian theologians was Christoph Wittich. He distinguished between Biblical passages which needed to be understood according to their vulgar sense and those which testified to doctrine. On the basis of this concept of accommodation, he defended the work of Copernicus.[48] But the Leyden theological faculty, standing in the tradition of Voetius, judged the Copernican system to be against Scripture.[49] Wittich further insisted that theology could not dictate the truth of philosophy. Philosophy did not exist merely to serve theology. But the most positive use of

---

[46] P. Petersen, *Geschichte der aristotelischen Philosophie im protestantischen Deutschland* (Leipzig, 1921), pp. 396-98.
[47] Partially this may also come from Descartes' own hesitation in the light of what happened to Galileo.
[48] *Consensus veritatis in scriptura divina et infallibili revelatae cum veritate philosophica a Renato des Cartes detecta* (1659).
[49] J. Bohatec, *Die cartesianische Scholastik in der Philosophie und reformierten Dogmatik des 17. Jahrhunderts* (Erster Teil; Leipzig, 1912), p. 43.

Descartes was made by Balthasar Bekker, who held a co-ordinate view of reason and Scripture. The Scriptures dealt with salvation, and reason with nature. This distinction made possible and necessary the abolition of everything which interfered with the essential order of either. Thus the superstitious world of spirits and devils had to go. On the basis of the mechanical world of Cartesianism, he was able to depopulate nature of its evil spirits. [50]

Although frequently forbidden, Cartesianism made its way in the Dutch scene. Among German Lutherans, however, the views of Descartes made little headway, though some German students studied Cartesianism in Holland. In Germany itself, Altsdorf was the only university at which Cartesianism was freely taught. Among the Reformed in the German scene the situation was the same as among the Lutherans. While representatives of Cartesianism were found in German universities toward the end of the century, there is no evidence that the influence on the theological scene was great. [51]

The reasons for theological opposition to Descartes are obvious enough. His positive views were unacceptable. They contradicted a basic Christian understanding. (The Roman Catholics placed his writings on the Index). Further, his complete separation of philosophy and theology was methodologically unacceptable. [52]

A number of other theologians unwittingly helped to undermine the authority of Aristotle. Afraid of the new science, they took refuge in the Bible and ignored all philosophical questions. Some, like Leonard Hutter, accepted neither Ptolemy, nor Aristotle, nor Copernicus. [53] As late as 1707, Hollaz still stood against Copernicus, primarily because the latter's system was unbiblical. Francis Turretin, while still

[50] For a discussion of Bekker, see E. Hirsch, *Geschichte der neuern evangelischen Theologie* (Gütersloh, 1949), Erster Band, p. 209 ff.

[51] J. Bohatec wrote the first part of his proposed two-volume work, *Die cartesianische Scholastik in der Philosophie und reformierten Dogmatik des 17. Jahrhunderts* in 1912. The first part deals with the philosophical tradition, but the part on the Reformed dogma never appeared. For an extensive account of the scene in the Netherlands, see E. Bizer; " Die reformierte Orthodoxie und der Cartesianismus," *Zeitschrift für Theologie und Kirche* (1958), pp. 306-72.

[52] For a discussion of the German opposition, see Gustav Frank, *Geschichte der protestantischen Theologie* (Zweiter Teil; Leipzig, 1865), p. 75 ff.

[53] Elert, op. cit., I, p. 377.

Scholastic in many ways, based his opposition primarily on Biblical grounds. Among such writers, Moses took on increasing authority, and the Book of Genesis was thought of as a book of science and of theology. Some found the theological articles of Lutheranism directly in Genesis.[54] But such individuals were definitely fighting a rearguard action.

It is hardly necessary to recapitulate the fateful development of the seventeenth century on the Continent. An inflexible Protestant Scholasticism dominated the scene, and even when it began to crumble, it left behind it the view of an inerrant Scripture. From this tradition, no new departure could be expected. At the same time, it must not be forgotten that philosophical and theological assumptions were inextricably bound to the new science and that even a more flexible Protestantism would have found them unacceptable.

[54] A. Pfeiffer, in *Pansophia Mosaica e Genesi delineata*, Leipzig, (1685), sees all twenty-eight articles of the Augustana in Genesis, and J. Deutschmann, *Theologia Primi Theologi Adami vere Lutherani* (Wittenberg, 1689), sees Adam as the first Lutheran theologian!

IV

The Convergence of Science and Theology
in Seventeenth-Century England

A: CONTROVERSIES THROUGH THE MIDDLE
OF THE CENTURY

The glory of seventeenth-century science belongs to England. After Galileo and Kepler, the great stars in science were to be found in England. Moreover, the relation between science and theology developed differently than on the Continent. The absence of the intense Catholic problem of the Continent and the breaking of the influence of Aristotle by the middle of the century created a different ethos.

But in the early decades of the century the situation was no different from that of the Continent. Richard Burton, in *The Anatomy of Melancholy*, argued that the Copernican view was contrary to reason and natural philosophy, and in fact, absurd. In 1612, Nicholas Fuller, the Prebendary of Salisbury, drew up a detailed list of Scriptural texts asserting the immobility of the earth and the mobility of the sun.[1] William Barlow opposed the new position in *A Brief Discovery of the Idle Animadversions of Marke Ridley*. Thomas Oberbury and Samuel Purchas also stood against the new science.[2] William Ames, while suspicious of metaphysics, still wrote in Scholastic Aristotelian form not dissimilar to that of the continental Scholastics. Alexander Gil's

[1] *Miscellaneorum Theologicorum Libri* III.
[2] Thomas Oberbury, *The Miscellaneous Works* . . . (London, 1856); Samuel Purchas, *His Pilgrimage* (London, 1617).

Sacred Philosophy of the Holy Scripture, written in 1625 but published after the author's death in 1635, was still a Scholastic volume.

The Ross-Wilkins controversy well describes the situation in England toward the middle of the century. Alexander Ross was known as "a divine, a poet, and an historian," and nothing lay outside his interests. John Wilkins became a bishop and combined his ecclesiastical affairs with an intense interest in science. He was the leading spirit in the small group which eventually became the Royal Society. The technical qualifications of both men can hardly be doubted, and hence they can serve as a barometer of how the issues appeared at the time. Ross wrote his *Commentum de Terrae Motu* (London, 1634) in reaction to two published volumes, *Geography Delineated*, 1625, by Nathaniel Carpenter, and *Commentationes in Motum Terrae Diurnum et Annuum*, 1630, by Philip Lansberg. While Carpenter did not present a completely Copernican position, he did bring Scriptural passages and aspects of the new science into some unity. Lansberg, on the other hand, rejected the authority of the Scriptural passages usually cited against the motion of the earth. But it was John Wilkins who carried on the debate. Wilkins' work, *That the Earth May Be a Planet*, brought forth the following volume from Ross:

The New Planet no Planet or, The Earth no wandering Star; except in the wandering heads of the Galileans. Here out of the principles of divinity, philosophy, astronomy, reason and sense, the Earth's immutability is asserted; the true sense of Scripture in this point, cleared; the Fathers and Philosophy vindicated; divers Theological and Philosophical points handled, and Copernicus, his opinion, as erroneous, ridiculous and impious, fully refuted by Alexander Ross. In answer to a discourse, that the Earth may be a planet.[3]

As on the Continent the debate raged around the question of the relative authority of philosophy, especially Aristotle, and Scripture. Ross did not contend that Aristotle was always to be followed; but he did believe that in attacking such a traditional authority the burden of proof rested with the aggressors. In that situation, he suggested, one did not start on equal terms, and more than the usual evidence

[3] London, 1646. In this period, the full title of a book revealed its contents.

was required. In fact, Ross used all the Aristotelian arguments; the heavy elements need to be at the lowest spatial place, hell must be situated at the centre of the earth, the earth must be placed at the centre of the universe for the sake of the drama of man, and the heavens must move about the centre, the earth.[4] Wilkins very perceptively suggested that this was a system in which theological affirmations rested upon proper physical position or place. The earth being the centre, Wilkins retorted:

> . . . is grounded upon the following uncertainties: 1. that hell must needs be situated in the centre of our earth. 2. that the heaven of the blessed must needs be concentrical to that of the stars. 3. that places must be as far distant in situation as in use.[5]

In short, Wilkins objected to the self-evident authority which was accredited Aristotle. Had not Aristotle himself made mistakes which churchmen already had to correct? Wilkins wrote:

> I must needs grant, that we are all much beholden to the industry of the ancient philosophers, and more especially to Aristotle, for the greater part of our learning; but yet 'tis not ingratitude to speak against him, when he opposeth truth; for then many of the fathers would be very guilty, especially Justin, who hath writ a treatise purposely against him.[6]

Moreover, Aristotle would certainly have accepted the evidence of the new science were he living then. The latter, we might add, is not an unfamiliar argument in the history of thought.

But Ross was afraid of the philosophical alternatives to Aristotle, and he realized that they were largely associated with the new science. With characteristic lack of refined language, Ross stated that Pythagoras was a sorcerer and pedlar of absurdities.[7] Further, his defence of the inerrant Bible was against those whose philosophical assumptions definitely ran counter to the Christian understanding.

For whosoever denied hell to be below, denied that there was any

[4] Alexander Ross, *The New Planet No Planet*, p. 58 ff.
[5] J. Wilkins, " That the Earth May Be a Planet," in *The Mathematical and Philosophical Works of the Right Reverend John Wilkins* (London, 1802), p. 190.
[6] J. Wilkins, " That the Moon May Be a World," in op. cit., p. 16.
[7] A. Ross, *The New Planet No Planet*, p. 6.

such place at all; as Pythagoras, Epicurus, Lucretius, Tully, Seneca, Lucian, Pliny, and some others; to whom I may add the Gnostics, who held there was no other hell, but this world, whom Irenaeus refutes.[8]

Ross insisted upon both the Aristotelian and the Biblical understanding because the alternatives appeared to him to deny the Christian view of life. It was in this context too that Ross could not accept the notion of accommodation, that the Holy Spirit, as Wilkins put it, spoke popular untruth in order that the truth might be understood.[9] Ross was willing enough to affirm that the Bible was not intentionally a book of philosophy. But this was no reason for refusing to accept the Bible as written or for saying that there was no philosophical truth in Scripture.[10] If there were no philosophical implications in Scripture, two disastrous implications followed. In the first place, it laid the Christian open to a diversity of philosophical assumptions with no way of deciding between them. Ross in fact found his own situation reminiscent of the early Church.

It is but a conceit of yours to say, that the Scripture accommodates itself to the vulgar conceits, in saying, the Sun riseth and falleth. I warrant you, if the vulgar should conceive that the heavens were made of water, as the Gnostics held; or that the Sun and Moon were two ships, with the Manichees; or that the world was made of the sweat of the Aeons, with the Valentinians; or whatsoever absurd opinion they should hold, you would make the Scripture say so, and to accommodate itself to their conceits.[11]

Just as the philosophical import of Scripture had to be used to reject Gnosticism in the early Church, so Ross believed it had to be used to reject the various unacceptable philosophical claims of his own time. But the situation is not entirely analogous. Behind and beneath the philosophical assumptions of the new science there had emerged an authentic methodology quite different from the mystery mongering of the ancients exhibited in the above passage.

[8] Ibid., p. 59.
[9] J. Wilkins, *That the Earth May Be a Planet*, pp. 159-60; *That the Moon May Be a World*, p. 19.
[10] A. Ross, *The New Planet No Planet*, p. 15.   [11] Ibid., p. 14.

In the second place, Ross saw in the new science and its philosophy an invasion into the prerogative of God's activity. That the earth stood still and that the sun moved was a testimony to the miraculous work of God's supernatural power. It was part and parcel of the conviction that there could be no independent motion or causation in the world.

You would have the earth to be both the efficient and final cause of its motion: But indeed it is neither the one nor the other, for if it move at all, it must be moved by another mover than itself: and God made the heavens not for the earth, but for man; so the diurnal and annual motions have man for their final cause, and heavenly movers for their efficient.[12]

Both extraordinary and ordinary happenings exhibited the power of God, but for Ross, the first was the basis for understanding the latter. The supernatural was the basis for understanding the natural, not the other way around. Hence, miracle guaranteed a dimension necessary for understanding the natural order. Thus the stage was set for a most unhappy development. It was rightly felt that the mystery of God's activity was threatened by the assumptions inherent in the new science; but the only way that seemed available to protect this mystery was a pronounced emphasis on miracle and prophecy.

Although Wilkins maintained the principle of accommodation, he too could not simply declare that Biblical passages so interpreted were to be left at that level. He created a number of problems for himself. He so naturalized the meaning of such passages that no theological point remained. It was possible to accept, as had been suggested by some on the Continent, that not everything in the Bible on the natural level was true, and still affirm a theological point in such passages. In such an interpretation, the passages could be said to point to a transcendent mystery beyond the natural. But while for Wilkins God was the author of the natural, his decisive focus was on nature or the natural order, not on Him who was the author of nature. That was why Ross found the following statement by Wilkins to be so offensive:

Astronomy proves a God and a Providence . . . (and) a more

[12] Ibid., p. 107.

accurate and diligent inquiry into their natures, will raise our understandings unto a nearer knowledge, and greater admiration of the Deity . . . Likewise may it serve to confirm unto us the truth of the Holy Scripture.[13]

The vigorous response of Ross was as follows:

But take heed you play not the anatomist upon these celestial bodies, (whose inward parts are hid from you) in the curious and needless search of them; you may well lose yourself, but this way you shall never find God. Whereas you say, that astronomy serves to confirm the truth of Holy Scripture: you are very preposterous, for you will have the truth of Scripture confirmed by Astronomy, but you will not have the truth of Astronomy confirmed by Scripture.[14]

The debate whether the world may be a moon, as the title of one of Wilkins's books expressed it, was here, as on the Continent, a symptom of the real problem. It had direct relevance only insofar as it raised a question concerning the extent to which the Bible contained knowledge about the whole universe. The endless debate about whether or not God would have mentioned the existence of other worlds in Scripture—an argument complicated indeed by the fact that there was no reference to the planets—was the fruitless form of debate for a much deeper problem. The real issue again was the relative authority of reason and nature versus Scripture. Ross was a conservative of the first order who was wrong on every point; but while he reacted defensively, he was right in sensing a threat to Christian understanding. Wilkins, though a bishop of the Church, inadvertently prepared the ground for the kind of natural theology which was not only independent of the Christian substance, but became a substitute for it. In fact, Wilkins wrote a book entitled, *Of the Principles and Duties of Natural Religion.* It was first published after his death in 1672 but by 1710 was already in its sixth edition. To such natural religion, Wilkins considered revealed religion to be an aid. It was exactly this type of approach which became evident in a more extreme form in deism and in a type of natural theology which gained

[13] Quoted by Grant McColley, " The Ross-Wilkins Controversy," *Annals of Science,* III (1938), p. 161.
[14] A. Ross, *The New Planet No Planet,* p. 117.

a foothold in Anglicanism and provided the context for the birth of Methodism.

Wilkins, as we have already indicated, was one of the moving spirits in the Gresham group and among those who formed the Royal Society. In this period, the new Royal Society, destined as it was to have such an illustrious history, was also a good barometer of the problem confronting the Church. Part of the opposition to the Society stemmed from rigid Aristotelians, and the Society, like Wilkins, had to defend itself against those who absolutized Aristotle. Part of the membership was composed of orthodox Christians.[15] Some were deists; and others had rationalized the nature of the faith in a fashion similar to that of Wilkins. Thomas Sprat, in his defence of the Royal Society, was quite revealing with respect to the latter position. His fundamental thesis was that the Church had nothing to lose but everything to gain from the Society. In the first place, the Society was engaged in the business of advancing the knowledge of God obtainable through natural philosophy. This part of divinity, he maintained, had rightly been taken from theology and given to experimental philosophy.[16] Sprat, like Wilkins and others of his day, was enamoured by the marvellous workmanship of God disclosed through the microscope.[17] A new world had come into being, and indeed the marvels of creation lay before anyone who cared to look. It was as if, through the telescope and the microscope, one had returned to the paradise of Adam.

Sprat argued that the Bible itself was replete with natural religion. To reject natural religion was to reject Genesis, Job, the Psalms, and parts of other books of Scripture.[18] Sprat was not at all aware that a Biblical understanding of nature could be different than that of natural philosophy or natural theology. In fact, the inability to see this was precisely the problem. Sprat himself was aware that the Society was accused of engendering a spirit of impartial philosophical inquiry

[15] Merton's study does show that statistically, the Puritans were the most significant group. But it is not clear in how far this is a theological or a sociological fact, nor precisely what the term Puritan includes. See R.K. Merton, *Science, Technology and Society in Seventeenth-Century England*, Osiris, 4 (1938), pp. 360–624.
[16] Thomas Sprat, *History of the Royal Society* (St. Louis, 1959), p. 82.
[17] Ibid., p. 348 ff.   [18] Ibid., p. 350.

which challenged the essentials of the Christian faith.[19] But Sprat saw nothing wrong in approaching the Scripture in the same way in which one derived knowledge from natural observation and experimentation. The conception of knowledge was the same in both cases.

Wherever this approach obtained, revelation was already defined in terms of reason. Where revelation had to be rational, the issues were clear enough; when it had to fit into the rational scheme by being placed above reason, it was still defined in terms of reason. Hence, revelation and natural theology could only be identical or in opposition. But in both instances, revelation was not understood in terms of itself. However ineffectively and mistakenly the more orthodox churchmen went about it, it was this reductionism which they rejected. To our eyes such churchmen present the pitiable situation of defending a level of truth through the perpetuation of old errors. On the other side, Sprat and others defended the distinctively Christian by an affirmation of miracle and prophecy which they considered valid alongside the preponderantly natural. It was their successors who saw that this was quite inconsistent or at least unnecessary.

The historical fact is that the defence of a literal Scripture began to crumble in England by the middle of the seventeenth century. Aristotle also had lost much of his authority, particularly among the scientists, though there were still pockets of resistance in the universities. After 1640, waves of Platonism and of Cartesianism were manifest. Certainly, the more rational spirit of More, Wilkins, or even of Glanville, dominated the remainder of the century and part of the next. By this time more traditional Puritans had already rejected Aristotle and they were generally favourably disposed to the fruits of the new science. They maintained their theological integrity and still accepted the new science. Nor were they afraid of the philosophical assumptions connected with it. We shall return to the Puritan development after looking at the scientific and theological implications in two of the great scientists of the second half of the seventeenth century, namely, Robert Boyle and Isaac Newton.

[19] Ibid., p. 353.

B: THE SCIENCE AND THEOLOGY OF ROBERT BOYLE

Robert Boyle was a great scientist. He laid the foundations for modern chemistry, made great strides in the comprehension of the nature of air pressure and its uses, and carried out many significant experiments of value to those who followed. But his scientific work made no direct impact on the theological scene, such as that created by Copernicus or Galileo. Boyle's scientific labours did not provide a grand new vision of reality. In fact, Boyle is important for this study precisely because he accepted many of the elements of the new science and tried to relate them creatively to Christian thought. Because Boyle himself wrote theological treatises, we have a more complete account of his religious ideas than in the case of the other scientists. Moreover, Boyle was equally interested in science and theology and therefore programmatically tried to do justice to both.[20]

Boyle agreed with Bacon in the rejection of the authority of Aristotle. He accepted a mechanical interpretation of the material aspects of reality, but he rejected the alleged atomistic implications. He stood more in the tradition of Henry More than of Descartes. He accepted the newer science himself, extended it, but disagreed with the current interpretation of those crucial points where the Christian drama was challenged.

Precisely because of this, Boyle was an excellent mirror of what was going on. Occasionally, Boyle is interpreted as one whose commitment to the Christian position was such that he would not draw the conclusions demanded by the new science. But for Boyle himself, his position represented the unity of two loves. One can even grant that for Boyle the religious side was the most important. He espoused missionary causes and established the Boyle lecture sermons. Nevertheless, he affirmed only that the religious affirmations were paramount for the meaning of life, and that in this sense, the scientific area must find its proper place in relation to religion. For Boyle, this did not mean that science was of secondary importance. His scheme of things

[20] The theological writings of Newton, as we shall see, cannot be put on this level.

expressed the subservience of science to theology; but this was not with respect to the method of attainments of science. It had to do only with a total understanding of life. It was, we might add, the old Medieval idea without its presumptuous claims.

Boyle was unwilling to accept the complete division of theology and science, or to accept the notion of double truth.[21] In this, he differed radically from Bacon. Boyle believed that the separation of the two areas created an easy way for scientists to dispense with religious problems or, as in the case of Hobbes, to reduce them to unreality. Boyle pointed out that the study of theology had greatly declined among the physicists.[22] Others, including some divines, talked of God as if He were some

> geometrical figure, or mechanical engine; as if the nature and per-
> fections of that unparalleled Being were objects of their intellect;
> and such abstruse Subjects, within the reach of human reason, or
> familiar objects of sense.[23]

God was the author of the book of nature and of Scripture. In this, Boyle repeated the traditional formulation. But what made Boyle fairly distinctive was his insistence that the two separate books were related to each other and yet did not contradict each other. Genesis and natural philosophy were different, but they had implications for each other. The time of creation belonged to the domain of natural philosophy, but Genesis gave hints about the origin of things which were true over against the speculations of the philosophers.[24] Likewise the Virgin Birth, as with Gerhard, was interpreted both biologically and theologically.[25] Boyle's general conclusion was that:

> if we lay aside all the irrational opinions, that are unreasonably
> fathered on the Christian religion, and all erroneous conceits repug-
> nant to Christianity, which have been groundlessly fathered upon
> Philosophy, the seeming contradictions betwixt Divinity and true
> Philosophy, will be but few, and the real ones none at all.[26]

---

[21] For a general discussion, see Harold Fisch, " The Scientist as Priest: A Note on Robert Boyle's Natural Theology," *Isis* XLIV (1953), pp. 252-65.
[22] Ibid., p. 259.
[23] *The Theological Works of the Honourable Robert Boyle*, ed. Richard Boulton (London, 1715), III, 211.   [24] Ibid., p. 9.   [25] Boyle, op. cit., I, 385.   [26] Ibid., p. 398.

The distinctiveness and yet interrelatedness of natural philosophy and theology was further illustrated in Boyle's analysis of causation and of purpose. He refused to banish final causes, as Descartes had done on the supposition that they were unknowable.[27] But Boyle argued that one started with efficient causes in physics and that investigation was confined to them.[28] But such concentration, he maintained, did not and could not exclude concerns beyond that level. For Boyle, the order and symmetry of the world argued for intelligent design rather than the concatenation of undirected atoms. This is but one illustration of Boyle's awareness of the necessity of seeing different levels of reality.[29] At the same time, he saw that such levels needed to be carefully distinguished.

Boyle did not accept the notion that everything in creation was made for man; nor did he exclude man from the purposes of creation. Some things were made for man's use and testified to his significance in the total drama of the cosmos. But an exclusive concern with man and this earth limited one's conception and made it impossible to conceive of God's design and purpose with reference to other planets.[30] He considered the whole matter of purposes and ends to be complex. It was equally wrong to see purpose everywhere, or not to see it at all. God indeed may have had many purposes.

And that Divine providence had several Ends, in making the World, and the several creatures that compose it, some of which are hid to us and others known, is evident, some being made for the manifestation of the Glory of God, others the usefulness of man, or the maintainance of the System of the world, with respect to particular Creatures or the propagation of their kinds.[31]

Or in another passage,

And here it may not be amiss to take notice, in relation to the opinion, that the whole material world was made for man, that though the arguments we have used may be more probable than others hitherto proposed, against the Vulgar Opinion, especially, as it relates to the Celestial region of the world, yet amongst the ends designed in

[27] Boyle, op. cit., II, 215. [28] Burtt, op. cit., p. 172. [29] Boyle, op. cit., III, 299-300.
[30] Burtt, op. cit., p. 190. [31] Boyle, op. cit., II, 131.

several of his works, especially planets, animals and metals, the usefulness of them were designed chiefly for men, yet God may design several ends in several creatures, which men are not yet aware of; so that men may find other, and more noble uses for several creatures than have yet been discovered.[32]

Boyle was more willing to abandon the notion of purpose in the field of astronomy than he was in that of biology. In physics, he argued, the question of "how" is central; but in biology the question of "why" arises.[33] Moreover, he considered the argument from design to be more convincing in biology than in astronomy.

The situation of the Celestial bodies afford not such strong arguments for the wisdom and design of God, as the bodies of animals and plants; for there seems more admirable contrivance in the muscles of a man's body, than the celestial orbs; and the eye of a fly seems a more curious piece of Work than the body of the sun.[34]

Boyle was particularly conscious of the intricacy of the human eye; more than anything else, the eye seemed to refute atomism.[35]

In contrast to the mystery he found in biology, Boyle also used the symbol of the world as a clock. This metaphor, which subsequently became more important, must be properly understood. Others in the English scene had already used it. For Mornay, it presented a picture of the world which stood against chance and randomness. It affirmed that the world was not capricious. John Robinson regarded the intricacy of a well-made clock as a testimony to the marvels of God's creation. But he added that the difference between God's relation to the world and that of an ordinary artisan to his labours, was that God, unlike the artisan, continued to have a relation, a *concursus*, to that which he had made.[36] In a similar way, Boyle used the metaphor of the clock with reference to the orderly course of the created world. The metaphor served as a weapon against all views in which God dipped into the world and called the discernible and dependable order into question.[37]

[32] Ibid., p. 235.   [33] Fisch, op. cit., p. 5.
[34] Boyle, op. cit., II, 220.   [35] Ibid., pp. 211-12, 221, 251.
[36] John Robinson, *Essays* (2d ed.; London, 1638), p. 31.
[37] Boyle, op. cit., II, 82-83.

Boyle did not believe that God was bound to order. Nevertheless, it was the order of the world which testified to the workmanship of God. But order was not considered a self-evident explanation, as in subsequent thought. Gravity, for example, was a fact; but it was not thereby explained. It remained a mystery. The whole order of nature was shrouded in mystery. For Boyle, and also for Sir Thomas Browne, the domain of nature and of Scripture were analogous in that there were elements of mystery and of clarity in both.[38] But the mystery was as evident in the discernible order as in the miraculous. In this conception, Boyle anticipated Schleiermacher.

Boyle's position was a creative attempt to relate science and theology. At no point did theology dictate the form of a scientific question or the content of the answer. His religious views entered only as he opposed philosophical assumptions which were not necessarily inherent in the new science and which appeared antithetical to a Christian understanding of the world. He saw the difference and yet the interrelatedness between science and theology with a clarity that was unusual for his time.

But his understanding of Christianity was less adequate. There was a sense in which the telescope and Scripture were on the same level for Boyle. This was not so much true in matters of content as of form. While the Bible provided information of a different order than that of the telescope, it was still information. Boyle spoke of true propositions which had been disclosed in Scripture. There were truths which could be said to be true information. Their authenticity was vouched for by the credibility of the original witnesses,[39] by the miracles which served to confirm revealed religion,[40] and by prophecies which had come true. He was confident that remaining obscurities of Scripture would be clarified when, in due time, unfulfilled prophecies would be realized.[41] Such prophecies included exact knowledge of the unknown future. That position, as we shall see, was widely held and created problems incapable of solution.

Still, Boyle was well ahead of his time in Biblical understanding.

[38] This motif, as we have already noted, will be utilized by Bishop Butler in the next century.
[39] Boyle, op. cit., II, 33.   [40] Ibid., pp. 33-34.   [41] Boyle, op. cit., III, 103.

He was not a Biblical literalist. He stated that one had to distinguish between what was said in Scripture and what the Scripture said. Some statements in Scripture were addressed just to its contemporaries, others to future generations.[42] But there was essential clarity in what the Scripture said, and hence, it was reliable. The Gospel and the light of nature taken together were sufficient for salvation.[43]

Boyle was a man of great piety. But it was the piety of a man who stood before two impressive orders of knowledge, namely, nature and Scripture. Both provided one with knowledge. For Boyle, the primary stress was not that the authority of Scripture resided in the mystery of God's redeeming activity made known to men as they were grasped by its power. It was rather that the Bible, like nature, was an attested book of knowledge.

In this Boyle, as the theologians on the Continent, was a creature of his time. His perceptive way of relating science and theology was undermined by his understanding of the Bible as a deposit of knowledge. Boyle was aware of many issues; but he never broke through to new solutions. He strengthened the views of those who defended the truth of Christianity through miracle and prophecy.

C: THE SCIENCE AND THEOLOGY OF ISAAC NEWTON

The scientific revolution begun by Copernicus, furthered so magnificently by Kepler and Galileo, was brought to comprehensive fulfilment through the genius of Isaac Newton. It is generally agreed that the various components of the Newtonian picture were known prior to Newton. But it was Newton's genius to have a vision of, and experimentally verify, a single, unified picture of what we might call scientific reality. Through the so-called universal law of gravitation, Newton was able to bring the disparate scientific achievements of his day into a total picture and to solve most attendant problems as well. He was able to bring order out of confusion, and with comparative simplicity at that. The heavens were indeed more complicated than had been believed, but the basic solution was simpler. In one stroke

[42] Ibid., p. 103.   [43] Ibid., p. 146.

of genius, combined with prodigious work, he had been able to combine the law of inertia of Descartes, the theory of universal gravitation of Roberval, and the centrifugal force of Borelli. It was now apparent that the new science of terrestrial mechanics, to which the experiments of Galileo contributed so much, was also applicable to the celestial spheres. The last hope of an appreciable difference between the terrestrial and the celestial spheres had disappeared.

Newton himself described his early discoveries as follows. He stated that he discovered

> first the binomial theorem, then the method of fluxions, (and then) began to think of gravity extending to the orb of the moon, and having found out how to estimate the force with which a globe, re-revolving within a sphere, presses the surface of the sphere, from Kepler's rule . . . I deduced that the forces which keep the planets in their orb must be reciprocally as the squares of their distances from their centres; and thereby compared the force requisite to keep the moon in her orb with the force of gravity at the surface of the earth, and found them to answer pretty nearly.[44]

This basic discovery became the basis for his scientific success and for the development of a scientific method which was rigorously single and simple in intent if not in actual execution. The fact of the matter was that the principle of universal gravitation served as an adequate description of the movement of the planets. His theory could not only be mathematically described in terms of the mechanical interaction of the planets with each other; it could also serve as a means for predicting as yet unknown planetary activities which were later telescopically confirmed. A single conception of motion, including speed and direction, could be formulated. All bodies had natural properties which made them react on each other. These could now be described in mechanical and mathematical form. Further, it did not matter whether the bodies had reference to something falling to earth, such as a stone from the top of a tower as in the supposed experiments of Galileo, or whether they referred to the influence of two planets on each other. Both instances obeyed the same law. The

[44] Quoted by F. S. Marvin, *The Living Past* (Oxford, 1931), p. 179.

description appeared like an explanation, and there seemed no need to add anything further. Newton wrote:

> We are to admit no more causes of natural things than such as are both true and sufficient to explain their appearances . . . Therefore, to the same natural effects we must, as far as possible, assign the same causes . . . We must . . . universally allow, that all bodies whatsoever are endowed with a principle of mutual gravitation.[45]

This matter of fact statement stood in marked contrast to Newton's predecessors. Gone were the arguments concerning the authority of Aristotle or of anyone in the past. Gone too were the occult qualities in nature. There were no hidden purposes to discover, and no explanations concerning the wherefore of motion were necessary. The basic programme was

> to subject the phenomena of nature to the laws of mathematics . . . from the phenomena of motions to investigate the forces of nature, and then from these forces to demonstrate the other phenomena.[46]

Everything could remain on the experimental, mechanical, mathematical basis.

And yet, Newton was puzzled by the fact of gravity. He entertained various explanations without success. He had delayed making his discoveries known, and finally abandoned the hope of developing a natural philosophy. He was forced to think of abolishing hypotheses from science because they posited qualities and causes which could be deduced from observation. Hence, with reference to the problem of gravity, he wrote:

> Hitherto I have not been able to discover the cause of those properties of gravity from phenomena, and I frame no hypotheses.[47]

This was in striking contrast to Descartes, for whom metaphysically deduced hypotheses had been fundamental. Scientifically, Newton felt it necessary to restrict himself to the description of observable, mechanical, mathematical laws of nature. All traditional hypotheses not

[45] Newton, *Mathematical Principles of Natural Philosophy*, *Great Books of the Western World* (Chicago: Encyclopædia Britannica, Inc., 1952), Vol. XXXIV, pp. 270-71.
[46] Ibid., p. I.
[47] Ibid., p. 371.

helpful in description, or in the discovery of laws, had to be abandoned.[48]

Newton's work was a grand synthesis of previous scientific work. But it was also more restricted, in that the more ultimate questions were deliberately laid aside. However, as Professor Burtt has so well shown, metaphysical questions cannot really be suppressed. The choice is always between a conscious metaphysics and metaphysical views which either make the method into a metaphysics or unconsciously absorb assumptions from the surrounding world.[49] Newton fell into the last category. He uncritically accepted the notion that the world was comprised of minute, solid, permanent particles called atoms. All change was the result of the " separations, associations, and motions of these permanent atoms."[50] Man and nature were interpreted in terms of these elements. In the case of man, the elements were combined with a soul which was identical with mind. Both were imprisoned within the brain and had only indirect contact with the outside world. With respect to the world of nature, for example, it was declared that rays of light called forth associations of colour; hence, secondary qualities had no reality. It was not the first time, we may add, that the loss of an adequate conception of man and of secondary qualities coincided.

Whatever Newton's intentions, his influence was on the side of those who held a mechanical view of the world. While he disavowed metaphysics, the metaphysical views of his predecessors showed through his own unexamined assumptions, and in the long run, his system was interpreted in ways he would have rejected. Professor

[48] In Newton, as in the whole history with which we have been concerned, there is some ambiguity concerning the meaning of hypothesis. Insofar as a hypothesis is an intuition which helps in description, or which can be confirmed, Newton could not escape it either. But a hypothesis as an extra quality or force behind the observable or necessary was rejected.

[49] Burtt, op. cit., p. 226. The assumption that the refutation of an anti-metaphysical bias can be refuted by calling that notion a metaphysical principle has never been very convincing to me. It is a logical trick. It is quite possible to be consistently anti-metaphysical in affirming that one is not even sure about one's method. A scepticism that is not sure about scepticism must be conceded as a possibility even if one does not agree with it. To call such a position metaphysical is not instructive.

[50] Burtt, op. cit., p. 228.

Burtt, with due acknowledgment that Newton would not have accepted the consequences, has written:

> It was of the greatest consequence for succeeding thought that now the great Newton's authority was squarely behind that view of the cosmos which saw in man a puny, irrelevant spectator (so far as a being wholly imprisoned in a dark room can be called such) of the vast mathematical system whose regular motions according to mechanical principles constituted the world of nature.[51]

Nevertheless, Newton the scientist had no intention of being anything else but a Christian. He not only had a conception of God's relation to the world; he also wrote theological treatises, as did Boyle. Newton simultaneously affirmed a mechanical world and God's free activity. The description of nature demanded a mechanical conception; but with respect to its origin or first cause, the world could not be mechanically understood. Questions of meaning and purpose again became relevant.

> The main business of natural philosophy is to argue from phenomena without feigning hypotheses, and to deduce causes from effects, till we come to the very first cause, which certainly is not mechanical; and not only to unfold the mechanism of the world, but chiefly to resolve these and such like questions. What is there in places almost empty of matter, and whence is it that the sun and planets gravitate towards one another, without dense matter between them? Whence is it that nature doth nothing in vain; and whence arises all that order and beauty which we see in the world?[52]

In a vein similar to Boyle and others, Newton believed that the biological mechanism of the eye could only be intelligible through reference to the Creator.

Newton assumed two levels of discourse which bore some relation to each other, the mechanical and the religious. In the light of their symmetrical proportions, Newton accepted the traditional arguments for the existence of God. But he affirmed that God was also actively related to the world of nature. Newton refused to accept that God

[51] Ibid., p. 236.   [52] Quoted in Burtt, op. cit., p. 284.

had created an independent machine, a clock which needed no further attention. For Leibnitz, a God who created a machine which needed further attention could not really be God. But for Newton, God continued to be active in a mechanical world. He joined More and Descartes in affirming the Creator's *concursus* with the order of the world. Moreover, God performed very definite tasks. Unfortunately, however, Newton called on God for the solution of problems which turned out to be scientific in nature. Newton believed that God actively kept the fixed stars in their positions. Newton was further troubled in that gravity explained the fact of planetary movement, but that it could not account for the precise orbs of the planets. He insisted that the paths of the orbs were directly determined by God. In both instances, one certainly could affirm that the creativity of God was operative; that is always possible in a proper theological delineation. But Newton had used the theological affirmation of the divine activity in order to solve scientific problems which demanded and received scientific answers.

Newton believed that the world, even if defined in terms of the movement of a clock, needed not only to be sustained, but also repaired, rebuilt, or renewed. God was considered to be the repairer and renewer of the universe. It was already obvious to many in his time that a more consistent mechanical conception of reality would make this argument look absurd. Newton's mistake, as we have indicated previously, was that he let his religious convictions intrude upon what were scientific problems. Nevertheless, his religious convictions were genuine.

Newton's religious instincts were nowhere more evident than in his conception of God's relation to space. He maintained that God was present everywhere, yet not suffused through space; that all things happened in the presence of God, that there was no place or space apart from Him, yet that God and space were not identical. Newton was grappling with this issue when he described space as the divine sensorium.[53] That description represented a serious concern for the presence of God, but he did not conceive it in a pantheistic sense.

[53] Ibid., p. 258.

Newton's aim was made clear in the *General Scholium* of the *Principia*.

> From his true dominion it follows that the true God is a living, intelligent, and powerful Being; and, from his other perfections, that he is supreme, or most perfect. He is eternal and infinite, omnipotent and omniscient; that is, his duration reaches from eternity to eternity; his presence from infinity to infinity; he governs all things, and knows all things that are or can be done. He is not eternity and infinity, but eternal and infinite; he is not duration or space, but he endures and is present. He endures forever, and is everywhere present; and, by existing always and everywhere, he constitutes duration and space . . . He is omnipresent, not *virtually* only, but also *substantially*, for virtue cannot subsist without substance. In him are all things contained and moved; yet neither affects the other: God suffers nothing from the motion of bodies; bodies find no resistance from the omnipresence of God. It is allowed by all that the Supreme God exists necessarily; and by the same necessity he exists *always* and *everywhere*. Whence also he is all similar, all eye, all ear, all brain, all arm, all power to perceive, to understand, and to act; but in a manner not at all human, in a manner not at all corporeal, in a manner utterly unknown to us.[54]

Or the following passage from the *Opticks*:

> . . . Does it not appear from phenomena that there is a Being incorporeal, living, intelligent, omnipresent, who in infinite space, as it were in his sensory, sees the things themselves intimately, and thoroughly perceives them, and comprehends them wholly by their immediate presence to himself; of which things the images only carried through the organs of sense into our little sensoriums, are there seen and beheld by that which in us perceives and thinks. And though every true step made in this philosophy brings us not immediately to the knowledge of the first cause, yet it brings us nearer to it, and on that account is to be highly valued.[55]

This was not a traditional way of speaking about God's relation to

---

[54] Newton, op. cit., pp. 370–71.
[55] Newton, *Opticks* (New York: McGraw-Hill, 1931), p. 370.

the world. It was more reminiscent of Nicholas of Cusa than of the deists; in fact, it was a most un-Newtonian way of speaking. Considerable opposition to Newton developed precisely over his way of putting this issue. Colin Maclaurin, an expositor and defender of Newton, has put the objections to Newton and his intention very clearly:

> Sir Isaac Newton, to express his idea of the divine Omnipresence, had said that the Deity perceived whatever passed in space fully and intimately, as it were in his Sensorium. A clamour was raised by his adversaries, as if he meant that space was to the Deity what the Sensorium was to our minds. But whoever considers this expression without prejudice, will allow that it conveys a very strong idea of the intimate presence of the Deity everywhere, and of his perceiving whatever happens in the completest manner, without the use of any intermediate agents or instruments, and that Sir Isaac made use of it with this view only; for he very carefully guards against our imagining that external objects act upon the Deity, or that he suffers any passion or reaction from them . . . The greatest clamour has been raised . . . by those who have imagined that he represented infinite space as an attribute of the Deity, and that He is present in all parts of space by diffusion. The truth is, no such expressions appear in his writings: he always thought and spoke with more veneration of the divinity than to allow himself such liberties . . . He adds indeed, that as the Deity exists necessarily, and by the same necessity exists everywhere and always, he constitutes space and duration: but it does not appear that this expression can give any just ground of complaint; for it is saying no more than that since he is essentially and necessarily present in all parts of space and duration, these of consequence, must also necessarily exist.[56]

Given the mechanical world and his religious faith, Newton had creatively related the two. But Newton's successors saw that the two did not necessarily imply each other.

A more serious problem in Newton's theological position was his

---

[56] C. Maclaurin, *An Account of Sir Isaac Newton's Philosophical Discoveries* (London, 1775), pp. 402, 403, 404.

rationalistic conception of Christianity. Newton was suspect among Christians for his views on the Trinitarian problem. Like many of his day, he maintained that the Trinity was not taught in the New Testament.[57] But it was not merely that the Trinity could not be found there; that many traditional theologians had also maintained. For Newton, as for Arians generally, the materials for a Trinitarian conception were not only lacking in the Scriptures, they were unnecessary. For orthodox churchmen, Newton's views were indeed heretical.

But on another point, Newton was traditional in the derogatory sense of that term. He was interested in discerning the future through Biblical apocalyptic literature. One must, in all honesty, add that his concrete speculations on such matters occurred late in his life. But they are not inconsistent with the speculation of many individuals in this period. It is certainly clear that for Newton the Bible contained the secrets of all future knowledge. Jesus Christ was pre-eminently a man of knowledge and that knowledge was primarily of the future. Jesus stood in the tradition of the prophets, but His teaching concerning the future was more reliable. The Word of God coincided with prophecy at the point of knowledge of the future. From an unpublished manuscript by Newton, one reads the following:

> The Father is omniscient, and hath all knowledge originally in his own breast, and communicates knowledge of future things to Jesus Christ; and none in heaven or earth, or under the earth, is worthy to receive knowledge of future things immediately from the Father but the Lamb. And therefore the testimony of Jesus is the spirit of prophecy, and Jesus is the Word or Prophet of God . . .[58]

Through such views, Newton reflected and encouraged the tradition in which prophecy was understood in terms of prediction fulfilled. That view became one of the last defences of Christianity in a world in which the successors of Newton saw no further need of God. For Newton himself, it was as if the past and present were known and fulfilled in knowledge of the functioning of the mechanical world, but

[57] Burtt, op. cit., p. 282.
[58] Brewster, II, p. 348 ff., quoted by Burtt, op. cit., p. 283.

that the future was to be divined from the prophetic tradition, primarily through the teachings of Jesus of Nazareth. In this way, the future was to be known, precisely as the mathematical present was known.

Just as the metaphysicians had made the knowledge of God akin to other forms of philosophical knowledge, so Newton had made the knowledge of God conform to the type of knowledge which he knew on the basis of a mechanical, mathematical understanding of the world. It was the form of the knowledge, the hidden presuppositions within it, which determined the way in which Christianity was understood. Christianity was not apprehended in terms appropriate to itself. Whatever Newton's intentions—and one can only interpret these positively—most theologians did not follow him. A notable exception was Samuel Clarke.

On the scientific side, the revolution begun in Copernicus appeared to be fulfilled in Newton. Only a number of isolated and peripheral problems remained. Something of the power of this completed revolution is evident in that the basic Newtonian world view remained unchallenged until late in the nineteenth century. Much eighteenth- and nineteenth-century thought was formulated in the light of it. It was not by accident that people spoke of the incomparable Mr. Newton. If understanding of the operation of things was itself an explanation—a tradition already articulated in Kepler and Galileo— then indeed Newton had solved both the immediate and more ultimate issues. Man's knowledge of the world, which was also knowledge of God, had been articulated. The problems which remained were certainly not essential mysteries. In fact, nature had lost its obscurities. Perhaps Scripture would be next.

From the standpoint of science, and on the basis of its impact on other areas of thought, the epitaph by Pope admirably expressed the mood:

Nature and Nature's laws were hid in night:
God said, Let Newton be! and all was Light.[59]

[59] A. Pope, " Epitaph on Newton," in L. Untermeyer, *Poetry* (New York: Harcourt, Brace and Company, 1934), p. 430.

Surely this was nothing less than the religious adoration of the accomplishments which men saw in the Newtonian synthesis.

An extensive adulation of the harmonious mechanical, ordered world machine was apparent everywhere. The characteristics of devotion and concern which once had gone to other aspects of life were now given to it. A great change had taken place when, for example, the rainbow was no longer described as God's rainbow, or even as the mystery and grandeur of colour, but simply as the refraction of light. Certain aspects of life now seemed less real. Burtt has described this well:

> The gloriously romantic universe of Dante and Milton, that set no bounds to the imagination of man as it played over space and time, had now been swept away. Space was identified with the realm of geometry, time with the continuity of number. The world that people had thought themselves living in—a world rich with colour and sound, redolent with fragrance, filled with gladness, love and beauty, speaking everywhere of purposive harmony and creative ideals—was crowded now into minute corners in the brains of scattered organic beings. The really important world outside was a world hard, cold, colourless, silent, and dead; a world of quantity, a world of mathematically computable motions in mechanical regularity. The world of qualities as immediately perceived by man became just a curious and quite minor effect of that infinite machine beyond. In Newton the Cartesian metaphysics, ambiguously interpreted and stripped of its distinctive claim for serious philosophical consideration, finally overthrew Aristotelianism and became the predominant world view of modern times. [60]

Philosophically, the world of Pythagoras and of the atomists had triumphed over Aristotle. This was true in spite of Newton's antimetaphysical leanings and his espousal of philosophical methods which would not have occurred to his philosophical predecessors. This philosophical heritage was not necessarily un-Christian; but Newton's philosophic successors and churchmen saw it as such.

With the advent of the Newtonian system, the ancient tripartite

[60] Burtt, op. cit., pp. 236-37.

world had been finally destroyed, God's functions had been drastically reduced, and only man's reason in a mechanical world saved him from nothingness. Such prospects brought both opposition and accommodation. A new theological direction did not come until the eve of the nineteenth century in the person of Friedrich Schleiermacher. But even that achievement was threatened when Darwinism attacked the shaky uniqueness of man in a Newtonian world.

D: THE LATER PURITAN ETHOS AND THE NEW SCIENCE

Initially, Puritans and the orthodox had much in common, but as the Puritan ethos developed, it proved to be more congenial to the new science than was the case with orthodoxy. As was previously indicated, the hold of Aristotelian thought on the English scene was broken earlier than on the Continent. The continued impact of Bacon and the logic of Ramus played a decisive role. Moreover, the concern with the Bible took on different characteristics than on the Continent. Biblical considerations took on more experiential and practical aspects in the context of the particular concerns of Church and State in England than the metaphysical form nourished by the continental debates between Protestants and Roman Catholics. Further, the Puritan concern for the Scriptural Word in preaching—an art which was particularly exercised in the social and political settings of English life— made them suspicious of the usefulness of Scholasticism. Richard Baxter, for example, opposed the study of Scholastic philosophy as a part of the preparation for the Christian ministry. This more practical approach to Scripture greatly modified the Continental view of the Bible as a book of knowledge. Hence, the philosophical undergirding of an inerrant Bible did not play so large a role. In spite of the contrary views of such men as the great John Owen, there were a good number of individuals who spoke out against an infallible Bible. In 1651, Vincent Wing replied to literalism as follows:

That this Copernican System is proved . . . I am certain . . . I know nothing of worth opposeth it; No: saith my adversary, what think you of the Scripture: Why, I answer, that whatsoever is there spoken of the Earth's Rest, or the Sun's motion. Psalm 92, Psalm 103, Ecclesiastes 1, Psalm 18, Isaiah 38, Ecclesiastes 48 is to be understood . . . as the philosophers say, according to our apprehension and vulgar manner of speaking, and not according to the nature of the things.[61]

And by 1673, Francis Osborne, in a volume which had already reached its seventh edition, challenged the infallibility of the patriarchal narratives and the usual interpretation of the book of Joshua concerning the sun standing still.[62]

These factors created a more favourable attitude toward the new science in England than on the Continent. But the situation was by no means totally positive. While active Puritan opposition was minor, Puritans raised questions about the field of science. Like some of the early Reformers, they feared that unbridled curiosity in the field of science would detract from the main question of destiny or of salvation. Because of this, John Cotton considered the pursuit of science to be an unacceptable occupation.[63] On the other hand, Richard Baxter considered the experimental philosophy, as he called it in contrast to the mechanical philosophy, to be an effective means for promoting the glory of God.[64] Many argued that the new science, when properly interpreted, could also serve a theological purpose.

For England, the middle of the seventeenth century can safely be designated as the point where the preponderant approach to science had become positive. Before this time, the new science had not widely penetrated into the universities. Cromwell had been instrumental in the creation of Durham University, where all the sciences were taught. Puritans had also been active in establishing the dissenting academies. Moreover, where the Puritan influence was strong, the new science made inroads into the universities.

Statistical evidence points to a predominant Puritan membership in

[61] *Harmonicon Coeleste* (London, 1651), To the Reader, quoted from *Annals of Science,* III, (1938), p. 181.
[62] Francis Osborne, *Works* (7th ed.; London, 1673), pp. 506-7, cited from *Annals of Science,* III, (1938), pp. 182-83.
[63] Miller and Johnson, *The Puritans* (New York: The American Book Company, 1938), p. 729.
[64] Merton, op. cit., p. 430.

the Royal Society. This does not mean that the Royal Society was unopposed by Puritans; but it does mean that the Puritans more than any other group contributed to the work of the Society. Some of the general opposition to, as well as ridicule of, the Royal Society is understandable. Many of its observations and conclusions were naïve, and in the aim to be of service to mankind, the Society promulgated many an old tale as if it were science. Only after the Society had been severely criticized for its indiscriminate mixture of science and fiction, was an attempt made to insure quality in its publications. However, from the very beginning, many considered the Royal Society to be that branch of man's learning in which the book of nature was seen as a book of God, now directly available for everyone who wished to see. Sprat, in his history of the Royal Society, referred to the Society and the Church as kindred agents. In its own way, he declared, each had carried through a reformation, the one in the field of science and the other in the field of religion.[65] Thus, one could be a member of the Royal Society and a man of God without serious questions arising.

The new science was widely accepted in the Puritan tradition in both Old and New England. Even before the time of Newton, the Copernican system was expounded at Harvard through Thomas Merton's *Compendium Physicae*. This text continued to be used there until 1725. Vincent Wing's *Astronomia instaurata*, (1656), which popularized Copernicus in English, was also used at Harvard. Hence, it was natural that the work of Newton would be met without resistance among most Puritan divines. Newton only supplied another element of evidence in a basic picture of the world which they had already widely accepted.

Many Puritans had accepted the orderliness of nature before Newton further substantiated it. Some had already made their adjustment to this by suggesting that miracles had ceased. Miracles, they said, were restricted to a special dispensation of the Spirit at work in the early Church. Faith demanded only that one accept the original miracles on the basis of the reliability of the witnesses. John Preston,

[65] T. Sprat, op. cit., p. 371.

for example, believed that miracles had ceased, and Samuel Nowell believed that God worked through natural means wherever possible. The Calvinist theologian, Antony Burgess, believed that God was bound to His own ordinances, that He could not go counter to nature because nature was a beam from His own wisdom.[66] John Preston too, believed that God altered no law of nature.[67] Some, as the independent Thomas Goodwin, felt that such views threatened the lordship of Christ and substituted for it a " constitutional head of a cosmic system."[68] But those who took the position that miracles had ceased and that God altered no law of nature did not believe that God had lost control of the world. God's providential work was now to be discerned in the order of nature. Hence, a thing or event was frequently described both in its natural and in its providential or theological sense. Samuel Danforth, for instance, believed that the comet of 1664 was subject to natural law and that it was a sign of disaster.[69] However naturally things might be described, theologians and philosophers affirmed a providential meaning for them as well. The collection of illustrations of divine providence appeared to be a particular pastime of theologians.[70] But for many within the scientific tradition, such an extended interpretation of the natural could be abandoned. But the documentation of God's providence among theologians rose to a crescendo before it declined.

The belief in the orderliness of nature was still accompanied by a belief in a world of spirits and of witches. While it was widely conceded that the Spirit had ceased with reference to miracles, it nevertheless appeared that there were powers which manipulated nature to their own ends or purposes. In retrospect, it is hard for us to understand this. We live under the sobering impact of a scientific tradition which has succeeded in depopulating the universe of such supposed spiritual entities. But in the seventeenth century, such diverging conceptions as a mechanical order and a belief in witches existed side by

[66] S. F. Mason, " The Scientific Revolution and the Protestant Reformation—I," *Annual of Science*, IX (1953), p. 86.
[67] Ibid., p. 71.   [68] Ibid., p. 86.
[69] Miller and Johnson, op. cit., p. 732.
[70] For example, Increase Mather, *Remarkable Providences* (London, 1890).

side. Richard Baxter, friendly to the experimental philosophy, wrote extensively on witches and spirits. And in quantity, such writing is astounding.[71] Henry More and Thomas Glanville believed in spirits. The scientist Robert Boyle " believed in the efficacy of the touch of Valentine Greatrix."[72] To the list of such respected Englishmen one need only add the spectacle of the witch trials of Massachusetts.

The belief in a world of spirits abated later than we are inclined to think in the light of the history of science. The seventeenth-century witch trials were not as isolated as is usually assumed. But all such phenomena, according to Hirsch, are a sign of a powerful heathenism which had crept into Christianity. But their persistence in this period was due in part to the fact that they provided a way of contending against a mechanical interpretation of reality. Men such as More and Baxter, while for the new science, were vigorously opposed to its mechanical interpretation. The belief in spirits, even in witches, was a last stand against mechanism by contending for another realm of reality alongside the natural. It is in this setting, too, that the Iatrochemist development in medicine and the continued interest in alchemy need to be understood.[73]

---

[71] R. F. Jones, *Ancients and Moderns* (St. Louis, 1936), p. 337.
[72] C. R. Weld, *A History of the Royal Society* (1848), I, 90.
[73] See Mason, " The Scientific Revolution and the Protestant Reformation—II," *Annals of Science*, IX (1953), p. 154 ff.

V

The Apologetic Defence of Christianity

A: THE NEW SCIENCE BECOMES A PHILOSOPHY

Prior to the time of Newton, the philosophical premises of the scientists were consciously related to their scientific theories. There was no attempt to hide such presuppositions. But Newton, on the other hand, had consciously laid metaphysical principles aside. This basic distinction is valid, in spite of the fact that the predecessors of Newton had philosophical assumptions of which they were unaware and that Newton did not really succeed in laying all metaphysical assumptions aside. But in the last quarter of the seventeenth century, a very different movement came into being. It made a philosophy out of the new science. This does not mean that the scientists necessarily believed in this development. Nevertheless, many saw implications in the new science which lent themselves to the popular philosophical movement.

The new philosophy had its roots in France. But it was quickly taken up in England. The achievement of the movement was that of bringing the ideas associated with the new science into a coherent world view and of popularizing the results. Its task was that of organization and of interpretation. The new ideas were brought into the orbit of a shared culture, and thereby indirectly into the orbit of the common man. This is what Locke characterized in his statement that no one read Newton, but everyone talked about him.

One of the books which widely disseminated and defended the new ideas, though written shortly before Newton published his *Principia*, was Fontenelle's *The Plurality of Worlds*. Originally published in French in 1686, it was already in English translation two years later. It went through at least a dozen editions in the ensuing century.[1] Fontenelle was not so much interested in the details of the new science, as in the vistas which it opened. No longer, he declared, was the centre of attention upon the earth and its puny drama; that was much too provincial. Fontenelle went so far as to admit that the vista of many worlds was a depressing thought to man, revealing to him his own insignificance. But if one contemplated the vastness of the universe and remembered that it was man who did the contemplating, it was a bearable thought.

Fontenelle was thrilled by the prospect of the plurality of worlds. He was aware that he could not prove the existence of life on other planets. But on the basis of analogy, he believed that it was highly probable. Had not the apparent difference between the earth and the other planets been discarded as a result of the repudiation of Aristotle and the discoveries of the new science? Was it not therefore logical to assume that what was true on earth was applicable to other planets as well? Was not science itself, when properly understood, a kind of theology?

Fontenelle was not alone in using this argument. Thomas Burnet argued that just as the knowledge gained in surgery on one man was applicable to other men, so knowledge gained in the exploration of our planet gave reliable knowledge of other planets. He went on to contend that the world of Aristotle was far too small to exhibit the wisdom of God in His creation.[2] God is made too small by thinking of life only on this planet. He said:

> We must not . . . admit or imagine, that all Nature, and this great universe, was made only for the sake of man, the meanest of all intelligent creatures that we know of; nor that this little planet, when we sojourn for a few days, is the only habitable part of the universe:

A. O. Lovejoy, *The Great Chain of Being* (Cambridge: Harvard University Press, 1953), p. 131; Butterfield, op. cit., p. 123.
[2] T. Burnet, *The Sacred Theory of the Earth* (London, 1816), pp. 359-60.

these are thoughts so groundless and unreasonable in themselves, and also so derogatory to the infinite power, wisdom and goodness of the first cause, that as they are absurd in reason, so they deserve far better to be marked and censured for heresies in religion, than many opinions that have been censured for such in former ages.[3]

Likewise Charles Blount, in *The Oracles of Reason*, published in 1693, argued that the plurality of inhabited worlds was more agreeable to the greatness and goodness of God than the notion of but one world.

Fontenelle, Burnet, and Blount no longer emphasized or acutely understood the Christian account of redemption. By contrast, Robert Jenkin, a more traditional theologian who was not adverse to the new science, was instructive if not altogether satisfactory. He tried to relate the concept of the plurality of worlds to the Christian view of redemption.

I observe, that though it should be granted, that some Planets be habitable, it doth not therefore follow, that they must be actually inhabited, or that they ever have been. For they might be designed, if mankind had continued in innocency, as places for colonies to remove men to, as the world should have increased, either in reward to those that had excelled in virtue and piety, to entertain them with the prospect of new and better worlds; and so by degrees, to advance them in proportion to their deserts, to the height of bliss and glory in heaven; or as a necessary reception for men (who would then have been immortal) after the earth had been full of inhabitants. And since the fall and mortality of mankind, they may be either for mansions of the righteous, or places of punishment for the wicked, after the resurrection, according as it shall please God, at the end of the world to new modify and transform them. And in the meantime, being placed at their respective distances, they do by their several motions contribute to keep the world at a poise, and the several parts of it at an equilibrium in their gravitation upon each other, by Mr. Newton's principles.[4]

Jenkin had obviously related the notion of the plurality of worlds to

[3] Burnet, op. cit., pp. 352-53.
[4] Robert Jenkin, *The Reasonableness and Certainty of the Christian Religion* (London, 1700) Book II, p. 222.

the possibilities inherent in the total sweep of the Christian drama. His views were pure conjecture. But so were the views of Fontenelle, Burnet, and Blount. While we have learned to keep the plurality of worlds as an open question, it was not so understood in the late seventeenth and eighteenth centuries. The debate hung on the assumption that human life existed on other planets. But while the externals of the debate were centred here, the fact of possible life on other planets was not as such the issue. The latter was neither affirmed nor denied in the Bible, and only those who believed that all truth had to be found in the Bible were theologically upset by the sheer fact of life on other planets. On this specific problem, as in most of those with which we have been concerned, the central issue was the question of natural knowledge, even a natural theology, versus the authority of the Biblical tradition. Specifically, the form which the problem took was that the plurality of worlds spoke more convincingly of God, the Creator, than did the Bible of God, the Creator and Redeemer.[5]

In the Bible, the redemptive work of God in Christ had appeared central. Creation was understood in the context of redemption. Now creation, interpreted as the wisdom of God in His works, was more significant than redemption. For some the concept of redemption itself was called into question. But even those who still believed that redemption was paramount had to admit that there was an entire realm where science was valid and where the Biblical tradition had nothing to say. For some time, a large group of writers had contended that the account of God's creative wisdom could more adequately be given in science than through Moses. But they still assumed a common realm of reality concerning which the Biblical tradition and the new science both spoke. When, by contrast, the notion of the plurality of worlds was seriously entertained, it became apparent that a whole area of reality had been opened concerning which the Bible said nothing at all. All at once, God the Creator had come into His own. Men were ecstatic concerning the wisdom and marvels of God expressed in the perfections of such an infinite world. Such a world

[5] Arthur Lovejoy and Marjorie Nicolson, who have made much of the threat to theology through the notion of the plurality of worlds, have not seen that the above was the real threat to Christians.

staggered the imagination and no provincial interpretation sufficed. Depressed in part by the discovery of such vastness, men were yet intoxicated by it, and saw their place in the scheme of things in tracing out the marvels of the Creator's world. In fact, this was their vocation as men. Nature and Nature's laws were everywhere, testifying to the marvellous wisdom of God. It was the task of everyone, and of the scientist particularly, to exhibit it to plain view. In this development, the concern with nature had become central for the knowledge of God. Heretofore, history and particularly the Biblical history, had been the central key to the knowledge of God. Natural knowledge of God had heretofore always been subservient to revelation, cither as a first step or in integral relation to it. Now natural theology was independent of revelation; it had come into its own.

This is not to say that the new independence of natural theology was the result only of the impact of the plurality of worlds in the latter part of the seventeenth century. The general direction was reinforced by related though fairly independent factors. The discontent of many with the confessional battles between the Lutheran and Reformed churches was also a major item in fostering disillusionment with a Biblically centred Christianity. Later, too, the knowledge of other religious cultures entered the picture. Nevertheless, the notion of the plurality of worlds, in spite of the long history of the concept, only came into its own in this period. It caught on as the natural expression of those who believed that philosophy and science must be wrested from the domination of those Christians who adhered so strictly to a Biblical tradition. It was such a powerful symbol because it provided an area of knowledge which testified to God apart from any strict Biblical dictation.

This new trend was firmly established by the early eighteenth century. It had an effect also on the more traditional theological circles. More and more natural theology became a first and independent section in theology with hardly any reference to the Biblical tradition. Those in the tradition of Derham, Burnet, and Ray, to Paley, maintained that natural theology was a prelude to revealed theology. The task of natural theology was to trace the marvels of God's works in nature. This, they believed, did not detract from revelation, though it must be pursued in independence of it. Among the deists, however, a truncated natural theology became a substitute for revelation. In all of these groups, the independence of natural theology was expressed. They were followed by a development in which natural theology was neither a first step in theology nor a substitute for revelation, but the avenue for understanding revelation. That development, which will concern us in the next chapter, is classically expressed in the transition in the Continent from Protestant orthodoxy to the Enlightenment.

We shall not undertake to trace the history of the groups we have mentioned. The influence of natural theology upon the orthodox will be included in the next chapter, where the transition to the Enlightenment will be delineated. Neither the tradition from Derham to Paley nor that of the deists can be said to be central enough to a positive Protestant tradition to warrant separate elaboration here. For our purposes, it is more important to note the type of apologetics used in the defence of Christianity by the orthodox and by those sympathetic to Christianity. Such apologists had now to meet the new philosophy as it expressed itself so cogently in such notions as the plurality of worlds, the views of the deists, and the French equivalents to both.

B: THE EVIDENCES FOR CHRISTIANITY

It was in the eighteenth century, prepared in decisive form in the latter half of the seventeenth, that the self-evidence of the Christian outlook was first challenged in post-medieval history. Until then one could assume interest in and knowledge of Christianity among those who were at all concerned about religious issues. Now began the bid for a religious understanding which placed Christians under the necessity of defending their views. Previously in Protestant history, the debates had centred in the issues which divided the Protestant fold internally and in the relation of Protestantism to Roman Catholicism. Insofar as the Christian claim previously had to be defended at all, it was against so-called atheism. But this type of defence assumed the superiority and dominance of the Christian understanding. Christians were sufficiently secure to be condescending in debate. Now, however, a new situation had arisen. While Christianity was not a minority movement, its hold on the minds of men, particularly in the traditional sense, could no longer be assumed. A new juncture in history had come. At one and the same time, Christianity had to defend its own understanding against all the new forms of thought, as in extreme orthodoxy, or to show, on grounds similar to the new philosophy, that it should not be ruled out, but rather accepted all the more enthusiastically.

The apologetic for Christianity primarily took four forms; the evidences through miracle and prophecy (which we shall treat together), the delineation of the wisdom of God in creation, and the argument from the analogy between nature and Scripture. Of these, the first two, miracle and prophecy, were considered absolutely essential for the defence of Christian revelation. And the amazing fact was that these arguments were utilized even by those whose Christian understanding had been rationalized to the point where one wonders how much Christian substance was left.

1. *Miracle and prophecy*. In this period it was almost universally accepted that the truth or falsity of Christianity depended upon the credibility of the Biblical miracles. The defence was always buttressed by reference to the Biblical tradition and to the early Church. Since the argument from miracle and prophecy had always had its place in Christian history, all could assume its significance. But, as we shall note, it was doubtful that it even had the pre-eminent position in the early Church which was now accorded to it. While the argument had been repeated by the orthodox theologians, it was now singled out for particular attention by orthodox and less orthodox alike.

The general thesis was that the authenticity and confirmation of Christ came through the miracles which He performed, and which the early disciples performed in His name. In the history of Israel, miracles too had their place. But in the course of history, they had stopped occurring. It was said that the Spirit had departed from Israel. But it was affirmed that when the Messiah arrived, He would be known through the miracles which He performed, that is, through the power of the Spirit. It must be added, however, that interpreters in this period stressed the *fact* of the miracles more than their association with the work of the Spirit. Indeed, there was some suspicion of the Spirit. Something as tangible and factual as miracles was demanded. Talk about the Spirit laid one open to the charge that one paid attention to the work of God in a private and therefore unconfirmable sense. Robert Jenkin argued that prophecy and miracles were more dependable than any immediate revelation from God. Imposture and scorn were removed, he declared, for miracles, unlike revelation and the Spirit, were public property.[6]

Our contemporary vogue of considering miracles in a way which takes attention away from whether or not they occurred as recorded, had not arisen in the minds of those thinkers. For them, the occurrence or non-occurrence of miracles was the issue. This left only one basis for decision about them, namely, the credibility of the witnesses. On this point all were agreed; for example, Robert Jenkin, the most traditional of theologians; Ralph Cudworth, in a more Platonist tradition; John Locke, in an essentially rational mould; Joseph Butler, in his mediating position; or William Paley, in a tradition of natural theology as late as the beginning of the nineteenth century.

For Locke, the reasonableness of Christianity rested on the confirmation of the messiahship of Jesus through the miracles which He performed. Although miracles had ceased among the Jews, they were expected of the Messiah.[7] Jesus had performed miracles, according to eye witnesses; consequently what could be more rational than that He was the Messiah? Locke was aware that everything depended upon the opinion of the spectators and that questions could be raised about the reliability of the witnesses. But in good rational form, he met such questions by suggesting that anyone who raised doubts about the credibility of the opinion of the spectators was beset with the same difficulty with respect to his own views.[8] He therefore concluded that

[6] Jenkin, op. cit., I, 29.
[7] Locke, *The Reasonableness of Christianity*, Works (12th ed., London, 1824), VI, 17, 18, 32.
[8] J. Locke, *A Discourse on Miracles*, Works (12th ed., London, 1824), VIII, 256.

the truth of Christianity rested upon a proper and reasonable understanding of miracles.

The type of argument used to confirm the credibility of the witnesses is readily illustrated in the work of Charles Leslie, *A Short and Easy Method with the Deists*. Accepting the notion that the truth of the miracles would establish the truth of Him who performed them, Leslie proceeded to argue for the credibility of the witnesses to miracles on the basis of three related rules. In the first place, we have to do with matters which can be confirmed by the outward senses, things which are seen and heard. Hence, miracles must be substantiated by the senses in the same way in which anything else in nature is open to verification. In the second place, in order to be authentic, miracles must be public. Everyone must be able to see them; in fact, it is necessary that they be seen by many people. In the third place, some customs or observances must follow in the wake of miracles, testifying to the impact which these events made upon subsequent history. The memory of Israel's miraculous delivery from Egypt was part of the observed and constant memory of the Church. Its impact upon the Church testified that it was an authentic event. It was not a freak event, as would be the case, Leslie points out hypothetically, if one made the claim that in the eighteenth century everyone cut off his middle finger. Since neither witness nor significant memories or actual cultic practices testify to it, such a claim can be called unauthentic. With respect to the first and second rules for the confirmation of miracles, Leslie gave himself to his descriptions with utter abandon. The Red Sea events, for example, are especially miraculous because the Sea was full and overflowing; moreover 600,000 men had witnessed the dividing of the waters. So many men could not be wrong. According to Leslie, those who interpreted the Red Sea story in the context of a Spring tide, or some such natural explanation, had capitulated to the point where Biblical truth was in doubt. He wrote:

I say this for the sake of some Christians, who think it no prejudice to the truth of the Holy Bible, but rather an advantage, as rendering it more easy to be believed, if they can solve what ever seems miraculous in it by the power of second causes; and so to make all, as they speak, natural and easy: wherein, if they could prevail, the natural and easy result would be, not to believe one word in all those sacred-oracles. For if things be not as they are told in any relation, that relation must be false. And if false in part, we cannot trust to it, either in whole, or in part.[9]

Leslie obviously believed in the inerrancy of the Bible; but in respect to miracles, the argument was no different on the part of those who no longer held a literalistic view.

In addition to the three rules Leslie elaborated for the confirmation of miracles, many writers added a fourth, namely, that of the willingness of Christians to suffer for their faith. The early Christians, it was stated, were so convinced by what they had seen that they could not and did not shrink from the consequences. This argument was still used as late as Paley.[10] But it was a supplemental argument, and therefore did not carry the weight of the more direct arguments. It must be added, however, that the interest centred, not in the miracles as such, but in what they confirmed. They testified to the Messiah. Writers were quick to point out that miracles were not unique. Many claimed to have performed them. Further, many individuals who had never performed miracles were considered as unique as those who had. The convincing point of the argument from miracles was that they confirmed the Messiahship. Things happened precisely as predicted; role and witness were conjoined, just as had been prophesied. Writer after writer pointed out that this was not the case of other religious figures. Mohammed was not confirmed by miracles performed or predicted.[11]

This line of argument was widely accepted, in spite of disagreement on whether miracles were still performed, occurred rarely, or had again entirely ceased. While there was no unanimity about such matters, there was unanimity that they had occurred in the past. Never-

[9] C. Leslie, *A Short and Easy Method with the Deists* in *The Theological Works* (Oxford, 1832), I, 23.
[10] W. Paley, " The Evidences of Christianity " in *Miscellaneous Works* (London, 1820), I, Part 1.
[11] J. Butler, *Analogy of Religion* (New York, 1870), p. 276; W. Paley, op. cit., p. 368.

theless, most theologians believed that miracles were now indeed rare or had ceased completely. In fact, the argument for their credibility partially depended upon the fact that they no longer occurred frequently. Bishop Butler maintained that miracles should be compared to rare events in nature, such as comets, rather than to the orderly course of nature.[12] Burnet suggested that one should stick to the level of secondary causation as long as possible and flee to miracles only as a last resort. Jenkin believed that miracles had entirely ceased; but that they were confirmed with reference to Christ and therefore were decisive in that setting.

> Faith in the miracles of Christ is required of men in all ages of the world, though miracles are ceased; and if this be reasonable now, it could not but be fitting then, that those who came to Christ, should believe in him for the sake of the miracles, which they had been certified that he had done upon others. For miracles, when they are fully attested, are as sufficient a ground of faith, as if we had seen them done; and to manifest that they are so, our Saviour might require belief in his former miracles, of those who expected any advantage from such as they desired him to do.[13]

By the middle of the eighteenth century, the role of miracles so understood was severely challenged. Men such as Christian Wolff suggested that Christians should concentrate on the order of nature as much as possible. He argued that God's power was more manifest in the orderly course of nature than through miracles. This way of thinking gained considerable support during the eighteenth century. The second major challenge came in Hume's criticism of miracles. After contending that all witnesses are at best secondary, and asserting that many contradictory and bizarre things are said about miracles, he concluded that:

> upon the whole, then, it appears that no testimony for any kind of miracle has ever amounted to a probability, much less to a proof; and that, even supposing it amounted to a proof, it would be opposed by another proof; derived from the very nature of the fact, which it would endeavour to establish. It is experience only, which gives

[12] Butler, op. cit., p. 219.   [13] Jenkin, op. cit., II, 489-90.

authority to human testimony; and it is the same experience, which assures us of the laws of nature. When, therefore, these two kinds of experiences are contrary, we have nothing to do but subtract the one from the other, and embrace an opinion, either on one side or the other, with that assurance which arises from the remainder. But according to the principle here explained, this subtraction, with regard to all popular religions, amounts to an entire annihilation; and therefore we may establish it as a maxim, that no human testimony can have such force as to prove a miracle, and make it a just foundation for any such system of religion.[14]

Hume's criticism was directed equally to miracles, to the laws of nature, and to a natural theology built upon design and the constancy of human nature. His own views were too radical to be taken seriously in his own time. Most theologians accepted both the laws of nature and the fact of miracles. The latter were but the expression of God's power over and above nature. Only the deists directly attacked miracles from the standpoint of the order of nature. The usual line of defence continued the old tradition, namely, whatever was above nature was as reasonable and certain as nature itself. In retrospect, the contention that miracles had occurred in the past but had ceased, only postponed facing the inevitable question of whether they could any longer be defined along traditional lines.

The traditional conception of miracle, as we have already indicated, was intertwined with the conception of prophecy. The miracles of Jesus and His near contemporaries were significant because they testified to the fulfilment of the Messianic prophecies. Hence, miracles in the restricted sense of the Messianic problems, pointed to the reality of fulfilled prophecy. In fact, the argument from prophecy had a distinct advantage over miracle. Irrespective of whether or not it was held that miracles had ceased or continued to happen, the miracles associated with the Messianic claim were past events. But prophecy had the strength of past prediction and subsequent fulfilment. Its significance increased in proportion to the length of time which

[14] Hume, *An Inquiry Concerning Human Understanding*, in *The English Philosophers from Bacon to Mill*, ed. Burtt (New York: Modern Library, 1939), pp. 664-65.

elapsed between the enunciation and fulfilment of a prophecy. Robert Jenkin wrote:

> Prophecies are generally of more concernment, and afford greater evidence and conviction in future ages, than when they were first delivered. For it is not the delivery, but the accomplishment of prophecies, which gives evidence of the truth of any doctrine: The events of things in the accomplishment of prophecies are a standing argument to all ages, and the length of time adds to its force and efficacy; and therefore when all that God saw requisite to be foretold, is delivered to us in the Scriptures, there can no longer be any need of new prophecies; which would be of less authority than the ancient ones, inasmuch as their antiquity is the thing chiefly to be regarded in prophecies.[15]

Ralph Cudworth from a different theological perspective also stressed the importance of prophecy. He suggested that prophecies were more valid than the recorded miracles.[16] The reason was that prophecies were written down and were fulfilled later. The Old Testament preceded the New Testament in time, and the latter fulfilled the former. By contrast, miracles were considered concurrent with the event to which they testified; prophecy included antecedent factors. The authority of the Bible finally rested upon the fact that what God had predicted in the old covenant had come true in the new.

On the basis of this assumption, theologians and non-theologians alike attempted to decipher the content of other predictions in the Bible which had not been fulfilled. Just as the prediction of the Messiah had been fulfilled, so too, the predictions of the end of the world would be fulfilled and were already recorded in the Biblical material. Just as God's thoughts were read after him in nature, so he who knew the Bible could discern God's thoughts and perhaps His infallible knowledge of the future. Knowledge of the future, it was believed, was certainly hidden in the Bible and could perhaps be discovered. Hence, Newton and others of a similar spirit, as we indicated previ-

---

[15] Jenkin, op. cit., II, 491.
[16] R. Cudworth, *The True Intellectual System of the Universe* (London, 1678), pp. 714-15.

ously, read both nature and the Bible, particularly the sections on prophecy, with an eye to uncovering knowledge of the future.

The argument from prophecy was challenged when it was discovered, particularly by those of a more rational bent of mind, that the prophecies had not always been fulfilled as predicted, that some were never fulfilled though the time for their fulfilment had passed, and that some predictions had been inaccurate. Those who were so minded could, of course, find explanations which saved the prophecies.

More important than the specific debates is the context for the arguments from miracle and prophecy. We have already indicated that the form of the apologetic stems from the ancient tradition of the Church. But it is doubtful that the seventeenth-eighteenth century context was the same as that of the early Church. The early Church, convinced that He who had come was the Messiah, affirmed that the expectations and predictions had been fulfilled. Convinced that He was the Messiah, the miracles were positive signs and proof of the event. Prophecy meant that the concrete expectation had been fulfilled and miracles were corroborative testimony that the new age had dawned. But it is doubtful that in the early Church the truth of the Christian claim rested on the form of the argument. Greeks and Jews alike shared the assumption that all knowledge of the future had already been disclosed in the past, and that the validity of truth was proportional to its antiquity. This was as true for understanding the myths of Homer as it was for understanding the Bible, and it indicates why Genesis was even more significant than Isaiah. In that way of thinking, the New Testament use of Old Testament passages in a predictive sense is intelligible and partially convincing. The fulfilled expectations now provided the possibility of seeing predictive allusions where they had not been seen before. Prophecy thus had a very significant role to play in the understanding of the early Church, whereas the question of the credibility of miracles was raised very early in the history of the Church.[17]

In the post-Reformation developments, the form of the argument

[17] R. M. Grant, *Miracle and Natural Law in the Graeco-Roman and Early Christian Thought* (Amsterdam, 1952).

was more significant than it was in the early Church. Hence, the analogy between the two does not hold. In the seventeenth and eighteenth centuries, one believed because of the miracles which occurred, and because prophecies as predicted, had been fulfilled. As we have indicated, miracle and prophecy were considered as objective facts, no different from those in the domain of science. Confirmation for the revelation of God in Christ was of the same order as that in the natural sciences. The Messiah had Himself become an object of ordinary knowledge and demonstration. He was no longer in the first instance the source of that new life which transformed old relations.

The fateful consequences of such a position are all too obvious. The defence of Christianity through miracle and prophecy in the seventeenth-eighteenth-century sense is an unfortunate chapter in the history of Protestant theology. It was already a mistake to discuss theological questions as if they were on the same level as the knowledge of nature. It was but a short and fatal step from understanding the messianic claims in categories appropriate to nature to rejecting them because the knowledge of nature made them appear incredible. On the old path, no new directions were possible. The latter occurred as late as Friedrich Schleiermacher in the early nineteenth century.[18]

2. *The wisdom of God in creation—the argument from design.* Just as was the case with reference to the interpretation of miracle and prophecy, so too the argument for a deeper understanding of God through the marvels of nature rested upon a Biblical foundation and the situation in the early history of the Church. Anyone who has read the Psalms or Job or Second Isaiah knows something of the power of those Biblical passages in which the marvels and mystery of God's creation are confessed and declared. But the world into which Christianity entered had no uniform conception of nature. It was variously assumed that the world, including nature, was subject to the power of inexorable fate and that chance was operative on every level. Frequently, both fate and chance were affirmed by the same person. It

[18] In anticipation, it should be said that the less dogmatic character of contemporary science and the abandonment of a concept of rigid order are no bases for a return to miracle in the old sense, though this seems frequently to be the assumption.

should be said here that fate was not the equivalent of inexorable law. It was a meaningless sway of a dark power from which there was no escape. In a world of fate and/or chance, Christianity affirmed the meaningful and purposeful character of all the events of nature and history. The powers of fate and fortune were challenged in the light of a destiny for man under God, even when that destiny was expressed in the most deterministic terms.

Cudworth felt a conscious kinship to the early Church as he undertook his own apologetic labours. Throughout the *True Intellectual System of the Universe* he contended against a mechanical view of the world and the concept of chance. He considered both to be atheistic views, which in different forms had already been met in the early Church. He recalled that Anaxagoras had said that man chanced to have hands. Cudworth found such a statement devoid of all meaning. Hands obviously have purposes, as do all aspects of reality. The concept of purpose was, in fact, the main argument against chance; in the last analysis, it was the defence against atheism.[19]

The argument from purpose which we encountered in a previous chapter was not only revived in this time; it was revived with new power, that is, with the support of all the insights and extensive knowledge which came from the science of nature. The intoxicating effect of this new knowledge was apparent in such a traditional theologian as Robert Jenkin.

Indeed infidelity could never be more inexcusable than in the present age, when so many discoveries have been made in natural philosophy, which would have been thought incredible to former ages, as any thing perhaps that can be imagined, which is not a downright contradiction. That gravitating or attractive force, by which all bodies act one upon another, at never so great a distance, even through a vacuum of prodigious extent, lately demonstrated by Mr. Newton; the Earth, together with the planets, and the sun and stars being placed at such distances, and disposed of in such order, and in such a manner, as to maintain a perpetual balance and poise throughout the universe, is such a discovery, as nothing less than a demonstration

[19] Cudworth, op. cit., p. 685.

could have gained it any belief. And this system of nature being so lately discovered, and so wonderful, that no account can be given of it by a hypothesis in philosophy, but it must be resolved into the sole Power and good pleasure of Almighty God, may be a caution against all attempts of estimating the Divine works and dispensations by the Measures of humane reason. The vastness of the world's extent is found to be so prodigious, that it would exceed the belief not only of the vulgar, but of the greatest philosopher, if undoubted experiments did not assure us of the truth of it.[20]

Similar sentiments were elaborated by such men as John Ray and William Derham. Ray, on the one hand, pointed to the immense size of the world and on the other, to the species in nature which are so small that they are unnoticed by most of us. He found it difficult to believe that this panorama was made for man alone.[21] The possibility of life on other planets intrigued him and he believed that such life belonged to the purposes of God. But even planets which have life, he declared, can be utilized by us to contemplate God's creative work. Likewise, the multitude of species can be viewed in different ways. By observing them, we can contemplate the wisdom and power of God and affirm that they have uses which we do not yet know.[22]

Derham, in a similar vein as John Ray, was impressed by the immensity of the universe. But he was equally enamoured by its apparent suitableness for the enrichment and purposes of man.

The motions the terraqueous Globe hath, are round its own axis, and round its fountain of light and heat, the Sun. That so vast a body as the earth and waters should be moved at all, that it should undergo two such different motions, as the diurnal and annual are, and that these motions should be so constantly and regularly performed for near 6000 years, without any the least alteration ever heard of (except some hours which we read of in Joshua 10: 12, 13, and in Hezekiah's time, which, if they cannot be accounted for some other way, do greatly increase the wonder; these things, I say, do manifestly argue some divine infinite power to be contained therein. But

[20] Jenkin, op. cit., II, 18-19.
[21] J. Ray, *The Wisdom of God Manifested in the Work of Creation* (11th ed., 1743), p. 177.
[22] Ibid., pp. 368-69.

especially, if to all this we add the wonderful convenience, yea absolute necessity of these circumvolutions to the inhabitants, yea all the products of the earth and waters. For to one of these we owe the comfortable changes of day and night; the one for business, the other for repose; the one for man, and most other animals to gather and provide Food, Habitation, and other necessities of life; the other to rest, refresh, and recruit their spirits, wasted away with the labours of the day. To the other of those motions we owe the seasons of summer and winter, spring and autumn, together with the beneficial instances and effects, which these have on the bodies and states of animals, vegetables, and all other things, in the torrid, temperate, and frigid zones. [23]

For Derham, the whole universe was still geared to the necessities and comforts of man. Approximately a century later, William Paley doubted the usefulness of astronomy in relation to natural theology.

My opinion of astronomy has always been that it is not the best medium through which to prove the agency of an intelligent Creator; but that, this being proved, it shows, beyond all other sciences, the magnificience of his operations. The mind which is once convinced, it raises to sublimer views of the Deity than any other subject affords; but it is not so well adapted as some other subjects are to the purpose of argument. We are destitute of the means of examining the constituition of the heavenly bodies . . . We see nothing but bright points, luminous circles, or the phases of spheres reflecting the light which falls upon them. Now we deduce design from relation, aptitude, and correspondence of parts. Some degree, therefore, of *complexity*, is necessary to render a subject fit for this species of argument. But the heavenly bodies do not, except perhaps in the instance of Saturn's ring, present themselves to our observation as compounded of parts at all. [24]

[23] W. Derham, *Physicio-Theology* (London, 1720), pp. 43-46.
[24] W. Paley, *Natural Theology* (London, 1836), II, 13-14.
Charles Raven makes much of the difference between the more organic and living biology of Ray and the more contrived, mechanical, and lifeless biological work of Paley. He believes that concentration upon the work of Ray provides a fruitful clue to a genuine partnership. Generally speaking, Raven believes that not enough attention has been given to the biological sciences in the science-religion question and that astronomy and

In spite of this difference between Derham and Paley, there was a remarkable similarity in the arguments which they employed. Derham saw in the astronomical realm precisely that degree of adaptation to purpose which made Paley more enamoured of biology. In fact, purpose was seen everywhere, and whatever was, was obviously meant to be as it was, in order to serve its purpose in the best way. Derham, contemplating the position of the eye, decided that it would have been more convenient to have the eye in one's hand because of the greater manoeuvrability of the hand; nevertheless, it was wiser to have it in one's head where it was not so susceptible to injury.[25] Writers continued to be intrigued by the marvellous workmanship and mystery of the eye. Paley suggested that if we had no other

example in the world of contrivance except that of the eye, it would be alone sufficient to support the conclusion that we draw from it, as to the necessity of an intelligent Creator.[26]

On the whole, however, one is struck by the tedious obviousness and lack of imagination in this literature. Two passages from Ray will suffice:

The great wisdom of the divine creator appears, in that there is pleasure annexed to those actions that are necessary for the support and preservation of the individual, and the continuation and propagation of the species; and not only so, but pain to the neglect or forbearance of them. For the support of the person, it hath annexed pleasure to eating and drinking, which else, out of laziness or multiplicity of business, a man would be apt to neglect, or sometimes forget; indeed to be obliged to chew and swallow meat daily for two hours space, to find no relish or pleasure in it, would be one of the

---

physics have received disproportionate attention. Certainly the opposition is less prominent in the field of biology, and in this sense Raven is right in stating that corrections need to be made. But it seems to me that he too easily pushes aside the fact that it was precisely in astronomy and physics that the original issues did occur and that they did, as he himself indicates, create problems in the field of biology. See Charles Raven's *John Ray, Organic Design,* and his two volumes, *Natural Religion* and *Christian Theology.*
[25] Derham, op. cit., p. 89.
[26] W. Paley, *Natural Theology,* I, 81. The conic structure of the eye is still one of the great mysteries of biology. But it is doubtful that the theological conclusions which such interpreters as du Noüy derive from it are valid.

most burdensome and ungrateful tasks of a man's whole life; but because this action is absolutely necessary, for abundant Security Nature hath inserted in us a painful sense of hunger, to put us in mind of it; and to reward our performance hath enjoined pleasure to it; and as for the continuation of kind, I need not tell you that the enjoyments which attend those actions are the highest gratifications of sense.[27]

Or again,

That whereas the breast is encompassed with ribs, the belly is left free, that it might give way to the motion of the midriff in respiration, and to the necessary reception of meat and drink as also for the convenient bending of the body; and in females for that extraordinary extension that is requisite in the time of their pregnancy.[28]

Two books even appeared in the eighteenth century with the titles, *Insect-Theology*, and *Water Theology*.[29]

Whatever was, was obviously right. (Basil Willey calls it Cosmic Toryism.) Believing that this was the best possible of all worlds, these men spelled out precisely the sense in which that was true. Ray reminded his contemporaries that the most pernicious insects provided us with medicine, and that sometimes God was pleased to send us scourges through insects, as in the case of the Egyptians, in order to chastise us.[30] Paley contended that mortal diseases reconciled us to death and thus ended the horror of it.[31] Derham admitted the inconvenience of volcanic action, but affirmed that a volcano supplied a necessary chimney for the fire burning in the earth.[32] Ray and Paley were so busy ascribing purpose and usefulness to everything that the agony and disproportionate character of human suffering did not seriously enter their horizon; and Derham never raised the question of imperfections in nature. Assuming the wisdom of God in creation, they elaborated the obvious positive uses of all things and even ascribed purposes to the most embarrassing aspects of the universe and of existence generally. It is not surprising that this type of natural

[27] Ray, op. cit., pp. 239-40.   [28] Ibid., pp. 287-88.
[29] F. C. Lesser, *Insecto-Theologie;* and J. A. Fabricius, *Wasser-Theologie.*
[30] J. Ray, op. cit., pp. 374-75.
[31] Paley, *Natural Theology*, II, 137.   [32] Derham, op. cit., p. 69.

theology was unconvincing in the long run. And just as he had done in the case of miracles, Hume mercilessly attacked it.

These writers, just as those who defended Christianity through miracle and prophecy, claimed that they were following the tradition of the early Church. But they too did not see that their situation was not identical, and that they had inverted the original apologetic.

To believers, according to the Biblical tradition and the early Church, nature manifested the glories of God the Creator. It was however, a subsidiary theme. Missionaries preached the drama of creation as a part of the drama of redemption. But in the period under discussion, the domain of nature was divorced from its Christological centre. The heavens no longer declared the glory of God to the eyes of faith. Rather, the heavens were used to argue for the wisdom of a Creator. It is understandable that such an apologetic should appear persuasive to those who were trying to interpret the new science in a religious sense. It is also understandable that such astounding discoveries should have taken on religious dimensions.

But in the long run, two factors were definitely against the usefulness of such an apologetic. First, as the scientific tradition continued to develop, scientists saw no need for such an interpretation of their work. In fact, many of them opposed it. Second, those interested in the wisdom of God in creation were so enamoured with what they saw that they practically subsumed the concern with revelation. The originally dubious charge of the theologians that too much attention given to science would take attention away from revelation had become more than a suspicion; it had become a fact. Reflection on this period raises the question whether a conscious apologetic is not usually a boomerang. If theologians and scientists had been less interested in writing apologetics for each other, their relationship might have been more creative in the long run. They might have been able to distinguish and then relate their concerns. As it was, they met on grounds detrimental to both.

3. *The analogy between nature and scripture.* The analogy between nature and Scripture, as we have noted before, meant that the affir-

mations and problems in each bore a proportionate relation to each other. The particular form of the usual analogy referred to the clarity and obscurity of nature and Scripture. Moreover, just as in the case of the arguments from miracle, prophecy, and design, it was maintained that the analogy was already used in the early Church. In setting forth his intention in the *Analogy*, Bishop Butler made this quite clear:

> From analogical reasoning, Origen has with singular sagacity observed, that " he who believes the Scripture to have proceeded from him who is the author of Nature, may well expect to find the same sort of difficulties in it, as are found in the constitution of Nature." And in a like way of reflection, it may be added, that he who denies the Scripture to have been from God, upon account of these difficulties, may, for the very same reason, deny the world to have been formed by him.[33]

While this passage immediately shows how conscious Butler was of standing in the old apologetic tradition, it also indicates that here, as in the other instances, a great reversal had taken place. Origen argued against those who would not take Scripture seriously because of its obscurities, and he maintained that Scripture was just like nature, that is, full of obscurities. He who objected to Scripture on the ground of obscurity, he argued, must logically reject nature, for here one encountered the same difficulties. Butler, on the other hand, confronted an entirely new situation. No longer did men feel that nature was obscure. That had to be argued. Butler had to contend that there were many true and real aspects of nature which could not be discovered by our natural faculties.[34] Origen had argued that Scripture was like nature, that is, like a view of nature which all accepted; but Butler had to argue that nature was like Scripture, with the disadvantage that neither nature nor Scripture were understood as he desired. The analogy which Origen utilized proceeded from the accepted to the unaccepted, maintaining that there were similarities between the two. Butler put himself in the position of arguing that nature as generally accepted was not really as orderly as assumed; of maintain-

[33] J. Butler, op. cit., p. 86.   [34] Ibid., p. 214.

ing that the analogy between nature and Scripture was valid; and of assuming that Scripture ought therefore to be accepted. Even if it were true, such an argument could hardly be convincing. Butler's *Analogy*, could not be the wave of the future. It was too widely held that nature was orderly and that its mysteries were being pushed aside by new discoveries. Butler was correct in sensing that the new science did not provide an adequate understanding of nature. But he attacked at the wrong point and was destined to fight a losing battle. In point of fact, the conception of analogy could more tellingly be used against him, particularly when, as in the case of Origen, one argued from the accepted to the unaccepted. Men were sure that nature had lost its obscurities. Obscurities remained only in Scripture. Hence, the inevitable hope was that they could be expunged from Scripture. And the obscurities of Scripture were indeed set aside, so that Scripture corresponded to the simplicity of nature. But since the principles for deciding what was obscure were derived from reason and nature rather than from Scripture, it was inevitable that the understanding of Scripture was drastically transformed in the process. This resulted in that increasing rationalization of Christian revelation which led directly to the Enlightenment.[35]

As we indicated previously, the most devastating attack on the arguments from miracle and prophecy came from David Hume. In his *Essay Concerning Natural Religion*, he also repudiated the argument from design and the conception of a definite and stable human nature upon which natural theology depended. The degree to which Hume was actually open to considering revelation as an alternative to natural theology, in the closing section of the Essay, is a debatable point; our only concern here is to stress that the philosophical method which included the certainty of the evidences and of natural theology was not so self-authenticating and convincing in the long run as its protagonists thought. While Hume was not accepted in his own time or extensively thereafter, his basic point was taken up by others in a less radical way. Natural theology was rejected as the pillar which sustained the Christian enterprise. In fact, it can be maintained that

[35] See next chapter.

natural theology was mainly responsible for the demise of Christianity in many areas.

C: SELECTED THEOLOGICAL FIGURES

Bishop Butler and John Wesley confronted the same problem within Anglicanism. They were deeply disturbed by the lack of a vibrant and living faith in the established Church. The contrast in the accomplishments of the two men suggests that the salvation of the Christian enterprise came not from the rearguard apologetics of Butler, but from the proclamation of the redeeming Word as preached by Wesley and his associates. Wesley's ideas were not held in opposition to the knowledge of his time; but the impact of the redeeming Christ upon the lives of men was its own apologetic. Wesley was so busy with his central mission of proclaiming Christ that many theological problems were lightly met rather than either carefully opposed or championed in new directions. The consequence is that we have a somewhat ambiguous picture of Wesley's relation to various forms of thought, including the natural sciences.

He shared the suspicion that science tended to take one's attention away from theological problems. In fact, he was not sure that it was always a proper way to spend one's time. In his Journal, he wrote:

> At the desire of some of my friends, I accompanied them to the British Museum. What an immense field is here for curiosity to range in! One large room is filled from top to bottom with things brought from Otaheite; two or three more with things dug out of the ruins of Herculaneum! Seven huge apartments are filled with curious books, five with manuscripts, two with fossils of all sorts, and the rest with various animals. But what account will a man give to the Judge of the quick and dead for a life spent in collecting all these?[36]

And in the light of experiments which he carried out, Wesley reported that he could not study mathematics, arithmetic, or algebra to an

---

[36] *The Journal of the Reverend John Wesley*, Curnock edition (Epworth Press, 1938), VI, 301.

appreciable extent without becoming a deist, if not an atheist [37] On the other hand, he declared that the study of nature humbled man's pride, showed forth the wisdom of God, warmed men's hearts, and filled us all with wonder, love, and praise.[38]

Whatever his attitude toward theoretical science, Wesley did popularize scientific results. His first concern was to make practical and useful information available. Two of his books belong in this category: one on medicine, entitled, *Primitive Physic*, and a book on electricity called, *Desideratum: or Electricity made Plain and Useful*. The former is full of helpful remedies for various recognized illnesses of the time, and it even suggests that psychological states have a bearing on bodily health. But by and large, these books were not original; they consisted of compilations of useful information taken from others. Much of the material was already out of date at the time Wesley published the books.

Wesley also published a volume entitled, *A Survey of the Wisdom of God in the Creation; or a Compendium of Natural Philosophy*. In it he expounded the traditional arguments from design; he quoted Ray, Derham, and many others, including Cotton Mather. Wesley himself said that his work was largely translated from the Latin work of John Francis Buddeus,[39] though he retrenched, enlarged, altered, and corrected it.[40] Originally published in two volumes in 1763, it was immensely popular and frequently republished. In the process, it grew to five volumes. Excerpts from it were reprinted in the *Arminian* magazine.

While Wesley's scientific writings were not original, they were highly successful in terms of circulation and republication. The situation with reference to his views on Copernicus and Newton is ambiguous. Dorothy Stimson has written that Wesley was one of the last opponents of the Copernican system.[41] But the evidence seems to me

---

[37] Sermon, " The Use of Money " in *Works of John Wesley* (1809), VIII, 384. (Incorrectly paginated as 284.)
[38] J. Wesley, *A Survey of the Wisdom of God in Creation; or, A Compendium of Natural Philosophy* (London, 1777), I, viii.
[39] *Elementa Philosophiae Practicae et Theoreticae.*
[40] Wesley, op. cit., p. v.
[41] Stimson, op. cit., pp. 93, 99.

to be that while Wesley believed that the Copernican view tended toward infidelity, he could not find Biblical reasons for denying it. He probably accepted Copernicus's views over against the Ptolemaic system. However, he was more sceptical of Newton than of Copernicus. This was due in part to his interest in the Hutchinsonians. In 1724, John Hutchinson published his *Moses's Principia*, obviously directed against the *Principia* of Newton. While Wesley did not fully accept the views of the Hutchinsonians, he was sympathetic to their charge that the Newtonian system tended toward atheism. Hence, Wesley's own position remained somewhat unclear. This was only natural. His interest in science was not genuinely theoretical in the sense of a concern for a true system of science. He was interested in the practical ways in which science assisted men in their pursuits and in the ways in which it disclosed the glory of God. On scientific matters, he felt dependent on the work of others and was not seriously perturbed by the competing claims; hence, his own vacillation on theoretical issues. Nevertheless, through his publications and practical interest, he helped to create a favourable attitude toward the scientific enterprise.

On scientific matters, Cotton Mather was more consistent than John Wesley. But Mather was no more original in his scientific and philosophical writings than was Wesley. He freely admitted his debt to John Ray and William Derham.[42] His interest was clearly expressed in the full title of the volume, *The Christian Philosopher—a collection of the best discoveries in Nature with Religious Improvements.*[43] This meant that he wanted the best of contemporary science understood in a Christian context. He believed his writing to be philosophical, but also evangelical.[44] He accepted the general distinction between the book of nature (creatures) and the book of Scripture, quoted Chrysostom in support of it, and added that the distinction stemmed from the Church fathers.[45]

Mather held the Copernican position, particularly the basic affirmation of the " stability of the Sun and the motion of the earth," to be beyond dispute. Only a complete reversal of all the causes of celestial

[42] C. Mather, *The Christian Philosopher* (London, 1721), p. 3.
[43] The parallelism to Wesley is clear.
[44] Ibid., p. 2.   [45] Ibid., p. 8.

motions as they were known could challenge the Copernican position, he declared, and that appeared unlikely.[46] Mather, too, exhibited something of the quasi-religious awe in which Newton was held in this period.

> But then comes the admirable Sir Isaac Newton, whom we now venture to call the *Perpetual Dictator* of the learned World, in the *Principles of Natural Philosophy*; and than whom, here has not yet shone among mankind a more sagacious reasoner upon the *Laws of Nature*.[47]

But Mather did not agree with a matter of central concern to Newton. He refused to assume the existence and power of gravity without further evidence. Nor was he willing to accept more favourable views of gravity. He agreed with Clarke that what passed for gravity was not to be understood as " motion originally impressed upon Matter."[48] And he agreed with the physician and quasi-theologian, Cheyne, that one should not resort to various principles of motion as propounded by the philosophers. Mather made his meaning clear when he wrote of Cheyne:

> He asserts, and with demonstration . . . that there is no such thing as an *universal Soul*, animating the vast System of the World, according to *Plato*; nor any *substantial Forms*, according to *Aristotle*; nor any omniscient *radical Heat*, according to Hippocrates; nor any *plastick Virtue*, according to Scaliger; nor any *hylarchick Principle*, according to More. These are mere allegorical terms, coined on purpose to conceal the ignorance of the authors, and keep up their credit with the credulous part of mankind. These unintelligible Beings are derogatory from the Wisdom and Power of the great God, who can easily govern the Machine He could create, by more direct Methods than employing such subservient divinities; and indeed those beings will not serve the design for which we invent them, unless we endow them with faculties above the dignity of secondary agents. It is now plain from the most evident principles, that the great God not only has the springs of this immense machine, and all the several Parts of it, in his own Hand, and is the first Mover;

[46] Ibid., pp. 75-76.   [47] Ibid., p. 56.   [48] Ibid., pp. 84-85.

but that without His continual Influence the whole Movement would soon fall to pieces. Yet, besides this, he has reserved to Himself the power of dispensing with these Laws, whenever He pleases.[49]
Mather was afraid of any emphasis upon secondary causes, or upon principles of explanation and movement which inevitably take on the status and functions of lesser divinities. Mather was contending for the grounding of all causation directly in the omnipotent cause.[50] Neither rest nor the motion of anything depended upon itself, but upon God directly. Hence, the concept of gravity could not be introduced as if it were a solution to the problem of motion. Even the old criticism of the Copernican system, that the speed of the earth in its path around the sun would result in the earth's disintegration, was still taken with seriousness. Mather contended that it did not fly to pieces because it was moved by God. While the laws of nature were real, Mather believed that they were anchored in the activity of God. They did not even have a semi-autonomous status.

Since Mather's aim was to provide a proper Christian interpretation of the new science, it is understandable that he wished thoroughly to ground causation in the pervasive activity of God, without the quasi-independence of laws or independent forces of motion, such as gravity. But when the logic of such a position was later applied in the field of biology, it led to the defence of the fixity of species. The power of God in every phase of creation and created existence can be assumed or proclaimed in faith. But it is doubtful that it can be argued successfully or legitimately.

Mather also reiterated the dictum that a preoccupation with the scientific enterprise could easily lead to the neglect of the Christological centre of Christian understanding. Still during the time of Mather most scientists considered themselves to be Christian. Having declared that the works of God are exhibited to us through nature, Mather hastened to add that the Christ of God must not be forgotten. Certain minimal Christological motifs for understanding creation are then elaborated. Early in the book, he declared that a small part of the wisdom of God was revealed in creation; but he added that those who

[49] Ibid., pp. 87-88.   [50] Ibid., p. 88.

did not admire wisdom itself—and by this he meant revelation—must be stark blind. And toward the end of the book, he declared:

This is not all we have to think upon; we see an incomparable Wisdom of God in his creatures; one cannot but presently infer, what an incomprehensible wisdom then in the methods and affairs of that redemption, whereof the glorious God has laid the plan in our Jesus.[51]

Mather distinguished between nature and Scripture; but he also interpreted events in the light of both. In his analysis of comets, he accepted the natural explanations of his time, including the predictions of Halley, but then added that comets had a theological meaning also. He stated that when he saw a comet, he thought of a wicked world made into a fiery oven in the time of God's anger, of what it would be like if our world were so afflicted, and of how wonderful it was that we were saved from such a calamity.[52] Likewise, after giving a natural account of the rainbow in Newtonian terms, Mather added that Christians should remember that the rainbow had been a covenant sign.[53] Thunder, too, was understood in natural terms; but it should remind us how quickly God can destroy us and that we are in need of the Saviour.[54]

Mather's instincts were correct, namely, that the same phenomena can be understood in a natural and in a theological sense. But the theological meaning was forced; at every point it reflected an old heritage in which the theological meaning was outlined in terms analogous to the natural meaning. Once the natural order was accepted, theologians should have conceived of the theological meaning in quite different terms. Here, too, the form of theological understanding was under the domination of nature. A decisive theological transformation had not yet taken place in either Mather or his contemporaries.

It is well known that Locke's psychology and Newton's conception of nature had their impact on Jonathan Edwards. Like Mather, Edwards had a sense for the central christological core in Christianity but also for the new science. Edwards particularly utilized Newton's concept of causation, in which sequences exist without knowing their

[51] Ibid., p. 301.   [52] Ibid., p. 45.   [53] Ibid., pp. 57-58.   [54] Ibid., p. 63.

mysterious connections, as a proper analogy to the complex of faith and regeneration.[55] He too believed that there was an analogy between the order of nature and of faith. But while Edwards related Christian insight to the currents of his time more astutely than most theologians, he did not determine the future in such matters. More creative than most, he did not slavishly reflect the past nor did he, as we have indicated, decisively influence the future at this level. For this reason, a fuller exposition will not be undertaken here.

[55] Perry Miller, *Jonathan Edwards* (New York: William Sloane Associates, Inc., 1949), p. 79.

VI

The Demise of Revelation

The arguments from evidences were held by conservative and liberal thinkers alike. Nevertheless, most of the thinkers whose thought we expounded in elaborating the evidences would not have passed muster among the more orthodox Lutheran and Reformed theologians on the Continent. The former were influenced by those rational currents of thought earlier associated with Socinianism and later with Arminianism. Rational notions and conservative motifs were inextricably intertwined among such thinkers. Whether we take theologians who challenged this conception, or those who delineated man's activity along Socinian and Arminian lines, we shall not find a new principle for the interpretation of Scripture. The more rational theologians were as literalistic in their interpretation of Scripture as the more orthodox. In some respects, they were even more literalistic. Precisely their inability to find a full-blown Trinitarian conception of God in the Bible contributed to their denial of the Trinity. By contrast, the orthodox in the period from 1560-1740 were not nearly so literal-minded. They saw the need for theological development. In spite of this, the more rational theologians were more open to the impending developments on the cultural front. They were not, as were the Protestant orthodox, in principle committed to the exclusive use of a consciously selected theological method. Hence, their theological views were not so defensively pursued and they could be more open to other currents of thought. But they were suspect among the more orthodox because a type of rational thought was making it impossible for them to accept the mysteries which the orthodox insisted belonged to the faith. It was in this sense, as we noted in chapter two, that the orthodox defence against such rational currents consisted in maintaining that the philosophical conceptions of such theologians were inadequate. Between the two groups no reconciliation was possible. But finally the power of reason, associated with the impact of the new science, made its inroads upon Christian thinking. All aspects of faith or of revelation had finally to be as clear or as self-evident as the order of nature. It was this widely held assumption which gradually led to the demise of revelation in any form akin to its more classical expression. At the same time, the orthodox did not rethink the concept of revelation; they merely continued the traditional defence.

A: A FINAL STRAND OF ORTHODOXY

The orthodox development continued with greater strength in the German and Swiss scene than in England or in America. Insofar as currents of orthodoxy were found in America, it was primarily traceable to a direct theological lineage from Europe. But by the latter decades of the seventeenth century and the early decades of the eighteenth, the traditional orthodox Aristotelians were on the defensive everywhere. In the Netherlands, Descartes had become important; in England, Aristotle had been successfully banished, and in America, his thought was even less in evidence. Also, in the German scene, the Aristotelian defence was rapidly breaking up. But the traditional position was still defended with some vigour, and even where this was not true, no ready substitute was at hand.

The more orthodox theologians on the Continent continued to oppose the new scientific conceptions. In Basel, for instance, the *Syllabus Controversiarum* of 1662, no more than two decades prior to Newton, affirmed that the stability of the earth and the movement of the sun was an article of faith. In 1675, a mathematician in Basel was forbidden to lecture on the Copernican system and in 1681, he was forbidden to publish his book there or elsewhere. It was however published in Amsterdam. And in the second decade of the eighteenth century, a mathematician in Zurich was having troubles over the Copernican system.[1] These instances show that the Swiss universities were even more conservative than the German ones. In Germany, the Copernican system was generally taught alongside other theories, and theological opposition to the new system was not nearly so influential as among the Swiss.

Nevertheless, the conservative position continued in Germany until well into the eighteenth century. In his *Examen Theologicum Acroamaticum* of 1707, the Lutheran David Hollaz, after carefully distinguishing between the significant and the less significant in Scripture, still did not concede the possibility of any mistakes in the Bible.

There are contained in Scripture historical, chronological, genealogical, astronomical, natural-historical, and political matters, which, although the knowledge of them is not actually necessary to salvation, are nevertheless divinely revealed, because an acquaintance with them assists not a little in the interpretation of the Sacred Scriptures, and in illustrating the doctrines and moral precepts . . . Divine inspiration, by which the subject matter and the words to be spoken, as well as those to be written, were immediately suggested to the prophets and apostles by the Holy Spirit, preserved them free from all error, as well in the preaching as in the writing of the divine Word.[2]

This was a defensive position. The assumption was that concession at any point opened the door for denials at all points. For his time, this fear was no doubt factually if not theologically correct. In any case, Copernicanism was rejected because it was not Biblical. All natural truth, which it was conceded had some basis apart from the Bible, must nevertheless conform to the Biblical view at every point.

The great eighteenth-century Reformed theologian, Francis Turretin, held views similar to those of Hollaz. The Bible was inspired and therefore correct in every respect. While he agreed that different books

[1] P. Wernle, *Der schweizerische Protestantismus im 18. Jahrhundert* (Tübingen, 1924), Zweiter Band, p. 3.
[2] D. Hollaz, quoted by Schmid, op. cit., pp. 56, 60.

in the Bible, like the stars, did not shine with equal brilliance, he still maintained that the original manuscript of each book was free of any error. The admission of any error, however small, was considered to be a repudiation of the authority of Scripture. Hence, Turretin's doctrine of creation was simply an exposition of Genesis and included the definite opinion that creation occurred in the Fall of the year. In short, the Bible was still a book of science and theological truth. The Dutch Reformed theologian, Van Til, held similar views.

The theologians who still opposed the new science toward the end of the seventeenth and early eighteenth century did so by resting the authority of the Bible on a concept of inspiration which insisted that the precise words of the Bible were true. While the original issue in the debate between theologians and scientists centred in the Aristotelian basis of orthodoxy and the quite different philosophical assumptions surrounding the new science, this issue was no longer in the foreground of discussion. The apparently inerrant Bible, the defence of which had previously been associated with Aristotelianism, had now become independently significant. It was maintained even when the Aristotelian arguments were no longer convincing. The problem of Protestant Biblical authority vis-à-vis the authority of the Roman Church and the collapse of the self-evident authority of Aristotle combined to leave an infallible Bible as the last line of defence. Hence, the orthodox were surely correct in sensing that to capitulate at any point would demand capitulation all along the line. Only a new beginning would do, and that they could not accept or see. It is important at this juncture to note that the literalistic defence of the Bible, which was the last stand of orthodoxy, was not nearly so central in its early·development. The views in the later development, which we have just touched upon, should not be read back into the earlier period. Philosophical views and Biblical inerrancy were assumed in the Reformation. But they only gradually became dominant and determinative in the subsequent development. It was therefore not by accident that the last battle between orthodoxy and the new science was to be over the Bible, and only indirectly over philosophy. But there was also a revival of the philosophy of the Scholastics in Leib-

nitzian form in the person of Christian Wolff; it was a revival powerful enough to become the direct target of Kant's antinomies.

B: OLD METAPHYSICS AND NEW SCIENCE: CHRISTIAN WOLFF

Historians of philosophy are divided over the question whether Descartes and Leibnitz belong more to the modern world or to the older
Medieval context. Carl Becker has made a convincing case that the
basic philosophical assumptions of these writers are still those of the
Medieval world, even though they are on the path to the modern
world.[3] They are certainly transitional figures. Leibnitz's basic concept
of monads was the key to an affirmation of individuality in a world
which was basically under the domination of a system of order, characteristic both of the world and of its Creator. Max Wundt maintained that the systems of Leibnitz and Wolff represent the old School
philosophy worked out in ways which brought it into unity with the
new mathematical science.[4] Wundt went so far as to say that it was
Leibnitz alone who saw that the philosophical assumptions of the new
science were unacceptable and therefore took it upon himself to
deepen them through motifs drawn from the School philosophy.[5]
By an affirmation of the basically rational character of all existence in its older sense, Leibnitz was able to safeguard meaning and
also accept the new mathematical order and the scientific world
view.

Christian Wolff, like many of his time, was distressed by the confessional strife among Protestant groups and particularly between
Lutherans and Roman Catholics. His ambition was so to demonstrate
theological truth that it could not be contradicted or become the
basis of strife. Such demonstration of infallibility, he had heard, was
made possible by the method inherent in mathematics. In fact, Wolff

---

[3] Carl Becker, *The Heavenly City of the Eighteenth-Century Philosophers* (New Haven:
Yale University Press, 1932).
[4] M. Wundt, *Die deutsche Schulphilosophie im Zeitalter der Aufklärung* (Tübingen, 1945),
p. 200.
[5] M. Wundt, *Die deutsche Schulmetaphysik des* 17. *Jahrhunderts* (Tübingen, 1939), p. 17.

took this so seriously that he taught mathematics and philosophy at Halle. But in his determination to find truth in its broad mathematical, rational form, he met the opposition of theologians, such as the pietist August Franke and the orthodox Joachim Lange. As a result, he lost his position at Halle, but was accepted at Marburg. He returned to Halle later as a result of a change in university policy there. The controversial literature about Wolff is enormous, including well over 200 pieces.[6]

A dramatic problem arose for the Church when Wolff, in his rectorial address, emphasized the significance of Confucius and maintained that man could attain human happiness without revelation. But this did not mean that Wolff opposed a Christian understanding of life. It meant only that he posited an area of meaning independent of the Christian drama, and that Christianity manifested a reality of which it was an illustration, perhaps even the most true. The problem for the Church, as so frequently before, was that a rational conception of reality and nature had become determinative for the understanding of Christianity.

For Wolff, God's plan or intention in the creation of the world was to reveal His majesty, that is, that man might apprehend the perfection and grandeur of God through the created order. The world as a whole was the image of God, mirroring God's perfections for man to behold.[7] Thus far, Wolff was traditional enough. And when he declared that the world was created with rational form in order to be the image of God's unseeable nature, he echoed an ancient tradition which placed the image of God in the rational capacity of man.[8]

But as in the instance of the evidences, the analogy with the early period of the Church did not hold. In the first place, the rational order or image was affirmed equally for nature and for man, whereas previously, the theological tradition had centred the image in man. In the second place, it had been clear that the rational image was the direct fruit of God's creation. Now, however, reason appeared to be

[6] See C. Wolff, *Jus Gentium Methodo Scientifica, Pertractatum*, Vol. II, trans. Joseph D. Drake (Oxford, 1934, *Introduction*).
[7] C. Wolff, *Vernünftige Gedanken, Physik* 2 (Halle, 1752), pp. 2, 6.
[8] Ibid., 2, p. 6.

the power and reality to which man, the world, and the Creator were subject. A drastic shift had taken place. God's nature and that of the world were derived from a particular philosophical conception of reality which embraced both.

This approach was given special cogency through the new science. The new science had enlarged the horizons of man's world. The rich diversity in the world served as a sign of the inexhaustible knowledge of God waiting to be explored.[9] By contrast, the ancient view of the world, with its limited views of space, was considered inadequate to disclose the perfections of God.[10] Copernicus, Kepler, and Galileo, it was declared, had contributed a view of the world that does more justice to the majesty of God than all previous views. Derham, Boyle, Clarke, and Cotton Mather were extolled and a debt of gratitude was expressed to the English who, it was noted, had been especially perceptive in such areas of exploration. The English, Wolff declared, had extended natural knowledge to the praise of God.[11]

Man's new knowledge of the world had a distinct advantage over previous science and philosophy. Such knowledge could be said to be clear and unambiguous. Clarity, declared Wolff, was a sign of genuine knowledge and therefore was applicable also to the knowledge of God. The clarity of nature provided certain knowledge which, it was maintained, was the basis by which other knowledge was to be judged.[12] Thus, the knowledge derived from nature was again superior to both Scripture and history. Wolff clearly articulated this approach in his contention that the attributes of God, derived from nature, could not be contradicted by revelation.[13]

The discussion of miracles exhibits the same difficulty. Wolff defined miracle as an event which did not have its ground in nature. But in order to know such an event, one must, by contrast, know the order of nature, particularly since, according to Wolff, miracles had not ceased to occur. He argued that by definition, however, miracles must be few in number. The order of nature, he declared, was the expression of the wisdom of God; miracles, of the power of God.

[9] bid., p. 16.   [10] Ibid., p. 56.   [11] Ibid., p. 58.   [12] Ibid., p. 66.
[13] C. Wolff, *Vernünftige Gedanken von Gott, der Welt, und der Seele des Menschen* (Halle, 1743), die neunte Auflage, p. 625.

Since the wisdom of God was greater than the power of God, he argued that the fewer the number of miracles, the greater the wisdom of God. Moreover, the wisdom of God in the order of nature also called for God's sustaining power in a way in which God's power exhibited in miracles did not call for His wisdom. Therefore, one must assume that the given, natural order was more significant than the miraculous. The disclosure of God was therefore greater in nature than in Scripture.[14]

Wolff had clearly articulated the assumptions which the theologians feared were implicit in the new science. After this, it did not matter how traditional Wolff might be in any particular delineation of a Christian doctrine. It was already of less significance than anything apparent in nature. The issue was not, of course, whether nature or Scripture as such was more important; it was whether nature or Scripture was more important for delineating a Christian understanding.

Wolff, like Derham, Ray, and Paley, gave detailed attention to tracing the wisdom of God in creation. He took great pains in showing the meaning of everything in creation. Choosing at random, one can point to Wolff's statement that the wisdom of God was evident in the rapid yet accurate movement of the tongue in speech.[15] Without depreciating one bit the miracle of the human body or any part of it, one can ask if it would not have been appropriate for Wolff to ponder what nonsense and irrelevancies the tongue can utter. Like many predecessors, Wolff also commented on the uses of day and night. The day provided a time for men to go about their duties, particularly those which they could not do so easily at night. But the night too had its special blessings. It was a time of refreshment for men and animals; it was also a time for such activities as one could not so easily perform by daylight, as catching birds and fishes. Likewise, the stars existed in order to provide man with directions and were very useful if one lost one's way at night. One can hardly resist the facetious remark of Ernst Cassirer:

[14] Ibid., pp. 639-40.
[15] C. Wolff, *Vernünftige Gedanken von dem Gebrauche der Theile in Menschen, Thieren, und Pflanzen, Physik* 3 (Halle, 1753), Neue Auflage, p. 178.

Now we know why sun, moon and stars, why day and night exist!
The stars, that we may find our way home, the day for work, the
night for sleep, and for catching birds and fish![16]

But while Wolff wrote of the purpose of the stars in this vein, he
did not believe that the stars existed just for man's use. The stars
existed also for providing light and directions for men on other major
planets. Some of the fixed stars were undoubtedly suns for other
planets. Surely on the basis of analogy, one must assume, he argued,
that there were plants, animals, and human beings on other planets.
It was as reasonable to believe that one planet was like another, as it
was to believe that the dissection of one dog would give reliable information concerning the internal structure of another.

It is all too apparent why Wolff was criticized by pietists and
orthodox alike. While he did not consciously oppose the distinctiveness
of Christianity, Wolff took his cue for the discussion of all aspects
of nature and even of God from what he believed to be true of nature.
Nature after all was the mirror of God and it was at every point the
key by which theological problems could be solved.

Wolff did not enjoy a reigning position for long. His particular
combination of the new science and of a rationalism still anchored in
the School philosophy could not be maintained in the light of the increasing repudiation of the older form of rational thought. The transformation of reason will need to receive some attention as we survey
the path from orthodoxy to the Enlightenment. Wolff had only taken
the first minimal steps in that direction.

C: FROM RATIONAL TO MORAL CHRISTIANITY

We indicated that the scientific genius of the seventeenth century
belonged to England. In the latter part of the century and in the
beginning of the eighteenth, the evidences for Christianity were
widely employed. The evidences were characteristically English in spirt.
In the meantime, the deist literature had also become prominent in
England, and an anticlerical philosophy was expressed in France. All

[16] E. Cassirer, *Rousseau, Kant, and Goethe* (Princeton, 1947), p. 67.

of these currents eventually made an impact on the German scene. None of them was indigenous to Germany, and there was a time lag before their influence was felt. In spite of this, the transition to the Enlightenment, culturally and religiously, took place in Germany. In England, the deist movement was largely overcome by Methodism and Evangelicalism. In America, the great awakenings made their way against the decaying Puritanism. Deist literature had its impact in America from the latter two decades of the eighteenth century into the first decade of the nineteenth. That too was met by a number of powerful religious revivals. Among the Germans the situation was different. Pietism had challenged and partially transformed orthodoxy. Except in one major instance, it did not break out of the Lutheran fold, as Methodism was forced to do from the established Church of England. Nor, as in America, did an evangelical impulse create new forms of the Church and transform traditional forms as well. In the strictly Continental scene the influence of English and French thought from the outside, and rational and pietist strands within orthodoxy, gradually led Protestant orthodoxy itself from its rigid tradition directly into the Enlightenment. In that transformation, the theological movement was not in the forefront. It followed in the wake of other developments. But two distinct theological movements can be noted. They are the transitional theologians and the innovators. Within both groups the new currents in science were variously assessed and sometimes still opposed in the light of a conservative tradition of Biblical interpretation.

This ambivalence underscores the fact that we are dealing with a period in which the currents of thought were sometimes separate and sometimes intertwined. But neither science, nor the philosophy associated with the science, was the chief problem any more. An entirely new rational tradition was being forged. Sometimes it was in alliance with the new science, sometimes it stood in opposition to it. In the last phases of the rational tradition, namely, the Enlightenment, opposition to the new science had been replaced by considerable indifference to its attainments. This did not mean that the new science was thereby less influential. Insofar as it was responsible for the exclusion of certain areas of knowledge from the arena of reason and of faith, it may have been all the more influential. It may be responsible for the reductionist character of much of moral theology, against which there was so quick a protest, Kant was a symbol of this theology and Schleiermacher already protested against it. But we are not yet concerned with the final destruction of the old picture of the world and the consequent attempt to start afresh in theology. Here we want only to indicate that the transition in the understanding of reason and revelation was determined by another conception of reason and by science becoming a philosophy. At the very time when scientists such as Newton had begun to be suspicious of the need for a philosophical heritage, Newtonianism arose as a philosophical position. Meanwhile, the independent currents of rationalism, which frequently had been allied with the new science, underwent a transformation. It is precisely because of this philosophical transformation that Barth believes that the impact of the scientific tradition should not be overexaggerated as a cause of the demise of the orthodox development.[17] But while the philosophical transformation now was a development ambiguously related to the new science and sometimes without direct reference to it at all, the development of the concept of reason did not take place without reference to what the scientific tradition implied. It is a significant fact that many of the philosophers and theologians felt it necessary to define their own problems in such a way as to be able to ignore the scientific developments. When one finds it necessary to keep one's eye on a tradition, one has not thereby ceased being influenced by it.

1. *A transitional phase.* The transitional theologians take their name from the fact that they stand between the orthodox development and the Enlightenment proper. It is difficult to see them in their own right because they do not represent a position which reigned for a long period of time. They stand between the times. This may argue that they were more relevant and significant than some theological figures whose influence was greater and more lasting; nevertheless,

[17] Karl Barth, *Die protestantische Theologie im 19. Jahrhundert* (Zurich, 1947), p. 81.

they were generally eclipsed from the history of thought because of the transitional character of their work.

They also stand between orthodoxy and pietism. While some were aloof to pietism, others show traces of its influence. In any case, the transformation of orthodoxy was the twin fruit of pietism and a change in the conception of reason. The relation of the pietist tradition to the new science was not particularly one of active concern. Pietists were conservative in their conception of Biblical inspiration and followed the orthodox position more often than not. But they did not defend the older position insofar as it manifested scientific and philosophical rather than Biblical influences. Thus Philip Spener, like others we have mentioned, understood comets in their scientific setting and also as harbingers of God's destructive powers. But, unlike his predecessors, he was reticent to elaborate either. His concerns were elsewhere. The pietists effected a revolution in the way in which Christians were called upon to concentrate on the Bible. They stressed the need for linguistic training, so that the Bible could be read in the original tongues for the sake of getting rid of foreign theological accretions. Their accent upon the Bible in this and in other ways was destined to transform Biblical study and free it from scientific and philosophical concerns. Further, the creation of new universities under pietist influence, such as that of Halle, was directly instrumental in furthering the new science. Without the burden of an ancient Aristotelian tradition, an open field for the new science was found within the new citadels of learning. (When piety rather than theology reigns, general learning frequently has a better chance. But such piety unwittingly is responsible for the secular independence of learning.)

As representative of the transitional theologians, we shall take John Franz Buddeus, Lorenz von Mosheim, Sigmund Jakob Baumgarten, and Christoph Matthäus Pfaff. All of them engaged in a battle against atheism, which they interpreted to be the practical, not the theoretical denial of God's relation to nature and to human affairs. Buddeus was interested in *Physiko-theologie* as a weapon against atheism. We noted previously that Wesley extensively used the work of Buddeus in his account of the wisdom of God in creation. Mosheim considered Cudworth's major work so important that he translated it into Latin in order to make it available to German readers, who had little knowledge of English in this period.[18] But Mosheim opposed Toland, and Baumgarten wrote against the deists. In short, these writers defended a total religious understanding against those philosophies which seemed to subvert it. They wanted to defend a conception of reason and of philosophy consonant with Christian understanding. That is why Cudworth was considered acceptable, but the deists were not.

For these thinkers reason and revelation stood in a harmonious relation to each other. Revelation did not contradict reason. For Buddeus, the Christian revelation fulfilled natural religion. He distinguished natural religion from those views of reason which approximated but did not lead to the Christian answer. Buddeus, for instance, rejected naturalism because it spoke of God, but not of Christ.[19] Natural religion must inevitably be fulfilled in Christ. Buddeus sensed that there was a mystery inherent in the Christian claim, and he objected to the Socinians primarily because they depended so much on reason that they destroyed the mysteries which belonged to true religion.[20] On the other hand, Buddeus also believed that reason rightly judged the adequacy of revelation. Here his view of philosophy as the handmaiden to theology was unacceptable because of the responsibility which he assigned to reason.

For Pfaff, too, the light of nature led to its fulfillment in revelation: but revelation had to be in accord with what one knew from natural sources. The dispute over the difference between the natural and revealed did not stir him. The net result, he believed, was the same, no matter where the lines were drawn.[21] Baumgarten elaborated a similar pattern of thought. Only Mosheim did not concern himself with natural religion or natural theology in his dogmatic work. But he expounded the equivalent of natural theology in his philosophical

---

[18] *Rudolphi Cudworthi Systema intellectuale huius universi* (Jena, 1733).

[19] *Historische und theologische Einleitung in die vornehmsten Religions streitigkeiten aus Herrn Johann Francisci Buddei*, bei Johann Georg Walch, (Jena, 1724), p. 696.

[20] Ibid., p. 83.

[21] C. M. Pfaff, *Einleitung in die dogmatische Theologie* (Tübingen, 1747), p. 27-28.

writings. In his dogmatic enterprise, he preferred to be entirely dependent upon Scripture.

Among these writers, natural religion had an intermediate position. It did not have an independent status; nor was it so bound to revelation that it was but a first step. Natural religion was significant apart from anything else; nevertheless, it was fulfilled only in revelation. Hence, these writers did not challenge the concern with redemption. But the orthodox extremes, which produced so much controversy, were softened. These men believed in reasonable essentials. As in the case of John Locke, it was considered reasonable that a Messiah had been sent to redeem men. But, as also in the instance of John Locke, the mystery of grace was increasingly understood in rational terms.

There were also signs of a middle position in the understanding of the Bible. Already in the seventeenth century, the traditional way of understanding the Mosaic authorship of the Pentateuch was questioned. One thinks of Spinoza and of Richard Simon, who, writing from different theological assumptions, were united on this point. Somewhat later, Henning Bernhard Witter called attention to the two creation stories. Pfaff, too, contended that parts of the Bible appeared bound to the comprehension, insight, and knowledge of man. He ignored the question of whether or not the Bible contained mistakes; but one can hardly doubt that he believed that there were some.

More important than such matters was the return to basic questions of Biblical interpretation. The orthodox had identified revelation and inspiration. Pfaff, Mosheim, and Baumgarten challenged this identification. In accord with the Reformers, they believed that a distinction needed to be made between the two. Baumgarten distinguished between believing in the Bible and believing in revelation. The Bible was the foundation or the original source for revelation. In considering whether the content of the Bible or the total Bible as written was inspired, Mosheim answered his own question by suggesting that just enough of the latter was inspired in order to guarantee the validity of its content.

If one does not judge these theologians by the subsequent demise of any hermeneutical principle in understanding the Bible, but looks rather at the orthodox position which they faced, one must admit that they had a genuinely creative thrust in their understanding of Scripture. For them, the inerrancy of the Bible was not the basis of its interpretation; nor would they admit that inerrancy and revelation were identified. But, as a point of fact, no new hermeneutical principle emerged. Although various distinctions and adaptations were made, there was no new pattern of Biblical comprehension. The consequence was that the literalistic understanding of some passages was rejected while others were not challenged at all.

This ambivalence was evident in the way in which some of the theologians encountered the new science. Pfaff, for example, was quite free in facing the new scientific theories. As a theologian, he did not wish to settle them. He wrote:

I do not wish here to develop, which system, the Ptolemaic, Tychonic, or Copernican is favoured by the Holy Scripture. It is true that a movement is ascribed to the sun, Joshua 10: 12-13; Psalm 19: 6-7; Ecclesiastes 1: 5; Isaiah 38: 8, while simultaneously the earth is ascribed as still, Psalm 18: 7; 24: 2; 104: 5, Ecclesiastes 1: 4; Job 38: 4; 2 Peter 3: 5; Revelation 6: 14. But one can only explain this on outward appearance, partly in other ways, and in theology there is no necessity to let oneself in for extensive astronomical clarification. But I must say one thing more. It appears that the Holy Scripture holds the stars are small, since it says, on the last day the stars will fall from heaven, just as a fig tree sheds off its figs, as moved by the wind, Matthew 24: 29 ff.; Revelation 6: 13. But are not, one would like to suggest, the fixed stars large suns, much larger than our earth, also which as such cannot fall without in a moment utterly destroying and burning the earth in even coming close? Here we are not concerned with genuine stars, but with meteors . . .[22]

But when it came to the question of how creation occurred and how many days it took, Pfaff pointed us to the Scriptures. For Pfaff, as for his contemporaries, those passages or sections of Scripture which had

[22] Pfaff, op. cit., pp. 85-86. (trans. J. Dillenberger).

not yet been directly challenged were accepted as statements of fact and their theological significance still included their literal truth.

Miracles were neither denied nor stressed. They were events thought to be above nature, just as in the case of revelation. But they were no longer used as "evidences." Writer after writer pointed to the infrequent occurrence of miracles in a universe which was predominantly orderly. Baumgarten was particularly impressed by the order of the created world, and suggested that miracles would have been unnecessary had there been no sin. Then he added, just as Wolff had, that the greatest display of God's goodness, wisdom, and power was in nature. Miracles displayed only God's power. But at times, he also referred to miracles when speaking of the order of nature. Both the order of nature and the order of grace were considered miraculous. The two orders of creation, that is, nature and grace, were both designated as miracles of God.

A more traditional view was expressed by J. G. Walch, who is remembered in Western history primarily for his German edition of Luther's writings. Miracle was defined as an act of God beyond the course of nature or its natural powers. But Walch was also influenced by the new currents of thought. He surveyed the scientific and philosophical developments since the time of the Reformation, and he pointed out that one of the main difficulties was that there was no unanimity as to what constituted the ordinary power or course of nature.[23] In one respect, he was more radical than his predecessors. He simply declared that Moses was not a physicist.[24]

2. *Enlightenment theologies.* Although there was a discernible trend toward the rationalization of many Christian concepts, the transitional theologians made every attempt to remain true to the Christian heritage. Among those theologians known as the "neologen" or innovators, the Christian substance was rather drastically transformed through the use of moral categories which they found so convenient for theological formulation. Here one finds the gate to the Enlighten-

[23] J. Walch, *Einleitung in die Philosophie* (Leipzig, 1730), pp. 214 ff.
[24] Ibid., p. 219.

ment. Still, one finds traditional and non-traditional ways of expressing the Gospel. Johann David Michaelis, one of the more conservative members of this group, still defended the New Testament miracles on the basis of the reliability of so many witnesses.[25] But miracles, he declared, now had to be infrequent if this was the best of all possible worlds.[26] Here Michaelis, like Wolff, followed Leibnitz. Miracles originally confirmed the man Jesus and His message, and made sense only then.[27] In all of this, miracle was still defined in the traditional manner as an activity of God beyond human possibility and the order of the world.

This was a fairly conservative interpretation of the Bible. On the basis of new historical information, such as his extreme knowledge of antiquity, and rational analysis, Michaelis asked some new questions. The Mosaic writings were analyzed with respect to their geographical, cultural, and political context. But the Mosaic authorship of the Pentateuch was defended on the basis of the number of individuals who had thought it to be genuinely Mosaic.[28] Michaelis, unlike his pupil Eichhorn, was not yet ready for literary criticism on such levels. He preferred Matthew to Mark and Luke in points of difference, but this was because of the alleged apostolic authority of Matthew. The concept of creation was expounded with reference to Genesis, but he said that it would have been helpful if Moses had given us more information. For instance, Michaelis wondered whether the fire under the earth heated it until the sun was created on the fourth day.[29] But Michaelis also announced that the fields of physics and astronomy were independent of theology, while men and animals belonged to it.[30] It is obvious that Michaelis combined things new and old. He had not broken through to a new Biblical and theological understanding.

The rational elements in Michaelis' understanding of Scripture are evident in how he dealt with embarrassing passages. That God should dispute for a half day, he declared, was neither credible nor appro-

---

[25] J. D. Michaelis, *Dogmatik* (Tubingen, 1785), p. 49.
[26] Ibid., p. 213.   [27] Ibid., pp. 38 ff.
[28] J. D. Michaelis, *Einleitung in die göttlichen Schriften des Alten Bundes* (Des ersten Teils erster Abschnitt; Hamburg, 1787), p. 79.
[29] J. D. Michaelis, *Dogmatik*, p. 200.   [30] Ibid., p. 217.

priate to God.[31] Likewise, the story of Adam and Eve appeared to Michaelis to have all the marks of a fable; but he was unable to bring himself to that conclusion.[32] In interpreting the story, however, he softened the traditional conception of original sin.[33]

A more radical conception of the nature of Scripture in the light of the new knowledge is found in J. F. W. Jerusalem. The creation account was considered to be an old story which explained the human plight. The story of the Garden of Eden was rejected as literal history. Only the philosophical or interpretative parts of these stories were ascribed to Moses.[34] In fact, Jerusalem suggested that the creation story bordered on the ludicrous in assuming that there was light before the sun was created.[35] He ridiculed the idea that millions of suns and stars were created in one day between the creation of plants and animals, as if such activity were merely a day's work like all the rest.[36] The first sentence of the Bible was true, namely, God created the heavens and the earth. But what followed in the Genesis account, suggested Jerusalem, was borrowed from the surrounding culture. Moreover, Moses said more than he should have about many things, particularly about nature. Of course, it could not have been expected that Moses would have known about Copernicus.[37] Israel was not yet ready for the wonders of Copernicus and of Newton.[38]

The concern with nature and natural religion had become dominant for Jerusalem. He commented on the contribution which Galileo, Leibnitz, and Newton made to the knowledge of nature and believed it to be immensely significant for religion.[39] God was not less active or

---

[31] J. D. Michaelis, *Einleitung* . . . . Hamburg, ed., 1787, p. 9.
[32] J. D. Michaelis, *Dogmatik*, pp. 254 ff.
[33] No attention is given here to the views of Johann August Ernesti, but his Biblical interpretation is essentially no different than Michaelis. Both insist upon the grammatical, historical sense, but are not yet critical in terms of sources.
[34] J. Jerusalem, *Betrachtungen über die vornehmsten Wahrheiten, Zweiter Teil Zweiter Band, oder Viertes Stück*, pp. 658 ff.
[35] Ibid., pp. 558-59.
[36] Ibid., pp. 587-88.
[37] Ibid., p. 590.
[38] Ibid., p. 600.
[39] J. Jerusalem, *Betrachtungen* . . . , (Zweiter Teil; Frankfurt und Leipzig, 1775), pp. 84-85.

apparent in nature than in revelation. Revelation corroborated the fruits of natural knowledge. It contradicted neither the order of nature nor of morality.[40]

In the thought of J. J. Spalding and Johann Salomo Semler, natural knowledge had become entirely independent. It was no longer a first step to revelation, not did it need confirmation by revelation.[41] The distinctiveness of revelation had disappeared, even when it was not denied outright. In this, as in other respects, Semler repudiated the older orthodoxy on many fronts. He considered theology to be a vocation which was neither necessary nor useful for Christians. This was a far cry from the orthodox writers, for whom theology had been the guarantee of an adequate Biblical witness and the defence against all error. For Semler, the Word of God and the Bible were severed. The Bible was meaningful insofar as it spoke to the internal life of man, and when it did this, one could speak of the inspiration of Scripture. Its content was no longer unique. Further, a sharp distinction was made between the Old and New Testaments. The message of the New was considered to be as far from the Old as it was from heathenism in general. The Old Testament was particular; the New Testament universal. The Biblical concern with a history of salvation was considered too concrete to be incorporated in universal concerns.

Such an interpretation demanded the abandonment or transformation of much of the history of the Church. For Semler and others of his persuasion, two traditional theological affirmations were particularly objectionable. Augustine's analysis and defence of original sin and his concept of predestination were rejected. A distinction was made between Augustine and the Reformers, to the credit of the latter. In retrospect it is clear that the Reformers were closer to Augustine than these writers assumed. Original sin and predestination were singled out for rejection because they were the pivotal points

[40] Ibid., pp. 90-91.
[41] J. J. Spalding, *Gedanken über den Werth der Gefühle in dem Christenthum* Neue verbesserte und vermehrte Auflage (Leipzig, 1764), p. 69. It is interesting to note that the analysis of feeling developed in this volume is not unlike that developed by Schleiermacher. It was also Spalding who translated Butler's *Analogy* into German.

at which the Enlightenment attacked the older Christian conceptions.

Since the centre of Christianity for Semler was no longer the traditional drama of man's redemption, the grace of God in Christ was equated with the spirit which made man alive. But this spirit was defined primarily as the encouragement which men discovered in the moral and ethical striving of Jesus. For Semler, the " moral " was a significant category of interpretation. It is, however, not to be understood in the later moralistic sense. It was a concept used primarily in contradistinction to modes of thinking which took their cue from nature or what became increasingly known as the physical world: hence, its importance for theology. The moral as a religious category meant measuring one's life by the perfections of God, followed by a concern for greater perfection in one's own life so that God's perfection might be reflected. The uniqueness of Christianity resided in the fact that it disclosed a moral religion not previously found in the world.

> To me it is a great truth, that God has revealed a universal, spiritual, perfect religion, through Jesus, and the apostles, a moral religion, which did not stand in the Jewish and heathenish religion.[42]

But in that conception, the classical Christian heritage had been largely abandoned.

The transition from a rationalistic to a moral conception of religion did not mean the end of reason; it was reason in a new form. In the older rationalistic tradition, Christian concepts and Scripture had been adapted to the new science insofar as individual writers were able to do so. In every instance, one had to face the question of what implications theology and science had for each other. This was true whether one was interpreted in the light of the other, or whether one managed to make some clear-cut distinctions between them. By contrast, the development we have just sketched presented a new conception. The two areas were not only distinguished; Christianity was so transformed that no problem of conflict could arise. Christianity was de-

[42] Johann Salomo Semlers neuer Versuch, die gemeinnüzige Auslegung und Anwendung des Neuen Testaments zu befordern (Halle, 1786), Vorrede, no pagination. (trans. J. Dillenberger).

fined as a moral realm, independently existing alongside of science. But such a drastic transformation implied the abandonment of the traditional Christian substance.

However, it must be added that the innovating theologians differed from those deists for whom natural religion had become a substitute for Christianity. The innovating theologians did not reject Christianity; they transformed it into their own image. Like many in their time, they believed in God, virtue, and immortality. But they also believed that these concepts were known supremely in the drama surrounding Jesus of Nazareth, that they were inextricably bound up with the Christian religion.[43] The innovators continued to hold to a concept of revelation, although they had abandoned the traditional content.

Lessing and Kant represent the transition to a religion independent of the Christian substance, or to a view which accepted Christianity as one illustration of the "religious." Lessing quarrelled with the " innovating theologians " because they were still concerned with the distinctiveness of Christianity and of revelation alongside their interest in the religions of the world. For Lessing and for Kant, revelation at best was the disclosure of what was potentially knowable through human reason. Revelation was necessary for the ignorant stage of mankind; it was the first stage in the education of the human race. For Lessing, as well as for Fichte later, the accent in religion had to be upon life, upon the acting, striving, moral nature of man which led individually and collectively from comparative ignorance and superstition to greater knowledge. Progress became significant. For Kant, also, reason with reference to religious matters was moral reason. While he also had some concern for development, Kant's concept of reason was formal rather than active. But in spite of this difference between Lessing and Kant, they had both left behind the older conception of reason. Gone was the notion that the universe had a pervasive structure of reason, in which the mind participated. Such a philosophical basis for guaranteeing knowledge and purpose was gone. Structural rationalism had been replaced by an active, moral reason,

[43] K. Aner, *Die Theologie der Lessingzeit* (Halle, 1929), pp. 301, 343.

in which *to do* was more important than *to know*, or in which knowing was discovered in doing.

The precise content of the religious views of Lessing and Kant lie outside our concern. They are merely indicative of the last stage in the transition from Orthodoxy to Enlightenment. But Kant is particularly important for the way in which he reconceived the philosophical and theological heritage, and thereby set the stage for the subsequent Protestant development. Kant's positing of two indubitable areas, the starry heavens above and the moral law within, set forth the implicit distinction already made by the innovating theologians between the domain of knowledge and that of religion. While the innovating theologians were fundamentally uninterested in the first, Kant was concerned to establish the significance of both. The starry heavens above referred to the Newtonian ordered world which was observable through the human senses. But such knowledge must be restricted and not extrapolated into other areas. Unlike the rationalists and the orthodox theologians, Kant restricted knowledge to the observable world in order to make room for the domain of moral, practical reason, that is, to make room for both. But the distinction between the two areas did not mean that they were essentially unlike; they were different, yet basically analogous. In fact, Kant had hoped to apply the notion of clarity and the method implicit in Newton to that of the moral realm. In an early work, *Allgemeine Naturgeschichte und Theorie des Himmels*, Kant's purpose was to extend Newtonian assumptions to other realms of experience. He went so far as to say that the proper method in metaphysics was identical with that introduced into the natural sciences by Newton.[44] But while the method, particularly with reference to clarity and precision, was considered the same for both, Kant was adamant in his insistence that the two areas be distinguished. He rejected the physico-teleological arguments for God, elaborated in the last chapter, precisely for this reason.[45] The traditional proofs for God's existence fell by the wayside, and were superseded by the moral arguments. The foundation and nature of

[44] E. Cassirer, *Rousseau, Kant and Goethe* (Princeton, 1947), p. 61.
[45] I. Kant. *Critique of Judgement*, Scribner Selections (1929), pp. 502 ff.

each realm was different, however analogous. Kant's starting assumption was the distinctiveness of each area.

Newton, it will be recalled, eschewed all speculation and ascribed the world just as it was directly to the creation of God. Kant suggested the nebular hypothesis, subsequently elaborated by Laplace, to account for its origin. But Kant did not draw the conclusion of the latter, who, when pressed as to the relation of theological dimensions to such a suggestion, allegedly replied that he had no need of the God hypothesis. According to the nebular hypothesis, the earth and our universe were the end product of swirling chaotic matter which now obeyed definite laws. Strictly within the domain of physics it is, of course, possible to say that one has no need of the God hypothesis; but Laplace undoubtedly meant more than that, namely, that the whole question of God was irrelevant.

Kant did not accept a simple mechanical interpretation of nature and of human life. Man's distinctiveness was at once so apparent, and the adaptations of nature so startling, that no mechanical assumption did justice to them. But Kant rejected the elaboration of purpose and adaptations by such figures as Christian Wolff. Man could not be said to be so favoured as to be the " special darling in nature," freed from all of its caprices.[46] Yet, creation had purpose and meaning through the uniqueness of man. Nor could the rest of the created order be explained in mechanical terms. Kant preferred a path between those who accepted a mechanical explanation of the world and those who abused the conception of purpose through its extravagant elaboration.

It is quite certain that we can never get a sufficient knowledge of organized beings and their inner possibility, much less get an explanation of them, by looking merely to mechanical principles of nature. Indeed, so certain is it, that we may confidently assert that it is absurd for men even to entertain any thought of so doing, or to hope that maybe another Newton may some day arise, to make intelligible to us even the genesis of but a blade of grass from natural laws that no design has ordered. Such insight we must absolutely deny mankind.[47]

46 Ibid., p. 495.   47 Quoted by Cassirer, op. cit., p. 65.

In the light of the overextended claims of rationalism and orthodoxy on the one side, and the difficulties of having knowledge at all along the empiricist lines, Kant's Copernican revolution existed in rehabilitating knowledge and faith, philosophy and theology. But in his thinking, the Christian substance remained only as the hidden foundation of absolute obligation. The religious dimension was excluded from anything which had to do with the world of knowledge; religious concepts were so narrowed that no content remained which could possibly create conflict. Kant represents the final product of a direction in which the issues between science and theology were solved by the virtual abandonment of the distinctive claims of the latter. In the next chapter, we shall give attention to the diverse protests against this Enlightenment development, and to new directions in theology. In the remainder of this chapter, we shall recapitulate the developments from the sixteenth century to the dawn of the nineteenth.

The sixteenth and seventeenth centuries were Christian in orientation and conception. But fairly independent movements, revived on Christian soil, began to make themselves known and felt. Nevertheless, the predominant ethos and understanding were Christian. The great scientists were consciously Christian, and they were certainly unaware that they stood on philosophical grounds which were destined to threaten and, for some, to undermine Christian thought. Further, they were unaware that their very discoveries would change the mode of Christian thinking even where it did not directly challenge its content. Hence, they could not understand why churchmen should be at all opposed to their discoveries. It is ironic that their defence against the attack of churchmen should have been the very thing which transformed theology, namely, the elaboration of an independent natural theology.

Thus far, we have traced various stages in this history. We have seen how science won the exclusive right to the delineation of nature, how the clarity of the method and results in science provided a methodological principle for understanding revelation; how the philosophical direction which emerged out of that method became a clue to the content of revelation; and how an entirely new tradition of reason and nature became a substitute for revelation. Certainly, that logic of events was not anticipated.

The theologians were only too afraid that the direction taken by the new science would destroy Christianity, and promote atheism as they understood it. They were remarkably right. But their own course of action was more shrouded in defensive and rearguard ways of thinking than in any creative advance through the problems. They were interested in holding the line, and had no inkling of new possibilities which could guarantee their basic position while adapting to the new currents. This was partly because they were so preoccupied with inter-Protestant strife and with clarifying their position vis-à-vis Rome. But it was also due to the fact that the new science, as we noted, was associated with a philosophy which ran counter to the prevailing Aristotelianism. Further, it was due to the fact that both theologians and scientists thought that their own conceptions of the world provided a literal picture in which meaning and detail coincided. There was little, if any, place for imagination and for what we today call symbol. Moreover, in spite of the advances which scientists *continued* to make, the prevailing mood was that scientific truth had dawned and that only details needed to be filled in. The Newtonian synthesis was believed to be an abiding picture of the world, demanding only minor corrections. The scientific tradition was a blending in which discoveries were accepted as final truth and in which new discoveries were always being made. Moreover, continuing new discoveries apparently did not call previous metaphysical assumptions into question. The sixteenth and seventeenth centuries were metaphysical centuries, in which doubt was but a methodological principle, not ontologically real. Even the battle about the authority of the ancients was not a challenge to basic certainty. It was the question of who should have authority among the ancients. Should the ancients who confirmed one's present position, however selectively they had to be taken, be preferred to groups and movements which contradicted it? Although it is true that the scientific tradition abandoned some cherished assumptions more quickly than did theology, this should not blind us to the fact that scientists were no more free of dogmatic convictions in the sixteenth and seventeenth centuries generally than were theologians.

The eighteenth century was a transitional period. At the very time when Newton exercised caution about the philosophical assumptions of his science, others were applying his basic outlook to other areas of knowledge and creating what we know as Newtonianism. Nevertheless, Newtonianism, while it made a philosophy out of the new science, abandoned the metaphysical superstructure and extensive philosophical elaborations which had accompanied science heretofore. Concurrently, those who had been influenced by the rationalism of Descartes and Leibnitz, developed tendencies of thought less sure of a structure of reason but more certain of the power of reason in life and in religion. Hence, from both the scientific and the philosophical traditions, a new conception of reason emerged. It was more modest in its claims, but more pretentious in its subject matter. Theology as the queen of the sciences had been superseded, not by the advent of one philosophy, but by a general philosophical spirit in which the various disciplines were assigned their place.

On the one side, the scientific tradition was converted into a new philosophy; and on the other side, the new philosophy of the eighteenth century frequently ignored science. Science had brought an independent power of reason to birth, which was now prepared to assume its independence. Thus, at times, eighteenth-century thinkers hoped to apply the method of science to all areas, along the lines originally suggested by Kant. That development took place in full strength in the nineteenth century. At other times, the new power in reason was confined to the domain of religion and of life as contrasted to the scientific tradition. That development was exhibited in Lessing and was given new form in the " Sturm und Drang " movement. Such thinkers objected to the new science because many aspects of life had been set aside through the mechanical, mathematical, indifferent order of nature. The worlds of nature and of man were beginning to be set against each other. Nature's participation in man's drama, or man's participation in nature, had guaranteed a bond which prevented man or nature from becoming an object. But in the tradition of Descartes, followed in this point by Kant, nature became an object or a stage upon which a drama was enacted. History was considered to be man's battle against nature. This objectification of nature circumscribed the role of human imagination. Where nature became an object to be surveyed rather than to be participated in, there conceptual thinking took on the characteristics of literalism and the horizons of thought were limited.

In the sixteenth and seventeenth centuries, the Christian understanding was too closely tied up with a particular picture of the world. (*Weltbild.*) In the eighteenth century, a new *Weltbild* became a *Weltanschauung.* Areas of experience which men had once felt to be significant, for example—in art and in religion—became unimportant or were so transformed that their former dimensions were lost. The Newtonian world of science and the moral universe of man, different but analogous, shrunk the horizons of men's experience. In the theological sense, this tended to eliminate or change much of what had been considered significant. Even where there was a sense for the traditional affirmations, adequate vehicles for formulation and expression were no longer at hand. In that situation, the orthodox had no alternative but to become more orthodox.

Whatever one's assessment of the older Aristotelian position, it provided the dimensions of life so essential to deal with purpose, destiny, and meaning in the Christian sense. That Aristotle had to be baptized in order to do this should not loom important in any assessment. Christians had always had to do that, since no philosophical system was ready-made or adequate. Such a problem was quite different from the one which now confronted Christians. There were no adequate categories to express the transcendent dimensions which belonged to revelation. In that development, the Church was not without guilt. It had succumbed to the temptation of defining revelation in terms not distinguishable from other forms of knowledge.

The older orthodox theology had now become impossible for those who wished to take their world seriously. On the other hand, since the middle of the eighteenth century, the new currents expressed by the innovating theologians were preached in pulpit after pulpit, and the Church was in danger of religious corrosion from within. A new direction was desperately needed, one which would still deal with the currents of the time, concern itself with the problems of the Church, and rehabilitate theology. That struggle was to occupy Protestantism for some time. Its initial genius was expressed in Schleiermacher. The Roman Catholic analysis of the period from the Reformation to Schleiermacher is that it represents the secularization of the West, variously brought on by Luther, Kant, and Descartes. For the Protestants, there seemed no alternative but to push through to a fresh beginning.

VII

Creative Theological Directions and New Problems

A: POSITIVE ALTERNATIVES TO A MECHANICAL NATURE

In the philosophy of the Enlightenment, the domain of nature was no more a sphere for religious understanding. The new intellectual assumptions had taken the world of nature out of religion and placed nature rather squarely and exclusively in the camp of scientific knowledge. As we have indicated, Kant accepted and gave classic formulation to this position. Fichte developed a conception of man and his progressive attainments over against the backdrop of nature, and Hegel, with his intense dislike for the whole Newtonian conception of science and nature, intentionally snubbed the field of science in the development of his philosophical system.

There were individuals for whom the Enlightenment conception of nature and reason were not adequate for the understanding of man or his world. Such persons believed that the dimensions of life and their religious significance were not adequately served in a religion of reason. Nor were they willing to accept the older orthodoxy, perpetuated as it was in isolated theological figures. The religious understanding must be broader than the prevailing Enlightenment conception but not consciously opposed to the new science of nature. Nature, too, must be understood in terms which did not reduce it to a mechanical, meaningless order.

Theologically, the " Sturm und Drang " movement and the later Romantic protest must be understood in this context. While some of its members did not adhere to Christianity, they fought against the reduction of life to sheerly moral aspects and had a feeling for nature and its vitalities beyond the barren order of the Newtonian world machine. It was not the order which bothered them; that, they readily accepted. But the objectification of nature and its remoteness from the life of man excluded a vital relation to the whole world process. The Newtonian world was the world of sense without an appreciation of its role in relation to ordinary experience and feeling. It was a world grown cold and dead. Against it, they protested with all the energy they could command. The excesses in their position were the dubious fruits of the urgency they felt.

The representatives of these movements lie outside our major concern. Some, like Johann Lavater and Johann Herder, were clergymen. Their works provide us with a picture of how they regarded some of the issues with which we have been concerned.[1] Herder, for example, regarded the Bible not as science or knowledge, but as poetry. He accepted the new science in its views of creation. He rejected all views which reconciled the new science and Genesis. For example, he stood against the views of Michaelis and Buffon, who believed that the six days of creation represented epochs of Nature.[2] Nor did the contradictory strands in the Genesis account bother Herder. One should not apply rationally consistent criteria to poetry, but rather read it in terms of its intention. Roy Pascal has written movingly of Herder's conception of Creation :

He sees it as a description of the dawn. The primitive shepherds of ancient Israel saw this miracle daily, and it was for them the supreme symbol of God's creative power; through it they were daily filled with the grateful consciousness of the divine force. This is not a " true " description of the origin of the universe or of God, for both appear in a form determined by the limited experience and nature of

[1] One of the most interesting figures is Johann Hamann. His concern with language is particularly relevant to the modern scene.
[2] Roy Pascal, *The German Sturm und Drang* (Manchester: Manchester University Press, 1953), p. 96.

the early Hebrews; but it is fuller, truer, than the modern metaphysical, rationalist conception of God, because God is a living reality for these shepherds, vibrating throughout their whole being, not an abstract construct of their minds. And for modern man, too, this symbol of God is truer, more significant and satisfactory than the Newtonian abstraction, since it sums up the totality of the creative force and appeals with intense power to man's imagination and feeling.[3]

The alternatives of considering God to be apart from the world (the deist view) or of God entirely in and through the world (a too consistent pantheism) did not please Herder. But in the last analysis, his views bordered on pantheism, and little of the traditional substance of Christianity was evident in his thought.

Friedrich Christoph Oetinger, while accepting the new science, had a more distinctly Christian orientation than either the "Sturm und Drang" movement or the romantics. Newton's work was positively interpreted in a Christian frame of reference.[4] God's concursus with the world was discussed in its various philosophical forms, but Oetinger concluded that the Biblical notion of God's relation to the world could not be expressed in such ways.[5] Oetinger regarded himself as a Biblical theologian.

Oetinger contended for a wider frame of reference in which to understand God, man, and world. He affirmed that there was a mystery to things in and beyond their natural properties, which consequently was not touched upon by the natural sciences. This level of reality was found where science and philosophy were carried beyond themselves, and, of course, supremely in the Biblical tradition. God spoke through nature and history, but beyond the confines of the empirical and the rational orders. Oetinger was noticeably influenced by Jacob Boehme and he prepared the ground for the philosopher, Friedrich Schelling.[6] But he also engaged in undue speculations; he

[3] Ibid., p. 97.
[4] F. C. Oetinger, *Die Theologie aus der Idee des Lebens* (Stuttgart, 1852), pp. 136 ff.
[5] Ibid., pp. 158 ff.
[6] Some of Oetinger's papers and writings have been collected under the suggestive title, *Die Heilige Philosophie* (München, 1923).

was interested in an alleged celestial chemistry or physics which had theological significance.

While Newton and his predecessors were scientifically accepted by the type of thinkers exhibited here, they revolted against the implied reductionist understanding of the world. The most creative theological figure in that setting was Friedrich Schleiermacher.

B: THE CREATIVE THRUST OF SCHLEIERMACHER AND RELATED FIGURES

Schleiermacher stands to the Christian tradition as Kant does to the philosophical. He recast and transformed the currents of the immediate past in a synthesis which marked a genuine new departure in Christian history. On the scientific side, he accepted the Newtonian world; but he refused to be bound to a doctrinaire conception of nature. He rejected both the rationalist philosophy and the rationalist orthodox systems of Protestant thought. Both, he inferred, destroyed life by system and by speculative thought. In this sense—though in this sense alone—Schleiermacher was antimetaphysical. Nor was he interested in natural religion or the religion of moral reason of the Enlightenment. They, too, destroyed religion and life. Positively, he was unduly influenced by both the pietist and romantic traditions; but they were primarily vehicles for his new comprehension rather than substantive influences. In fact, Schleiermacher was interested in nothing short of a reconception of the life and thought of the Christian church. He knew that the traditional theological systems were no longer viable, and that the new religious currents were sub-Christian. In spite of the differences between the *Speeches* and the *Christian Faith*, in both Schleiermacher affirmed aspects of life and experience which had been ignored in the Newtonian world, and which he believed to be essential in any explication of the Christian faith. Since the time of the Enlightenment, we can no longer escape the question whether the thought forms and patterns of a period provide dimensions of thought adequate to a full-blown Christian understanding. Schleiermacher was the victim of this very problem; but that in no way detracts from his significant attempt to overcome it. Schleiermacher has been judged too much by the inadequacies of his own positive theological statements, and not sufficiently in terms of the problems of his own time.

Schleiermacher was acutely aware that the Christian faith was being understood in thought patterns more appropriate to other disciplines. This is what lies behind his insistence that religion was the third between practice (duty) and science (knowledge).

> Piety does, indeed, linger with satisfaction on every action that is from God, and every activity that reveals the Infinite in the finite, and yet it is not itself this activity. Only by keeping quite outside the range both of science and of practice can it maintain its proper sphere and character. Only when piety takes its place alongside of science and practice, as a necessary, an indispensable third, as their natural counterpart, not less in worth and splendour than either, will the common field be altogether occupied and human nature on this side complete.[7]

Obviously Schleiermacher did not say that religion was independent of practice and science; it was more primordial and in this sense inclusive of the other two. He stated that religion must be understood in terms appropriate to itself. In his own way, Schleiermacher was saying what has increasingly come to be accepted—that a level of reality must be judged first of all by principles of validation arising out of the subject matter itself and by other criteria only after intrinsic boundaries have been taken into account.

In the *Speeches*, Schleiermacher asked the cultured of his time to abandon their traditional conceptions of religion as rational knowledge or as principles of obligation and duty. He called upon the cultured despisers of religion to see, instead, that the religious was akin to their own conceptions of the depth of feeling engendered by the stimulus of the world about them. For Schleiermacher, the religious was the apprehension of the infinite in and through the finite. It was the givenness and immediacy of such discovery which distin-

[7] F. Schleiermacher, *On Religion*, trans. Oman (New York: Harper Torch Books, 1958), pp. 37-38.

guished it from reflection, or induction from sense experience. Religion was essentially revelational in character, even when its content was not Christologically grounded.

Schleiermacher saw no significant gap between the *Speeches* and the *Christian Faith*. The former was a phenomenological description of the essentially revelational nature of all concrete religions, while the latter was the particular elaboration of the uniqueness of the Christian faith. Precisely because of the distinctiveness of Christianity, Schleiermacher did not consider it an instance of religion but its ful filment and essential embodiment. By intention, and to a great extent in fact, Schleiermacher did not reduce the Christian claim to an instance of "the religious." Christianity was the perfect religion.

While Schleiermacher's relation to the romantic tradition and his pietist heritage kept him from seeing many aspects of the Christian faith, his intended faithfulness to its position is not in question. He considered the theological enterprise to be inextricably bound up with the Church. It was the experience of the Christian community which alone provided the context of theological inquiry. Everything extraneous to that did not belong to dogmatics. But the criteria for correct theologizing in the Church was genuine religious experience. Such a concept of experience was not to be equated with being subjective. Experience, in Schleiermacher's sense, always included objective components.

Schleiermacher's concept of experience did mean that theological discourse was not about God and His activity, but concerned the *experience* of God and the *experience* of His activity. For this reason, Schleiermacher relegated the Trinity to an abbreviated appendix in *The Christian Faith*. He considered it a theological concept made up of various elements of experience, rather than directly grounded in experience. He believed that in the long run a theology which was not anchored in Christian experience was abstract. Schleiermacher tried to avoid the orthodox presumption of the identification of language and knowledge; but in so doing he refused to accept the risk of speaking about God in the light of His disclosure.

Schleiermacher was averse to speculation and was acutely sensitive to reality in its immediate embodiment. The concrete, the poetic, or the figurative expressed things in their primordial character, while abstract thought was always in danger of being one step removed from the centrality to be expressed. For Schleiermacher, theological statements were definitely secondary. While one could not do without them, the danger was always that they expressed a particular school of philosophy rather than the immediacy of the redemptive role in Christ.[8] The danger of dogmatics was that it could lead to a formalism divorced from the immediacy of life in the Christian church.

Schleiermacher's insistence upon the unique and concrete against the abstract and speculative was most evident in his scorn of natural religion.

The so-called natural religion is usually so much refined away, and has such metaphysical and moral graces, that little of the peculiar character of religion appears. It understands so well to live in reserve, to restrain and to accommodate itself that it can be put up with anywhere. Every positive religion, on the contrary, has certain strong traits and a very marked physiognomy, so that its very movement, even to the careless glance, proclaims which it really is . . . And if a religion is not to be definite it is not a religion at all, for religion is not a name to be applied to loose, unconnected impulses. Recall what the poet says of a state of souls before birth. Suppose someone were to object to come into the world because he would not be this man or that, but a man in general! The polemic of natural religion against the positive is this polemic against life and it is the permanent state of its adherents.[9]

It is evident from these passages that for Schleiermacher the common denominator in religion, a so-called moral and natural religion, was not only the refutation of religion; it also violated what we know of life itself. Schleiermacher contended for dimensions in

[8] F. Schleiermacher, *The Christian Faith*, eds. Mackintosh and Stewart (Edinburgh, 1928), pp. 81–83.
[9] F. Schleiermacher, *On Religion*, pp. 214, 234.

Christianity and in life which natural religion and deism had pushed aside.

Schleiermacher addressed himself most creatively to the problem of miracle. He vigorously rejected the traditional use of miracles as evidences. He rightly insisted that proofs of any kind did not precede or produce faith. In the Biblical tradition, faith produced miracles, not miracles faith.[10] If the purpose of miracles was to produce faith, Schleiermacher concluded, they were a failure. Miracles had a context, and apart from that context they were misunderstood. The Scriptures did not distinguish as such between the miracles performed by Christians and those performed by non-Christians. In the instance of Jesus of Nazareth, the witnesses to miracles were enjoined to keep silent about them, ostensibly lest His mission be understood in the wrong frame of reference.[11] Moreover, in the Biblical context, the use of miracles as proof had a definite context.

It is never asserted that faith sprang from the proof, but from the preaching. Those proofs were applied among the Jews, with reference to their current ideas of the coming Messiah, in order to repulse the opposition presented by these ideas to the witness of the Gospel, or to anticipate any such opposition.[12]

While this ancient apologetic may have been useful in the period of the early Church, Schleiermacher, unlike his predecessors, rejected its usefulness for posterity.

The question remains, what did Schleiermacher himself mean by miracle? In the *Christian Faith*, he indicated that the supreme divine revelation in Christ introduced spiritual estates among men which could not be explained in terms of ordinary antecedents. States of this type were given the designation of miracles.[13] They rested on the supreme miracle, Jesus of Nazareth, whose life could not be explained in terms of the environment in which and out of which He came.[14]

[10] F. Schleiermacher, *The Christian Faith*, p. 71.
[11] I once had a student who insisted that the injunction to tell no one was a deliberate device to insure the word getting around. This has always seemed to me to be too psychological in the bad sense.
[12] Schleiermacher, Ibid., p. 70.
[13] Ibid., p. 72.
[14] Ibid., pp. 380-81.

Miracle was that which was known as qualitatively different. Hence, the way certain events were seen or perceived made them miracle. It was not that the events themselves were strange and entirely different to those who looked at them. In the *Speeches*, Schleiermacher declared:

> Miracle is simply the religious name for event. Every event, even the most natural and usual, becomes a miracle, as soon as the religious view of it can be the dominant. To me all is miracle. In your sense the inexplicable and strange alone is miracle, in mine it is no miracle. The more religious you are, the more miracle would you see everywhere.[15]

Indeed, for Schleiermacher, it can be said that faith itself was the miracle through which all things were miraculously seen.

For Schleiermacher, miracles were in no way connected with the breaking of natural order. He wanted nothing to do with debates concerning which events could properly be called miracles. Miracles, in short, had nothing to do with physics.

> The strife about what event is properly a miracle, and wherein its character properly consists, how much revelation there may be and how far and for what reason man may properly believe in it, and the manifest endeavour to deny and set aside as much as can be done with decency and consideration, in the foolish notion that philosophy and reason are served thereby, is one of the childish operations of the metaphysicians and moralists in religion. They confuse all points of view and bring religion into discredit, as if it trespassed on the universal validity of scientific and physical conclusions . . . Religion, however loudly it may demand back all those well abused conceptions, leaves your physics untouched, and please God, also your psychology.[16]

But Schleiermacher was not as doctrinaire in his conception of nature as some of the scientists and theologians. He was aware of the changes which had frequently occurred in the views of nature and of the need to explore the problem of the influence of spirit upon the physical order.

[15] F. Schleiermacher, *On Religion*, p. 88.   [16] Ibid., p. 88.

That is to say, it is natural to expect miracles from Him who is the supreme divine revelation; and yet they can be called miracles only in a relative sense, since our ideas of the susceptibility of physical Nature to the influence of the spirit and of the causality of the will acting upon physical Nature are as far from being finally settled and as capable of being perpetually widened by new experiences as are our ideas of the forces of physical Nature themselves.[17]

This was a genuine expression of openness to new knowledge and widening horizons of thought. It certainly did not mean that Schleiermacher interpreted nature in such an open way as to make room for accepting the Biblical materials just as recorded. That would be to misunderstand both his views of Nature and of Scripture. His views were more akin to what we today know more adequately through psychosomatic medicine.

On the whole, therefore, as regards the miraculous, the general interests of science, more particularly of natural science, and the interests of religion seem to meet at the same point, that is, that we should abandon the idea of the absolutely supernatural because no single instance of it can be known by us, and we are nowhere required to recognize it. Moreover, we should admit, in general, that since our knowledge of created nature is continually growing, we have not the least right to maintain that anything is impossible and also we should allow, in particular (by far the greater number of New Testament miracles being of this kind), that we can neither define the limits of the reciprocal relations of the body and mind nor assert that they are, always and everywhere, entirely the same without the possibility of extension or deviation. In this way, everything—even the most wonderful thing that happens or has happened—is a problem for scientific research; but, at the same time, when it in any way stimulates the pious feeling, whether through its purpose or in some other way, that is not in the least prejudiced by the conceivable possibility of its being understood in the future. Moreover, we free ourselves entirely from a difficult and highly precarious task with which Dogmatics has so long laboured in vain, that is, the discovery of definite signs

[17] F. Schleiermacher, *The Christian Faith*, p. 72.

which shall enable us to distinguish between the false and diabolical miracle and the divine and true.[18]

By conception and definition, Schleiermacher's view of miracles has much to commend it theologically. It is the content of Schleiermacher's understanding of the Christian faith rather than the formal conception of miracle which is the root of the problem.

Schleiermacher interpreted prophecy as he did miracle. The Old Testament prophecies had validity only among believers who expected redemption and fulfilment. Their validity depended on appropriating the Old Testament views, where faith was rightly prior to all other evidence. Moreover, even from the Old Testament background, there was no direct correlation between expectation and fulfilment. Christ was different from the preparatory expectations.

> . . . It can never be proved that those prophets foresaw Christ as He really was, and still less the Messianic kingdom as it really developed in Christianity. Thus it must be admitted that a proof from prophecy of Christ as the Redeemer is impossible . . . A clear distinction must, therefore, be made between the apologetical use which the apostles made of the prophecies in their intercourse with the Jews, and a general use which might be made of them as evidences. When, however, faith in the Redeemer is already present, then we can dwell with great pleasure on all expressions of the longing for redemption awakened by earlier and inadequate revelations.[19]

Schleiermacher had a radically different conception of Scripture from that of the orthodox. The traditional concept of the inspiration of Scripture was unacceptable. The Old Testament prophetic utterances were accepted by Christians because of the use which Christ and the apostles made of them and not because the documents allegedly came from the hand of God. Moreover, men became Christian long before the New Testament books were assembled. Schleiermacher believed that the concept of inspiration provided an impulse toward a better knowledge of Christ. It is obvious that while he pointed out the inadequacy of the traditional doctrine of inspiration, he did not himself develop a significant view of it.[20]

[18] Ibid., pp. 183-84.   [19] Ibid., p. 74.   [20] Ibid., p. 75.

Schleiermacher also opened up new directions in the understanding of creation. He maintained that the distinction between the act of creation and the sustaining activity of God was grounded in myth, rather than in an adequate theological understanding. The two were united in the concept of the world's absolute dependence on God. But this does not mean that Schleiermacher had a totally negative view of myth. While he believed the creation story in Genesis to be mythological, Schleiermacher also believed that the Hebrews did not understand the creation story in a literalistic sense. For Schleiermacher, the dogmatic task was to transcend myth, while repudiating all speculation which had lost its religious ground. Schleiermacher saw unwarranted speculation in the problems of form and matter in respect to creation, the question of time prior to or subsequent to creation, the issue of the temporal or eternal creation of the world. He considered all such problems as inappropriately conceived and therefore incapable of being answered.

Schleiermacher brought the Newtonian world and the religious dimensions together without obscuring or mixing them. It was axiomatic that for Schleiermacher it could never be " in the interest of religion so to interpret a fact that its dependence on God absolutely excludes its being conditioned by the system of Nature."[21] And conversely, natural science was not to be hampered by the " assumption of the absolutely supernatural."[22] For Schleiermacher, everything depended upon the apprehension of another order of reality in and through the natural order without conceiving of such an order in a spatial sense.

In such matters, Schleiermacher was indeed creative. In retrospect, we can easily see that his positive theological views were far too much under the influence of the very Enlightenment he wished to overcome. Neither the problem of man nor the redemptive process was developed with full urgency. For that reason, Schleiermacher has not received his due in the contemporary scene. He was culturally and methodologically significant, even if theologically wrong. This is said

[21] Ibid., p. 178.
[22] Ibid., p. 193.

in the full awareness that method and content are not entirely separable.

Wilhelm M. L. de Wette, whose fame in theological thought rests upon his work in the Biblical field, approached theological issues in a way closely akin to that of Schleiermacher. He too was aware of the need for fresh directions in theology. He was among the first, not only to see, but also to comment on the disastrous influence of Aristotle's thought on the orthodox development and the formalistic character of such theology.[23] Further, he did not accept the theological moralism of Kant nor the pantheistic dangers inherent in the thought of Fichte and Schelling. The philosophers here mentioned, he maintained, kept much of the form of Christianity, but not its substance.[24]

In a manner similar to Schleiermacher, de Wette defined the essence of the religious in terms of piety or feeling. He frequently used the word " Ahnung," which later became important in the philosopher Jakob Fries and indirectly in the thought of Rudolf Otto. " Ahnung " meant a premonition, a presentiment, a discernment of the order of God prior to its conceptual expression. For de Wette, conceptualization was inescapable and positive as long as it did not become speculative. He defended the use of concrete Biblical imagery, rejecting the negative attitude of theologians and philosophers generally toward such imagery.[25] In fact de Wette assumed that all language was best recognized as an exercise in imagery. Language pointed to a mystery beyond comprehension, though not thereby beyond reason.[26] Human language was the rational expression of a mystery that was not lifted as mystery.

De Wette was acutely aware of the limitation of all categories of thought. That all things have their being through God was more

---

[23] W. de Wette, *Ueber Religion und Theologie, Erläuterungen zu seinem Lehrbuche der Dogmatik* (Berlin, 1815), pp. 137-38.

Also, *Dogmatik der evangelisch-lutherischen Kirche nach den symbolischen Büchern und den älteren Dogmatikern* (Zweite verbesserte Auflage; Berlin, 1821), pp. 19-24.

[24] W. de Wette, *Ueber Religion und Theologie*, p. 138.

[25] Ibid., pp. 32 ff.

[26] He distinguishes between *Verstand* and *Vernunft; Dogmatik* . . . (Berlin, 1821), p. 54.

adequately known in feeling than in concepts, he declared.[27] But this did not mean that concepts could be abandoned. It meant only that it was necessary to recognize the actuality of truth prior to all expression. Descriptively, the concept miracle apparently demanded freedom beyond order; but in actuality, miracle was the apprehension of God in and through nature.[28] A miracle was like a new creation; it was something extraordinary. For the Hebrews, miracle referred to God's activity everywhere in and through nature. But the Biblical accounts of miracle were exaggerated stories which occurred long after the event.[29]

De Wette considered the traditional use of miracle and prophecy for the accreditation of revelation as a dubious enterprise. Just as Schleiermacher had, so de Wette maintained that miracle and prophecy already depended upon the truth to be shown or proven.[30] The traditional arguments from design, as for example, the purposeful creation of animals and plants for the sake of man's need, were abandoned in favour of a conception of the beauty and variety in nature. The fact of design and purpose was not denied; but the direct ascription of purpose to every aspect of nature was discouraged.[31]

De Wette, as we indicated, was significant for his advanced Biblical work. Some of this was translated into English for American readers by the Unitarian Theodore Parker. De Wette referred to Richard Simon as the first representative of the critical-historical approach to the Bible. He also referred to Semler, Eichhorn, and Michaelis; but his own approach to the Scriptures was free of their rationalistic interpretations. Many of de Wette's obvious conclusions were similar to theirs; but he set them in a more positive frame of reference. De Wette viewed the historical books of the Bible as compilations of

[27] De Wette, *Lehrbuch der christlichen Dogmatik* (Erster Teil, Die Biblische Dogmatik, Dritte verbesserte Auflage; Berlin, 1831), p. 79.
[28] Ibid., p. 79.
[29] W. de Wette, *Lehrbuch der historisch-kritischen Einleitung in die kanonischen und apokryphischen Bücher des Alten Testaments* (Vierte, verbesserte und vermehrte Auflage; Berlin, 1833), pp, 183 ff.
[30] W. de Wette, *Dogmatik* . . . (Berlin, 1821), p. 36.
[31] W. de Wette, *Ueber Religion und Theologie*, pp. 46-47.

materials,[32] and the genealogies as combinations of dogmatic and mythological elements.[33] The creation story was composed of two strands; the accounts of the work of each day and of the Sabbath were obviously mythological. But God's omnipotence was such, de Wette further declared, that creation could have occurred as delineated in Genesis. Further, in the second strand of the creation story, God's omnipotence was not as forcefully expressed as it was in the first story.[34]

In the theological works of the next decade, the Genesis story of creation was less and less interpreted as literal history. Philipp Marheineke, a theologian considerably influenced by Hegel, did not even bother to raise the question of historical elements in the Genesis account. The determination of how much myth, poetry, and philosophical speculation (and in the latter the Hegelian influence is evident) was present in the story, Marheineke considered to be the task of critical work. But the main intent of the Biblical story was to affirm that God had created the world.[35] A similar attitude was expressed by such theologians as Alexander Schweizer and Richard Rothe, who were influenced by Schleiermacher. For them, Genesis was no longer accepted as history.[36]

Nor was God's relation to the world understood in philosophical or scientific terms.[37] For Schweizer, the Ptolemaic versus the Copernican system was not a theological issue. He added that the simplicity of the Copernican system with reference to the swift movement of the planets was most attractive.[38] He frankly stated that the Church had made mistakes on the problem of astronomy. But the fundamental point was that

[32] W. de Wette, Lehrbuch der historisch-kritischen Einleitung in die kanonischen und aprokryphischen Bücher des Alten Testaments, p. 178.
[33] Ibid., p. 187.
[34] W. de Wette, Lehrbuch der christlichen Dogmatik, Die Biblische Dogmatik (Berlin, 1831), p. 76.
[35] Philipp Marheineke, System der christlichen Dogmatik (Berlin, 1847), p. 140.
[36] Alexander Schweizer, Die christliche Glaubenslehre nach protestantischen Grundsätzen (Erster Band; Leipzig, 1863), p. 241; R. Rothe, Dogmatik (Zweite Ausgabe, Erster Teil; Heidelberg, 1870), pp. 126 ff.
[37] Schweizer, op. cit., p. 102.
[38] Ibid., pp. 201-2.

the world is God's, whether the earth moves or not, whether we comprehend it more or less rightly; in both cases we can indeed be both religious and Christian, but we will marvel at the creator more, the more correctly we know his works.[39]

An example of the creative way in which some of these theologians attempted to deal with the Newtonian world is evident in Schweizer's interpretation of the order of nature.[40] The traditional problem created by the rigid Newtonian order was that one had either to affirm that God was bound to the order or that God also acted apart from it, either in contradiction to it, or above or beyond it. Before Newton, such statements presented no problem. A rigid order, however, created a problem. But for Schweizer, this was to misinterpret the situation. To define the laws of nature in this way, he believed, was to bow to the deist understanding of nature.[41] The deists had made the laws of nature into an independent power standing over against God, as if men were not dependent for their being—existence and continuation in existence—upon God Himself. God cannot be bound by anything apart from Himself, as the deists in fact implied. But Schweizer did not mean that God's activity in the world could be expressed in violation of the very order which expressed His activity. Hence, he opposed a conception of absolute miracle set over against a given order.[42] Schweizer knew that the mystery of God's working in and through nature had to be expressed without contradicting nature or reducing God's activity to the observed order of nature. Precisely how this could be done in a Newtonian world was not made clear; but the hope that it could was a sensitive and creative response to the Newtonian view.

Many streams of thought entered into the thinking of Richard Rothe.[43] Since a good deal of them are not significant for our purposes and others are similar to those expressed in Schweizer, we shall mention only one unique and crucial concern. For Rothe, the uniqueness

[39] Ibid., p. 202 (trans. J. Dillenberger). Though this edition is written after Darwin, he is not mentioned. In relation to nature, the problem is still that of the Newtonian world.
[40] See also R. Rothe, *Dogmatik* (Heidelberg, 1870), Erster Teil, pp. 126 ff.
[41] Schweizer, op. cit., p. 205.
[42] Ibid., p. 206.
[43] See the chapter on Rothe in K. Barth, *Die protestantische Theologie im 19. Jahrhundert.*

of man's personality manifested itself in nature. Man was not man apart from nature; yet he was the personal in and through nature. Here the lines were laid down for the liberal defence of man in the Darwinian world.[44] The slogan became "man over nature."

Schweizer and Rothe continued the tradition started by Schleiermacher. They rejected both the repristination of the old orthodoxy and the rationalist or moral interpretation of Christianity.[45] Like Schleiermacher too, Schweizer and Rothe were sufficiently under the grip of the Enlightenment so that they did not see the radical problem of man in all its depth, nor that of redemption in all its power.

It is evident from the preceding that there were definite attempts to overcome the reductionist understanding of Christianity occasioned by the Enlightenment philosophy. The concern with dimensions of life and thought deeper than the Enlightenment reason, reflected most dramatically and forcefully in Schleiermacher, was not affirmed against the scientific tradition as such. There were figures, such as Hegel, for whom the Newtonian development was anathema. Generally, however, the struggle was for dimensions of life and depth of understanding beyond the scientific views, but not in contradiction to them. There were also, as we have seen, some creative ways of coming to grips with the Newtonian world. The struggle to recover the integrity of the Biblical message in the Church also provided opportunity for a more creative relation to other disciplines, including philosophy and science.

C: NEW SOLUTIONS TO OLD PROBLEMS IN ENGLAND AND AMERICA

The pattern on the Continent was similar to that in England. Samuel Taylor Coleridge was contending for dimensions of meaning beyond the mechanical philosophy and abstract reason. For him, the concept

---

[44] Cf. Reinhold Neibuhr's contention that man is immersed in nature, but transcends it.
[45] Both of which fall outside our concern, since they are not creative thrusts toward the future.

of imagination was essential in poetry. It was the way whereby one could be a creative artist in the present and transcend the meaningless imitation of past themes. Coleridge used the concept of reason for religion in the same way that he used imagination for poetry. But it must immediately be added that reason was not understood in the Enlightenment sense; it had imagination within it. With the risk of oversimplification, one can say that the position of Coleridge was between that of Schleiermacher and of Kant.

Coleridge was convinced that both the poetic and the religious areas involved affirmation, an entering into, which was also a being entered into; neither was susceptible to proof nor to evidence in the usual sense. Coleridge wrote of evidences:

I more than fear the prevailing taste for books of natural theology, physico-theology, demonstrations of God from nature, evidences of Christianity and the like. Evidences of Christianity! I am weary of the word. Make a man feel the want of it, rouse him, if you can, to the self-knowledge, of his need of it; and you may safely trust it to its own evidence.[46]

It was a matter of life, not proof.

In this way of thinking, the Bible was not regarded as primarily information or knowledge; it was not a book of evidence. Its truth arose from the truth to which it bore witness and which it engendered in the lives of people. This interpretation of Scripture maintained a position beyond both the critical-historical questions—Coleridge himself ignored such questions except for the admission of minor errors of fact—and the ensuing science-religion battle of the Darwinian period.

While Coleridge, as the romantics and as Wordsworth before him, protested against a mechanical, dead conception of nature, it is wrong to see such writings simply as an over-romanticizing of nature. Indeed, they were that. But such statements miss the point that the views were an affirmation of the genuinely human, of human spirituality, of the demand for a richer world than Newton had provided.

On the theological front, the defence of Christianity through evi-

[46] S. Coleridge, *Aids to Reflections* (New York: N. Tibbals and Son, 1872), pp. 317-18.

dences did not easily abate. In the early decades of the nineteenth century, Paley's *Natural Theology*, in spite of acknowledged inadequacies, was still widely read. The degree to which the scientific tradition appeared to threaten Christian understanding was analogous to the extent to which the urge presented itself to defend Christianity. Not only was it said that there remained no opposition between science and theology; it was further maintained that a proper understanding of science suggested a Christian view of the world. The terms for the Bridgewater Treatises, published by a bequest left to the Royal Society, stipulated precisely the latter approach. While these works are widely ridiculed, a deeper perusal of some of the volumes as well as additional writings of some of the authors do indicate that remarkably new lines of exploration were suggested. We can ignore Kirby, who attacked Lamarck and defended a literalistic conception of the Bible, and Buckland, who was severely attacked for rejecting the traditional account of creation. William Whewell, in his *Astronomy and General Physics Considered with reference to Natural Theology*, was acutely aware of the difficulties inherent in natural theology. He knew that the opinion that design must point to a designer was convincing only to those already impressed with the concept of design. The argument made sense only if one already came to it predisposed toward accepting it.[47] Moreover, Whewell insisted that the creator of the physical world was also the creator of the moral world, and that this should never be forgotten by those who gave so much attention to astronomical matters.

The Scottish divine, Thomas Chalmers, also stressed the limits of natural theology. For him it played a positive but preliminary role. It was the precursor of revelation, but stood outside the temple. Chalmers wrote of natural theology:

> It can state the difficulty, but cannot unriddle the difficulty—having just as much knowledge as to enunciate the problem, but not so much as might lead to the solution of the problem. There must be a measure of light, we do allow; but, like the lurid gleam of a vol-

---

[47] W. Whewell, *Astronomy and General Physics Considered with reference to Natural Theology* (London, 1833), p. 344.

cano, it is not a light which guides, but which bewilders and terrifies. It prompts the question, but cannot frame or furnish the reply. Natural theology may see as much as shall draw forth the anxious interrogation, " What shall I do to be saved? " The answer to this comes from a higher theology.[48]

Here, and in other passages, Chalmers utilized a classical and contemporary terminology, namely that of natural religion longing for its completion in revelation. It is imperative to note that this type of approach was not identical with the independent natural theology of Paley.

Chalmers' creative approach is also evident in another of his works, entitled, *Discourses on the Christian Revelation viewed in connection with the Modern Astronomy*, but usually simply called, *Astronomical Discourses*.[49] In this volume, he addressed himself imaginatively and directly to issues raised in the light of astronomical discoveries through the time of Newton. He was convinced that most difficulties arose from assumptions made by Newton's followers rather than by Newton himself. The most serious was the transfer of the method and truth claims discovered in one area of concern to other areas. The Newtonian order, he maintained, did not directly or necessarily have any implications for history or philosophy.[50] But right as he was in such matters, Chalmers, regrettably we may add, defended the content of Newton's commentary on the Book of Revelation.[51]

Chalmers was aware that Christianity was no longer a viable possibility for many individuals because it apparently centred attention on this planet. The problem was not that the Copernican system had moved the earth from the centre. It was rather that telescopic instruments had apparently made it possible to think of the plurality of worlds as more than a theoretical possibility. Chalmers did not underestimate scientific possibilities here or in other areas. He believed that the invention of more adequate instruments would confirm much

---

[48] T. Chalmers, *The Bridgewater Treatises on the Power, Wisdom, and Goodness of God as Manifested in Creation* (London, 1834), II, p. 286.
[49] New York, 1851.
[50] T. Chalmers, *Astronomical Discourses*, pp. 53-55.
[51] Ibid., pp. 60 ff.

which was only theoretical. He believed that there were undoubtedly other worlds and galaxies, and suns whose light was not the reflection of our sun but indigenous to themselves. Nor did such suns exist just for this planet. Chalmers was further aware that the argument from analogy indicated the possibility of life on other planets. But he was neither willing to affirm nor to deny that this was true. It was open to future verification; for the present, one had to accept the limits of knowledge. But Chalmers was conscious too that the possibility of life on other planets was much greater than those who had formerly speculated on it had imagined.[52] Moreover, he maintained, within the Christian tradition there had been assumptions concerning the existence of intelligences other than our own. These may or may not have a relation to other planets.

Chalmers therefore believed that the infidels were mistaken in assuming that Christianity was a religion which had reference only to this planet.

> The assertion is, that Christianity is set up for the exclusive benefit of our minute and solitary world. The argument is, that God would not lavish such a quantity of attention on so insignificant a field . . . How do infidels know that Christianity is set up for the single benefit of this earth and its inhabitants? How are they able to tell us, that if you go to other planets, the person and religion of Jesus are there unknown to them? We challenge them to the proof of this announcement.[53]

He conceived of the possibility that other " mansions of infinity " may marvel at the mercy of God expressed in our world.[54] In short, Chalmers maintained that speculation could also be used to the benefit of Christianity. Christians might not know the true situation; but neither did the infidels.

The problem of the opponents to Christianity, suggested Chalmers, was that they found it impossible to combine the vastness of the world and God's particular concern for man.[55] But it was precisely the nature of God to encompass such extremes. The problem, stated Chalmers, existed even for science. Man had paid so much attention

[52] Ibid., Discourses 1 and 2.   [53] Ibid., p. 56.   [54] Ibid., p. 137.   [55] Ibid., p. 76.

to the vastness disclosed by astronomy that he had closed his eyes to the minuteness revealed under the microscope. In the latter, God's concern with the small and concrete was also apparent. In almost Pascalian form, he wrote:

By the telescope, they have discovered that no magnitude, however vast, is beyond the grasp of the Divinity. But by the microscope, we have also discovered, that no minuteness, however shrunk from the notice of the human eye, is beneath the condescension of His regard. . . . In a word, by the one I am told that the Almighty is now at work in regions more distant than geometry has ever measured, and among worlds more manifold than numbers have ever reached. But, by the other, I am also told, that with a mind to comprehend the whole, in the vast compass of its generality, He has also a mind to concentrate a close and a separate attention on each and on all of its particulars; and that the same God, who sends forth an upholding influence among the orbs and the movements of astronomy, can fill the recesses of every single atom with the intimacy of his presence, and travel, in all the greatness of His unimpaired attributes, upon every one spot and corner of the universe He has formed.[56]

More theologically, he expressed it this way:

The more we know of the extent of nature, should not we have the loftier conception of Him who sits in high authority over the concerns of so wide a universe? But is it not adding to the bright catalogue of His other attributes, to say, that, while the magnitude does not overpower Him, minuteness cannot escape Him, and variety cannot bewilder Him; and that, at the very time while the mind of the Deity is abroad over the whole vastness of creation, there is not one particle of matter, there is not one individual principle of rational or of animal existence, there is not one single world in that expanse which teems with them, and that His eye does not discern as constantly, and His hand does not guide as unerringly, and His Spirit does not watch and care for as vigilantly, as if it formed the one and exclusive object of His attention.[57]

[56] Ibid., pp. 81, 82.　　　　[57] Ibid., pp. 74-75.

In both cases, he concluded his argument by maintaining that those who think otherwise had already reduced God to the level of human comprehension.

> They, therefore, who think that God will not put forth such a power, and such a goodness, and such a condescension, in behalf of this world, as are ascribed to Him in the New Testament, because He has so many other worlds to attend to, think of him as a man. They confine their view to the informations of the telescope, and forget altogether the informations of the other instrument . . . To bring God to the level of our own comprehension, we would clothe him in the impotency of a man. We would transfer to his wonderful mind all the imperfection of our own faculties.[58]

In short, the knowledge of God had been destroyed because God was no longer thought of as God. This was because He was no longer known as God in the Biblical sense, and had instead become the dead image of man's own impotency and lack of information.

There were thus many on the Continent and in Britain who had come to a creative response to the new astronomy and the Newtonian world machine. We indicated earlier that Newton had been widely accepted in America. In the early nineteenth century, Timothy Dwight praised Newton and marvelled at the heavens as disclosed in the new science. In the new astronomy, the sun was the centre of many worlds and the stars twinkled not only for our gratification; in fact, all suns shone for numerous systems of worlds, all under God's kingly rule.[59] Thus, the plurality of worlds was not a problem everywhere for the Christian mind.

D: NEW PROBLEMS FOR CHRISTIANITY IN GEOLOGY AND BIOLOGY

While the Newtonian world created certain problems for the Christian mind, it did not basically challenge the Biblical conception of creation. That could still be interpreted as an event, almost precisely dateable,

[58] Ibid., pp. 82, 75.
[59] R. Bainton, *Yale and the Ministry* (New York: Harper & Brothers, 1957), p. 74.

in which the world sprang full blown into being. Buffon had suggested that the earth resulted from a comet falling upon the sun, and Kant had suggested the nebular hypothesis. But these views made no appreciable impact on the minds of men. Laplace, by combining Kant's suggestion with the Newtonian world view, developed a theory which demanded long periods of time and change. Creation was neither so recent nor so quickly completed as Genesis would indicate. While the celebrated question of Napoleon as to the place of God in Laplace's views (if asked) may have received the reply, " Sir, I have no need of that hypothesis," there was nevertheless some ambiguity as to what Laplace intended. It is not clear whether the reply referred only to the descriptive process of the scientist's work, or to a philosophical affirmation of the chance development of the earth in the gyrations of time and space. Many interpreted Laplace in the latter sense. More important is that such a statement played into the hands of those for whom any departure from the Biblical account was considered atheism by definition.

Laplace's views, concerning the time factor in the creative process, provided a fresh context for work in the geological field. The problem had long been how to interpret so-called fossil remains. Already in the pre-Christian era, one explanation had been that a plastic force existed in nature which formed imitations both of bones and shells. Another was that fossils were the result of some strange force emanating from the stars. But for our purpose, it is important only to note that, in spite of occasional questions, there had been no drastic change in theories since antiquity.

The problem of the age of the earth was further complicated by the assumption that there was one uniformly valid law of gradual change for the whole process of creation. This view did not originate with Lyell; but it was most dramatically set forth in his *Principles of Geology* at the beginning of the third decade of the nineteenth century. The gradual erosion of our planet, with its distribution of strata, was accepted as a key which pointed to gradual development on other fronts as well.[60] Moreover, the laws in operation now were those

[60] As we shall see, it could also be applied to biology.

which also accounted for the past. Geological change was to be explained by constant natural causes or forces operating over a long span of time.

The traditional theological interpretation not only dated creation at 4000 B.C.; it also explained the fossils. The most popular explanation was a universal flood which destroyed all life—except that in the Ark—and deposited the remains over the earth. This view had finally to be abandoned because it could not explain how fossils actually became parts of rocks embedded deep in the earth. Among others, a theory of successive catastrophes was adopted, after which God again populated the earth. This seemed to have the virtue of both maintaining the direct creative activity of God and of explaining the fossils. But it did demand some tampering with the Biblical text. Men such as Benjamin Silliman, the great Yale scientist; Edward Hitchcock, Congregationalist Professor and President of Amherst; and William Buckland, writer of one of the Bridgewater Treatises, posited epochs which they tried to reconcile with the Biblical account by suggesting that the six days were eras. This was a serious yet wishful harmonization of the scientific discoveries and the Biblical account. It was an attempt to accept scientific certainty, without abandoning the view that the Bible contained accurate scientific descriptions.

There were two alternatives to such views. While Silliman insisted that fossils millions of years old could be found in stones in the Grove Street cemetery in New Haven, Nathaniel Taylor replied that God could create fossils.[61] Archbishop Ussher had maintained that God created fossils in order to test our faith. But the more enlightened protest came from such men as Moses Stuart, who pointed out that the Hebrew word for day could not possibly be interpreted to mean anything other than twenty-four hours. For him, the attempt to harmonize science and the Bible had to be abandoned. Geology must be permitted to draw its own conclusions.

In the American scene, Horace Bushnell became impatient with the debates and difficulties and decided that Genesis was definitely

[61] Bainton, op. cit., p. 107.

mythological. But this did not deter him from a rhapsodic description of geologic change.

How magnificent also is the whole course of geology, or the geologic eras and changes, taken as related to the future great catastrophe of man, and the new-creating, supernatural grace of his redemption. It is as if, standing on some high summit, we could see the great primordial world rolling down through gulfs and fiery cataclysms, where all the living races die; thence to emerge, again and again, when the Almighty fiat calls it forth, a new creation, covered with fresh populations; passing this, through a kind of geologic eternity, in so many chapters of deaths, and of darting, frisking, singing life; inaugurating so many successive geologic mornings, over the smoothed graves of the previous extinct races; and preluding in this manner the strange world history of sin and redemption, wherein all the grandest issues of existence lie. This whole tossing, rending, recomposing process, that we call geology, symbolizes evidently, as in highest reason it should, the grand spiritual catastrophe, and Christian new-creation of man . . . What we see, is the beginning conversing with the end, and Eternal Forethought reaching across the tottering mountains and boiling seas, to unite beginning and end together. So that we may hear the grinding layers of rocks singing harshly—

> Of man's first disobedience and the fruit
> Of that forbidden tree—

and all the long eras of desolation, and refitted bloom and beauty, represented in the registers of the world, are but the epic in stone, of man's great history, before the time.[62]

This type of view was one of the ways in which theologians responded to Darwinism. But this is ironic, since Bushnell saw so many difficulties for theology in the notion of evolution that he could not accept it.[63]

Just as the traditional interpretation of geology was based on the Mosaic account, so biological theory, with respect to the origin and

[62] H. Bushnell, *Nature and the Supernatural* (New York: Charles Scribner's Sons, 1858), p. 206.
[63] Bainton, op. cit., p. 124.

fixity of species, was based on Genesis. It was believed that the species each stemmed directly from the hand of God, and for our history, directly from Noah's Ark. This view had been given biological credibility in the hands of the great Swedish naturalist, Linnaeus, who had affirmed: " We reckon as many species as issued in pairs from the Hands of the Creator."[64] The only change in this view was in number, not in kind. There was no conception that species evolved from each other.

The destruction of the Mosaic views on geology also had implications for biology. Already men like Geoffroy Saint-Hilaire had suggested species might have developed into other species through environmental changes. He had affirmed this in opposition to Georges Cuvier, who accepted geologic ages but insisted upon the fixity of species. The fullest theory of the evolution of species had been given by Lamarck, who had built it upon the thought of Buffon. But the basis for a genuinely irrefutable position was still lacking. This came through the painstaking observations and imaginative theorizing of both Alfred Russell Wallace and Charles Darwin. It was through the latter, of course, that the new position was widely made known both to the scientific world and to the general public.

One may well ask why, at the very time when a new astronomical cosmology had been widely accepted, it was not possible to adapt more readily to developments in both geology and biology. Part of the difficulty was due to the fear of a further erosion of Biblical authority. But the cause lies deeper. It appeared to many as another step by which God was being pushed out of the created order. In the Newtonian world, it was still possible to relate God the Creator to the world machine. In Laplace, and in the geological and biological theories which followed, there was no apparent need for the God hypothesis. It was not that He could be excluded. No one could prove that. But for all practical purposes, He seemed unnecessary; and that was most damaging. Moreover, it was difficult to relate God to a process of such endless duration and such apparently chaotic and un-

[64] Quoted by H. F. Osborn, *From the Greeks to Darwin* (2d ed.; New York: Charles Scribner's Sons, 1929), p. 187.

structured development. In one sense, one was left only with faith, without the usual evidence for God to which men had grown accustomed. Every need for God as a necessary source of explanation had disappeared. That shock brought an end to the possibility of a natural theology. Something that drastic threatened Biblical understanding and thousands of years of Christian history. But the crisis about God was hardly apparent, when the full impact of the Darwinian theory already introduced the crisis of man.

VIII

The Darwinian Impact

A: EVOLUTIONARY THEORIES AND THEIR PROBLEMS

1. *Darwinism.* There are striking similarities between the work of Newton and Darwin. Each brought separately known areas of scientific knowledge into a new unity. Through painstaking work, imaginative powers and insight, each revolutionized his field through a new vision which appeared to have the virtue of scientific confirmation. Like all reconceptions, each theory was more than a summation of the elements which went into it. Hence, each theory was fruitful, but also fraught with danger. In both cases, new explanations for observed phenomena were found; conclusions were drawn which did not follow from a more limited view of scientific evidence. The theories of Newton and of Darwin, respectively, proved so fruitful as to be considered more permanent than was justified. The very power of successful explanation in one area led to claims of truth which shocked some individuals and seemed to threaten the independence of other disciples.

One difference between Newton and Darwin made it more difficult for the latter to gain ready acceptance. While Newton's theological views were not widely acceptable, he professed that the world had a Christian foundation. This was true, despite the fact that such a view was unnecessary for Newton's scientific description. On the other hand, Darwin's views appeared to challenge a Christian understanding of the world. Moreover, it was known that Darwin was an agnostic. The intense concentration on the observation and interpretation of scientific materials had drastically shrunk Darwin's own interests and vision. While Newton had written unacceptable commentaries on certain Biblical books, they nevertheless testified to his wide interests. In the case of Darwin, the Reformation warning that a too exclusive concern with scientific affairs would lead to a loss of interest in Him, who is the Creator, appeared more than justified. Undoubtedly, Darwin's intense concentration produced results; but one shudders, nevertheless, on learning that Darwin lost his sensibilities for literature as a result of his scientific concentration.[1] However, one must immediately add that the issue is not the man, but the theory.

We noted previously that the accepted theory had been that each species stemmed in pairs directly from the Creator. This accounted for the distinctiveness of each species in the created order and was in accord with the account in Genesis. If one coupled such a view with the notion that catastrophes had occurred in nature, one could, as we indicated in the previous chapter, account also for fossil remains. This close connection between biology and geology shows that the abandonment of the older view of catastrophes in geology, in favour of a long periodic development, immediately had implications for the field of biology. One now had a long time span, with the possibility of understanding it through a law or principle of development. Lyell had accomplished precisely this in his *Principles of Geology*. In addition, the principle of development received impetus elsewhere. The notion of development or of evolution was in the air. While Herder, Fichte, Lessing and Hegel applied it to man and his affairs, the idea of development had already been applied to the entire domain of natural history, including biology, by such men as Buffon—who retracted his views under Roman Catholic pressure—and Geoffroy Saint-Hilaire, the opponent of Cuvier. Further, Alfred Russell Wallace had come to rather precise views concerning the development of species. His conclusions were so similar to those which Darwin drew

---

[1] *Life and Letters of Charles Darwin* (New York, 1919), I, 81, 82. For Darwin's letters and comments on his own view of the religious question, see pp. 272–86.

from extensive researches, that the dissemination of the views of Wallace was responsible for Darwin's publication of the *Origin of Species*. Darwin, unlike his predecessors or contemporaries, had amassed overwhelming evidence for his position.

Darwin rejected the view that each species had been independently created in favour of the idea that all beings are the lineal descendants of some few beings or some one being. Over a long span of time, confirmed by geology, a development of species took place from the lower to the higher animals with many a loss in between. A principle of Natural Selection was at work, in which those variations which were favourable for survival were preserved and continually led to new species. Darwin has written about his initial discoveries in these terms:

In October, 1838, that is, fifteen months after I had begun my systematic enquiry, I happened to read for amusement "Malthus on Population," and being well prepared to appreciate the struggle for existence which everywhere goes on from long-continued observation of the habits of animals and plants, it at once struck me that under these circumstances favourable variations would tend to be preserved, and unfavourable ones to be destroyed. The result of this would be the formulation of new species.[2]

Darwin elaborated this basic idea in the *Origin of Species* in 1859. There he wrote:

It is interesting to contemplate a tangled bank, clothed with many plants of many kinds, with birds singing on the bushes, with various insects flitting about, and with worms crawling through the damp earth, and to reflect that these elaborately constructed forms, so different from each other, and dependent upon each other in so complex a manner, have all been produced by laws acting around us. These laws, taken in the largest sense, being Growth with Reproduction; Inheritance which is almost implied by reproduction; Variability from the indirect and direct action of the conditions of life, and from use and disuse: a Ratio of Increase so high as to lead to a Struggle for Life, and as a consequence to Natural Selection, entailing Divergence of Character and the Extinction of less-improved

[2] Ibid., p. 68.

forms. Thus, from the war of nature, from famine and death, the most exalted object which we are capable of conceiving, namely, the production of the higher animals, directly follows. There is grandeur in this view of life, with its several powers, having been originally breathed by the Creator into a few forms or into one; and that, whilst this planet has gone cycling on according to the fixed law of gravity, from so simple a beginning endless forms most beautiful and most wonderful have been, and are being evolved.[3]

In this passage as in others, it is apparent that Darwin did not specifically reject the notion of a Creator. But he introduced a principle of laws or powers which worked through chance variations, apparently independent of the Creator. For many, this violated not only the Mosaic account of the creation of man; it could not be reconciled with the assignation of design and purpose in all things—a view which was still powerful as the result of Paley's works. Darwin's views did not directly deny God the Creator; but he so defined the developmental process that it seemed hardly appropriate as the work of a Creator. The end product appeared to be not man, but man as animal. It was a sign of bad manners when, in 1860, Wilberforce wanted to know whether Huxley was descended from an ape through his maternal or paternal grandfather. But in one sense Wilberforce was correct. He sensed that for Darwin man did not seem to be distinct from the animal world. In the *Descent of Man*, written almost a dozen years later, Darwin wrote:

In the class of mammals the steps are not difficult to conceive which led from the ancient Monotremata to the ancient Marsupials; and from these to the early progenitors of the placental mammals. We may thus ascend to the Lemuridae; and the interval is not very wide from these to the Simiadae. The Simiadae then branched off into two great stems, the New World and Old World monkeys; and from the latter, at a remote period, Man, the wonder and glory of the Universe, proceeded.

Thus we have given to man a pedigree of prodigious length, but not, it may be said, of noble quality. The world, it has often been

[3] C. Darwin, *Origin of Species*, Modern Library, pp. 373-74.

remarked, appears as if it had long been preparing for the advent of man: and this, in one sense is strictly true, for he owes his birth to a long line of progenitors. If any single link in this chain had never existed, man would not have been exactly what he now is. Unless we wilfully close our eyes, we may, with our present knowledge, approximately recognise our parentage; nor need we feel ashamed of it. The most humble organism is something much higher than the inorganic dust under our feet; and no one with an unbiased mind can study any living creature, however humble, without being struck with enthusiasm at its marvellous structure and properties.[4] Darwin was aware of the distance which separated the inorganic and the organic realms. Nevertheless, it is clear that for Darwin man belonged to a general class, and consequently could hardly claim to be so distinct. Thomas Huxley, for example, suggested that there was less difference between man and the highest apes than between the highest and lowest apes. Physiologically considered, or in terms of cranial capacity, this may be true. But Huxley's statement was deceptive, inasmuch as no levels of discussion were distinguished. From one perspective, it made no difference whether man was descended from the apes or whether both had a common ancestor in the distant past. The problem was that a biological description of man had become a statement concerning the nature of man. Hence, both biologists and theologians fought over man as if man's *descent* determined his *nature*. Neither transcended their acceptance of the problem in this form. For the Darwinians, man was not unique in nature. He was essentially animal, though more highly developed than most animals. For the more conservative theologians, man was considered to be essentially distinct and unique. This view was undergirded by the Mosaic conception of the fixity of species. Fundamentally, the Darwinian problem was the problem of the nature of man, and the many evolutionary theories which arose manifested diverse ways of speaking about him.

In the period between Copernicus and Newton, theologians had witnessed a change in men's thinking, whereby God's relation to the

[4] C. Darwin, *The Descent of Man*, Modern Library, p. 528.

cosmos had become more and more limited. For many, it was no longer necessary to think of God at all. Now man himself was no longer unique; he was essentially animal. He was the product of forces working without design or purpose, a being who essentially belonged to the nature from which he had emerged. Insofar as Darwinism was the end product of a long development in which not only the meaningful conceptions of world and God, but also of man, had been called into question, it was inevitable that the battle should be bitter. Only those who could inject spiritual dimensions into Darwinism could directly come to terms with it. For others, Darwinism produced conflicts in which the real issue was frequently obscured. In essence, one can say that Darwinism could be reinterpreted or transformed. But no rapprochement was possible between Darwinism as such and Protestantism as such. The conceptions of man were too divergent.

Among Darwin's scientific contemporaries, the principle of natural selection was not readily accepted in the form suggested by Darwin. In fact, Darwin expected opposition from fellow scientists rather than from the Church. Wallace, who had independently come to the same conclusions concerning the development of one species from another, defended the principle of natural selection but doubted that it provided a total explanation.

This power is " natural selection "; and, as by no other means can it be shown, that individual variations can ever become accumulated and rendered permanent so as to form well-marked races, it follows that the differences which now separate mankind from other animals, must have been produced before he became possessed of a human intellect or human sympathies. This view also renders possible, or even requires, the existence of man at a comparatively remote geological epoch. For, during the long periods in which other animals have been undergoing modification in their whole stucture, to such an amount as to constitute distinct genera and families, man's *body* will have remained generically, or even specifically, the same, while his *head* and *brain* alone will have undergone modification equal to theirs. We can thus understand how it is that, judging from the head and brain, Professor Owen places man in a distinct sub-class of mammalia, while as regards the bony structure of his body, there is the closest anatomical resemblance to the anthropoid apes, " every tooth, every bone, strictly homologous—which makes the determination of the difference between *Homo* and *Pithecus* the anatomist's difficulty." The present theory fully recognizes and accounts for these facts; and we may perhaps claim as corroborative of its truth, that it neither requires us to depreciate the intellectual chasm which separates man from the apes, nor refuses full recognition of the striking resemblances to them, which exist in other parts of his structure. [5]

Briefly to resume my argument—I have shown that the brain of the lowest savages, and, as far as we yet know, of the prehistoric races, is little inferior in size to that of the highest types of man, and immensely superior to that of the higher animals; while it is universally admitted that quantity of brain is one of the most important, and probably the most essential, of the elements which determine mental power. Yet the mental requirements of savages, and the faculties actually exercised by them, are very little above those of animals. The higher feelings of pure morality and refined emotion, and the power of abstract reasoning and ideal conception, are useless to them, are rarely if ever manifested, and have no important relations to their habits, wants, desires, or well-being. They possess a mental organ beyond their needs. Natural Selection could only have endowed savage man with a brain a little superior to that of an ape, whereas he actually possesses one very little inferior to that of a philosopher. [6]

Thus, while Wallace accepted natural selection as a necessary explanation, he was not convinced that man in his full powers as a reasoning, feeling human being could be explained in terms of it. Wallace insisted upon the uniqueness of man; but he elaborated his biological side in essentially Darwinian terms. It would be interesting, though fruitless, to ponder whether history would have been different if the impact of

[5] A. R. Wallace, *Contributions to the Theory of Natural Selection* (2nd ed.; New York: The Macmillan Co., 1871), pp. 328-29.
[6] Ibid., pp. 355-56.

the new biology had come through Wallace rather than through Darwin.

Among biologists, the greatest opposition to Darwin came from the Englishmen, John Owen and Edmund Gosse, and the formerly continental, then Harvard scientist, Louis Agassiz. The three objected to Darwin on religious grounds. In his opposition, Gosse combined his biological and geological interests, and rejected the new theories in both on the basis of their incompatibility with Genesis. He accepted the idea that the totality of creation occurred in a series of catastrophic acts rather than through the slow development of organic forms. But even this admission forced him into the position of having to accept that it seemed as if life had been on earth a long time ago. This state of affairs precipitated the overhasty conclusion, (not, as such, the words of Gosse) that God hid fossils in these catastrophic acts in order to tempt the geologists and test the faith of men.[7]

In the American scene, the great mediator in assessing Darwin's contribution was Asa Gray. He had befriended Darwin through an extensive review of the latter's work. For Gray, as for Wallace, the development of species through a long evolutionary process was essentially correct. Theologically, however, he was drawn to the theological views of Agassiz. But he refused to defend them, as Agassiz had done, in terms of the older biology. He believed that the science of Agassiz was " theistic to excess." But he admitted that there were dangers in Darwin's naturalistic explanation. Gray vacillated in his own analysis of the relation of theism to science. He argued that Darwin's views were not essentially atheistic, but he admitted that they could be so interpreted. But he stated that Darwin's views were less atheistic than were the nebular hypothesis and the Newtonian theory.

It would be more correct to say that the theory in itself is perfectly compatible with an atheistic view of the universe. That is true; but it is equally true of physical theories generally. Indeed, it is more true of the theory of gravitation, and of the nebular hypothesis, than of the hypothesis in question. The latter merely takes up a particular,

[7] See Edmund Gosse, *Father and Son* (New York: Charles Scribner's Sons, 1907), pp. 111-18.

proximate cause, or set of such causes, from which, it is argued, the present diversity of species has or may have contingently resulted. The author does not say necessarily resulted; that the actual results in mode and measure, and none other, must have taken place. On the other hand, the theory of gravitation and its extension in the nebular hypothesis assume a universal and ultimate physical cause, from which the effects in Nature must necessarily have resulted. Now, it is not thought, at least at the present day, that the establishment of the Newtonian theory was a step toward atheism or pantheism. Yet the great achievement of Newton consisted in proving that certain forces (blind forces, so far as the theory is concerned), acting upon matter in certain directions, must necessarily produce planetary orbits of the exact measure and form in which observation shows them to exist—a view which is just as consistent with eternal necessity; either in the atheistic or the pantheistic form, as it is with theism.[8]

In still another passage, Gray referred to Darwin as belonging to that group which could no longer accept revelation, but had developed a notion of design as the product of natural forces or natural selection. The eye and the hand, those perfect instruments of optical and mechanical contrivance and adaptation, without the least waste or surplusage—these, say Paley and Bell, certainly prove a designing maker as much as the palace or the watch proves an architect or a watchmaker. Let this mind, in this state, cross Darwin's work, and find that, after a sensitive nerve or a rudimentary hoof or claw, no design is to be found. From this point upward the development is the mere necessary result of natural selection; and let him receive this law of natural selection as true, and where does he find himself? Before, he could refer the existence of the eye, for example, only to design, or chance. There was no other alternative. He rejected chance, as impossible. It must then be a design. But Darwin brings up another power, namely, natural selection, in place of this impossible chance. This not only may, but, according to Darwin, must of necessity produce an eye. It may indeed co-exist with design, but

[8] Asa Gray, *Darwiniana* (New York, 1876), pp. 54-55.

it must exist and act and produce its results, even without design. Will such a mind, under such circumstances, infer the existence of the designer—God—when he can, at the same time, satisfactorily account for the thing produced, by the operation of this natural selection? It seems to me, therefore, perfectly evident that the substitution of natural selection, by necessity, for design in the formation of the organic world, is a step decidedly atheistical. It is in vain to say that Darwin takes the creation of organic life, in its simplest forms, to have been the work of the Deity. In giving up design in these highest and most complex forms of organization, which have always been relied upon as the crowning proof of the existence of an intelligent Creator, without whose intellectual power they could not have been brought into being, he takes a most decided step to banish a belief in the intelligent action of God from the organic world. The lower organisms will go next.[9]

In this passage, Gray suggested that the logic of Darwin's position, whatever Darwin's own belief in the matter, implied an atheistic interpretation of the world.[10] But Gray also believed that the Darwinian hypothesis, or something like it, could be interpreted in such a way as to introduce teleology on a wide basis. Properly understood, it could interpret the emergents in nature in broad, purposeful terms and show that, whatever the waste, the process was economical.[11]

In the last analysis, Gray interpreted religion in evolutionary terms. The traditional Christian concerns were relegated to the periphery.

I accept Christianity on its own evidence, which I am not here to specify or to justify; and I am yet to learn how physical or any other science conflicts with it any more than it conflicts with simple theism. I take it that religion is based on the idea of a Divine Mind revealing himself to intelligent creatures for moral ends. We shall perhaps agree that the revelation on which our religion is based is an example of evolution; that it has been developed by degrees and in stages, much of it in connection with second causes and human actions; and

---

[9] Ibid., pp. 68-69.
[10] This, as we shall note, is one of the points insisted upon by the conservative theologian, Charles Hodge.
[11] Asa Gray, Darwiniana, pp. 375, 378.

that the current of revelation has been mingled with the course of events.[12]

T. H. Huxley was the most powerful figure in the early evolutionary camp. In " The Reception of the ' Origin of Species ' " in the *Life and Letters of Charles Darwin*, he wrote of the situation to which Darwin provided the key, as follows:

As I have already said, I imagine that most of those of my contemporaries who thought seriously about the matter, were very much in my own state of mind—inclined to say to both Mosaists and Evolutionists, "a plague on both your houses!" and disposed to turn aside from an interminable and apparently fruitless discussion, to labour in the fertile fields of ascertainable fact. And I may therefore suppose that the publication of the Darwin and Wallace paper in 1858, and still more that of the " Origin " in 1859, had the effect upon them of the flash of light which, to a man who has lost himself on a dark night, suddenly reveals a road which, whether it takes him straight home or not, certainly goes his way. That which we were looking for, and could not find, was a hypothesis respecting the origin of known organic forms which assumed the operation of no causes but such as could be proved to be actually at work. We wanted, not to pin our faith to that or any other speculation, but to get hold of clear and definite conceptions which could be brought face to face with facts and have their validity tested. The " Origin " provided us with the working hypothesis we sought. Moreover, it did the immense service of freeing us for ever from the dilemma—Refuse to accept the creation hypothesis, and what have you to propose that can be accepted by any cautious reasoner? In 1857 I had no answer ready, and I do not think that anyone else had. A year later we reproached ourselves with dullness for being perplexed with such an inquiry. My reflection, when I first made myself master of the central idea of the " Origin " was, " How extremely stupid not to have thought of that! " . . . Whether the particular shape which the doctrine of Evolution, as applied to the organic world, took in Darwin's hands,

[12] Asa Gray, *Natural Science and Religion* (New York: Charles Scribner's Sons, 1880), pp. 106-7.

would prove to be final or not, was to me a matter of indifference.[13] This passage shows the emancipatory effect which Darwin had on Huxley. It did not matter to Huxley how much Darwin might be wrong in detail.

Reference has already been made to Huxley's statement that in body and brain man was not significantly different from the higher apes. This is less important than that the logic of Huxley's understanding denied the possibility that conscious purpose operated in the evolutionary process. His scientific analysis made man appear as animal. Yet Huxley affirmed the intelligence of man. " The intelligence which has converted the brother of the wolf into the faithful guardian of the flock ought to be able to do something towards curbing the instincts of savagery in civilized man."[14] Man became a unique product in nature and was destined to go somewhere. But the rationale for his emergence was not clear. At best, Huxley remained agnostic about ultimate meaning. He rejected materialism, spiritualism, or any metaphysical conception. While Huxley did not as rigorously reduce man to animal as did other interpreters, he denied that man had any final claim to significance. He conceded that, when judged by Christianity, the world was justified in considering him an atheist or infidel.[15]

Another vigorous defendant of Darwinism was John Fiske, lecturer in Philosophy at Harvard and renowned as a popular lecturer throughout the country. His views were close to those of Herbert Spencer, though on the relation between science and religion, Fiske believed that he had moved beyond Spencer. The Church's real difficulty with Darwinism, maintained Fiske, lay not in any attack on the dignity of man or on Biblical cosmology, but in the destruction of a natural theology built upon harmony and design in the world.

From the dawn of philosophic discussion, Pagan and Christian, Trinitarian and Deist, have appealed with equal confidence to the harmony pervading nature as the surest foundation of their faith in an intelli-

[13] Life and Letters of Thomas Henry Huxley (New York, 1901), I, 182-83.
[14] T. H. Huxley, Evolution and Ethics (New York: D. Appleton and Company, 1914), p. 85.
[15] Life and Letters of Thomas Henry Huxley, I, 260.

gent and beneficent Ruler of the universe. We meet with the argument in the familiar writings of Xenophon and Cicero, and it is forcibly and eloquently maintained by Voltaire as well as by Paley, and, with various modifications, by Agassiz as well as by the authors of the Bridgewater Treatises. One and all they challenge us to explain, on any other hypothesis than that of creative design, these manifold harmonies, these exquisite adaptations of means to ends, whereof the world is admitted to be full, and which are especially conspicuous among the phenomena of life. Until the establishment of the Doctrine of Evolution, the glove thus thrown, age after age, into the arena of philosophic controversy, was never triumphantly taken up. It was Mr. Darwin who first, by his discovery of natural selection, supplied the champions of science with the resistless weapon by which to vanquish, in this their chief stronghold, the champions of theology. And this is doubtless foremost among the causes of the intense hostility which all consistent theologians feel towards Mr. Darwin. This antagonism has been generated, not so much by the silly sentimentalism which regards the Darwinian theory as derogatory to human dignity; not so much by the knowledge that the theory is incompatible with that ancient Hebrew cosmogony which still fascinates the theological imagination; as by the perception, partly vague and partly definite, that in natural selection there has been assigned an adequate cause for the marvellous phenomena of adaptation, which had formerly been regarded as clear proofs of beneficent creative contrivance.[16]

Fiske was right in interpreting Darwinism as a drastic blow to natural theology. But theologians were not all as outmoded as Paley. Fiske did not see the problem created by Darwinism for those theologians who had already abandoned the concepts of design and of natural theology. His own religious views would hardly enable him to see that problem. Fiske was interested in a cosmic philosophy which transcended the mythological and the anthropomorphic in religion. For him, the heavens did declare the glory of God, but in a very real sense, Fiske could make such statements only because he assumed

[16] John Fiske, *Outlines of Cosmic Philosophy* (Boston, 1875), II, 396-97.

that the Divine initiative and natural law were identical.[17] God could be said to be the cause of everything, but the explanation of nothing.[18] The drama of revelation in the Christian sense was not central for Fiske. In fact, " the fourth gospel completes the speculative revolution by which the conception of a divine being lowered to humanity was substituted for that of a human being raised to divinity."[19] Fiske clearly belonged to the tradition in which evolution was fulfilled in the emergence of humanity, interpreted at its best in terms of divinity. Darwinism had been turned into an optimistic direction. Religion and science worked toward the same positive end.

Nor was Darwin's interpretation readily accepted among those who did accept the basic view of evolution. The concept of development was accepted, and it was agreed that Darwin had collected undeniable supportive biological evidence. But many did not accept the hypothesis that chance variations and natural selection, on the basis of the survival of the fittest, explained the process. Lamarck had suggested that adaptation to the environment was the basic factor. Later, Weismann propounded the germ-plasm theory, which completely excluded environmental and chance factors. Ernest Haeckel, the German scientist, developed a materialistic interpretation in which everything was explained through the chance combination of chemicals. He believed that when that combination was solved, the mystery of the world will have been disclosed. Haeckel was so adamant in his views that Huxley and Darwin did not encourage direct personal contact with him. His interpretation of the Darwinian position was unacceptable to those who were sure that man was more than a summation of chemicals and who believed religious factors could not simply be the hoax Haeckel believed them to be.

2. *Subsequent developments.* There were evolutionary theories in which mechanistic and materialistic interpretations were excluded. Hans Adolf Driesch's vitalism, for example, was a means of positing an *entelechy* operating alongside the natural order. But it was a state-

[17] Ibid., II, p. 428.
[18] Ibid., p. 383.
[19] J. Fiske, *The Unseen World and Other Essays* (11th ed.; Boston, 1876), p. 125.

ment concerning the necessity of another dimension rather than a solution to the evolutionary problem. Driesch did not go beyond positing an *entelechy* as a mysterious, operating factor which could not be explained on natural grounds. In the last analysis, it was a way of accepting the natural order and positing another parallel order. The intent was clear enough, but as a solution, it was hardly convincing.

A more fully worked out theory in opposition to mechanistic interpretations was Bergson's *Creative Evolution*. Beneath all adaptations, Bergson saw the mystery of a life force, which could be described in its growing, evolving pattern. No preconceived plans were involved in evolution; rather there was a kind of groping, with trials and errors. Three stable points had been reached in the process—torper (plants), instinct (insects), and intelligence (man). However, they are not to be understood in an advancing scale. In man, the process of life has become self-directive, with matter as the deposit left in its wake. In this line of interpretation, the divergence from Darwin is all too obvious. But Bergson's broad philosophical position was not accepted widely among scientists or theologians.

The most novel view was expressed in Lloyd Morgan's emergent evolution. The concept of emergence meant that genuinely new levels came into being which were not explainable in terms of previous levels. Life and mind were such new emergents. But while this was the case, they were in continuity with the lower levels. Morgan believed that his theory escaped the problem of mechanism, in which there could be no higher levels, and of vitalism, which drew too sharp a line between life and matter. The process of evolution, he believed, was the result of the divine activity within nature. But it was essentially an immanentist conception, with no clear picture of purpose, direction, or goal. Morgan was acutely aware that new forms did emerge which were qualitatively different from other levels, though they incorporated them. The overly immanentist views inherent in Morgan's views kept them from being accepted by most theologians.

In the preceding views, the Darwinian contribution was accepted but transformed. There were fields of study which were directly influenced by the spirit of Darwinism. Behaviourism in psychology and utilitarianism in social philosophy certainly expressed it. Social Darwinism came to be a term applied to the conservative political trend which justified economic struggle and the survival of the fittest.[20] Thus, Darwinism was used both in an optimistic and in a pessimistic sense; not infrequently its negative side was considered to be a necessary part of the struggle for progress and for the greatest good.

The evolutionary hypothesis was also directly applied to the study of religions. The origin of religion was discussed in terms of Tyler's animism, Durkheim's totemism, Marrett's preanimism, and in Frazer's much publicized work, *The Golden Bough*. The hypothesis was applied even to the study of the Old and New Testaments. In each instance, stress was laid on the development from primitive to higher forms. This led to two diverging but allied paths of interpretation. The first emphasized the glory of the achievements of the present. Man had come a long way from the primitive stage. A second interpretation had the opposite effect. Some contemporary ideas were discredited by disclosing the primitive character of their origin. Either alternative could be taken, and one could, on different questions, take one or the other. Those under the impact of such thinking were unaware that there was no obvious criterion in any given situation which provided the clue to whatever interpretation one took.

While there is truth in the idea of development, the notions of progress and of evolution had been in the cultural milieu before Darwin; but they were immensely strengthened by their success in the biological field. In the light of that success, they pervasively influenced other fields. In terms of the popular poem one could say, " some call it Evolution, and others call it God."[21] A conception of evolution reigned supreme in many areas, and if one was minded to think of God, one thought of Him in such terms. For some, evolution had become the only adequate way in which to think of God's relation to the world.

[20] See Richard Hofstadter, *Social Darwinism in American Thought* (Philadelphia: University of Pennsylvania Press, 1945.)
[21] W. H. Carruth, *Each in His Own Tongue*, in the *World's Great Religious Poetry*, ed. Hill (New York: The Macmillan Co., 1941), p. 145.

B: DIVERGING THEOLOGICAL RESPONSES

The theological response to Darwinism was as diverse as that among scientists and philosophers. On the Continent, where the Darwinian view was largely identified with the views of Haeckel, theologians mostly snubbed the development. The emerging liberal Protestant tradition tried to overcome the inherent dangers in Darwinism, while accepting evolutionary development and the general notion of progress. In England and in America, the response was diverse. One of the early positive responses came from Charles Kingsley.

But if it be said, " After all, there is no why; the doctrine of evolution, by doing away with the theory of creation, does away with that of final causes," let us answer boldly, " Not in the least." We might accept all that Mr. Darwin, all that Prof. Huxley, all that other most able men have so learnedly and acutely written on physical science, and yet preserve our natural theology on the same basis as that on which Butler and Paley left it. That we should have to develop it I do not deny. Let us rather look with calmness, and even with hope and goodwill, on these new theories; they surely mark a tendency toward a more, not a less, Scriptural view of Nature.

Of old it was said by Him, without whom nothing is made, " My Father worketh hitherto, and I work." Shall we quarrel with Science if she should show these words are true? What, in one word, should we have to say but this: " We know of old that God was so wise that he could make all things; but, behold, he is so much wiser than even that, that he can make all things make themselves."[22]

Rabid opposition to Darwinism and to evolution began rather late and had all the earmarks of a rearguard action. The so-called monkey issue played a role in the dismissal of Crawford H. Toy from the Louisville Baptist Seminary and James Widrow from the Southern Presbyterian Seminary in Columbia, South Carolina. The most dramatic instance, of course, was the famous Scopes trial in Tennessee

[22] Asa Gray, *Darwiniana*, p. 282.

early in this century, featuring Clarence Darrow and William Jennings Bryan. In reading the court transcript of the trial, one encounters an arrogant attack upon the Biblical tradition on the one side, and a well-meaning, but utterly uninformed outlook on the other. The Fundamentalist attack on evolution obscured the genuine problem which evolutionary thought presented to the churches. But we must also add that the Fundamentalist passion was a reaction to a modernist theory which still carried the Christian name but had lost the Christian substance. In the light of the claim of Biblical inerrancy, heresy trials arose in very respectable denominations. Chief of these are undoubtedly the charges brought against Charles A. Briggs, a Presbyterian, late in the nineteenth century, and against Harry Emerson Fosdick, a Baptist, in this century. Fosdick's later views are of course quite different than those of the period under discussion. Today, one would want to defend the right of Briggs and of Fosdick in his earlier period to hold their views; but one does not need to read far to see how much Briggs and Fosdick, in his earlier days, diluted the Christian substance. The evolutionary theology of a Lyman Abbott, for example, represented the abandonment of the Christian heritage in a genuinely recognizable sense.

It would be historically unjust to concentrate on the late nineteenth- and early twentieth-century reactionary opposition to Darwinism. Moreover, the tendency to read the previous history in the light of the latter, obscures the underlying problem as well as some of the more informed reactions, positive and negative, of an earlier period. In the instance of Charles Hodge, as we shall see, we have a responsible, urbane, and learned conservative, whose position contrasts sharply with its fundamentalist derivatives. There were such responsible scholars as Charles Kingsley and F. J. A. Hort, both of whom enthusiastically welcomed the general Darwinian position and interpreted it in a positive Christian sense.[23] For our purposes, we shall briefly

[23] In relation to scientific currents, general thought patterns, and Biblical interpretation, it is interesting to compare *Essays and Review* with *Lux Mundi*. The earlier essays are generally creative, though they show the influence of the *Zeitgeist*. The latter volume is more distinctly Christian and defensive. Some writers look backward, rather than forward, through the new intellectual currents.

examine the views of three diverse figures: Charles Hodge, James McCosh, and Henry Drummond.

Charles Hodge was the most influential theologian in the Presbyterian Church of his time and the star of Princeton Theological Seminary. He had accepted the new theories in astronomy and reconciled them with Scripture. He belonged to that orthodox group which had found it possible to adjust in astronomical matters, but for whom the Darwinian theory presented an insuperable hurdle. An examination of his views on the new astronomy, miracle, and God's relation to the world—themes which have frequently recurred in our exposition—will provide a spectrum of the way in which orthodox thought had developed by the middle of the nineteenth century.

The interpretation of Scripture was central to Hodge's position. In terms of a distinction accepted by many of the orthodox writers, Hodge defended plenary as opposed to mechanical inspiration. He maintained that mechanical inspiration, namely, that the writers of Scripture were like machines in whom no self-consciousness or cultural conditioning was at work, was never held by the Church. Inspiration had to do with the notion that their words " are to be received not as the words of men, but as they are in truth, as the words of God."[24] Plenary inspiration referred to the total inspiration of the entire Bible, as opposed to partial inspiration or to the inspiration of parts of the Bible.

But inspiration was confined to what was *taught*, whether of doctrine or of fact. What was taught or enjoined to be believed was to be distinguished from all other knowledge. Infallibility had to do with the former, not with the latter. Hence,

> as to all matters of science, philosophy, and history, they stood on the same level with their contemporaries. They were infallible only as teachers, and when acting as the spokesmen of God. Their inspiration no more made them astronomers than it made them agriculturists. Isaiah was infallible in his predictions, although he shared with his countrymen the views then prevalent as to the mechanism of the universe. Paul could not err in anything he taught, although

[24] C. Hodge, *Systematic Theology* (New York: Charles Scribner's Sons, 1872), I, 157.

he could not recollect how many persons he had baptized in Corinth.[25]

Hodge distinguished between what was *taught* and what was *thought* at a particular time. Previous writers had called the latter an accommodation to vulgar capacities, For Hodge, the question was not whether parts of Scripture were incorrect, but whether error was taught. " For example, it is not the question Whether they thought that the earth is the centre of our system? but, Did they teach that it is?"[26] And the form of the question was already its answer. In the same way, " They may have believed that the sun moves round the earth, but they do not so teach."[27]

Hodge further distinguished between facts and theories, between the Bible and our interpretation. Facts and the Bible were of God; theories and interpretation were of men.

There is also a distinction to be made between the Bible and our interpretation. The latter may come into competition with settled facts; and then it must yield. Science has in many things taught the Church how to understand the Scriptures. The Bible was for ages understood and explained according to the Ptolemaic system of the universe; it is now explained without doing the least violence to its language, according to the Copernican system. Christians have commonly believed that the earth has existed only a few thousands of years. If geologists finally prove that it has existed for myriads of ages, it will be found that the first chapter of Genesis is in full accord with the facts, and that the last results of science are embodied on the first page of the Bible. It may cost the Church a severe struggle to give up one interpretation and adopt another, as it did in the seventeenth century, but no real evil need be apprehended. The Bible has stood, and still stands in the presence of the whole scientific world with its claims unshaken.[28]

But having said this, Hodge nevertheless attempted to reconcile specific Biblical accounts with science, instead of frankly distinguishing the interests of each. Inasmuch as Genesis mentioned light prior to the creation of the sun, he distinguished between an initial " cosmical

[25] Ibid., I, 165.   [26] Ibid., I, 169.   [27] Ibid., I, 170.   [28] Ibid., I, 171.

light " and the light emanating from the sun.[29] On geological matters, he distinguished between the original creation of matter and its subsequent organization. He interpreted a day as being longer than an ordinary day, and he referred to Biblical passages outside of Genesis for support, such as the " day of your calamity " and the " day of judgment."[30] In short, Hodge did not consign anything to a cosmology which could simply be abandoned. All Biblical passages could be divided between those which were bound to their own time or were deeply in accord with science. Hence, no passages contradicted science. Hodge boasted that the Bible, alone of the ancient books, was in accord with natural science.[31]

The laws of nature and their relation to God's activity was discussed with reference to three levels. According to the Bible,

The chief question is, In what relation does God stand to these laws? The answer to that question, as drawn from the Bible, is, First, that He is their author. He endowed matter with these forces, and ordained that they should be uniform. Secondly, He is independent of them. He can change, annihilate, or suspend them at pleasure. He can operate with them or without them. "The Reign of Law" mnst not be made to extend over Him who made the laws. Thirdly, as the stability of the universe, and the welfare, and even the existence of organized creatures, depend on the uniformity of the laws of nature, God never does disregard them except for the accomplishment of some high purpose. He, in the ordinary operations of his Providence, operates with and through the laws which He has ordained. He governs the material, as well as the moral world by law.[32]

In a subsequent section, he distinguished between the ordinary processes of nature in which God worked through secondary causes, as in the movements of heavenly bodies, and those processes under the influence of the Holy Spirit, such as regeneration. But there were also events which belonged to neither level, the distinguishing characteristics of which were:

First, that they take place in the external world, i.e., in the sphere

[29] Ibid., p. 570.   [30] Ibid., p. 570.   [31] Ibid., p. 573.   [32] Ibid., p. 607.

of the observation of the senses; and Secondly, that they are produced or caused by the simple volition of God, without the intervention of any subordinate cause. To this class belongs the original act of creation, in which all co-operation of second causes was impossible. To the same class belong all events truly miraculous. A miracle, therefore, may be defined to be an event, in the external world, brought about by the immediate efficiency, or simple volition of God.[33]

Biblical miracles were of the latter kind. When Lazarus was called from the grave, the chemical forces of decomposition ceased, and when Jesus walked on the sea, the law of gravitation was counteracted. But this, wrote Hodge, happened all the time.

After all, the suspension or violation of the laws of nature involved in miracles is nothing more than is constantly taking place around us. One force counteracts another; vital force keeps the chemical laws of matter in abeyance; and muscular force can control the action of physical force. When a man raises a weight from the ground, the law of gravity is neither suspended nor violated, but counteracted by a stronger force.[34]

After insisting that miracles were different from the usual or ordinary course of things, he also tried to show that they were not unusual. But it is doubtful that the latter attempt was useful or convincing. Further, while Hodge maintained that miracles were subordinate to the truth of the Gospel, he also affirmed that miracles proved the reality of Christ.

Hodge also addressed himself to the older tradition of God's *concursus*. He rejected the notion of continuous creation because it denied the existence of secondary causes, so that the heaven and the earth " are but the pulsations of the universal life of God."[35] But a secondary cause had meaning only in that it was acted upon. The idea of God's *concursus* related the priority of God's activity to every secondary cause without denying its reality. But Hodge was also so conscious of the difficulties in the notion of secondary causation that he referred to it as an attempt to explain the inexplicable. Hodge finally declared that one must be content with the simple declaration

[33] Ibid., p. 618.   [34] Ibid., p. 621.   [35] Ibid., p. 579.

of the Bible, that "God does govern all his creatures and all their actions."[36]

However one may disagree with his statements, Hodge adapted himself to the new scientific theories of the cosmos. But with respect to the theory of evolution, the situation was different. In the discussion of evolution, he reiterated that with reference to scientific matters one had to make careful distinctions. He commented again on the movement of the planets and recalled that it was once felt they were moved by spirits, then by vortexes, and then through self-evolved forces. He then quite properly asked if one was required to change one's faith with every new moon. It is true that many theologians were blamed for opposition to scientific theories which later were proven wrong from a scientific standpoint. That fact does not justify the opposition of the theologians. But it made Hodge's concern for patience intelligible. He judged that the Church had been correct in going slowly in judging astronomical matters and in waiting for full evidence. The same, he believed, held for many facets of the theory of evolution.

Hodge applied his distinction between theory and fact to the question of evolution. He conceded that there may be phases of development, but not that one phase stemmed from another. The former was a fact, the latter was a theory.

Religious men believe with Agassiz that facts are sacred. They are revelations from God. Christians sacrifice to them, when duly authenticated, their most cherished convictions. That the earth moves, no religious man doubts. When Galileo made that great discovery, the Church was right in not yielding at once to the evidence of an experiment which it did not understand. But when the fact was clearly established, no man sets up his interpretation of the Bible in opposition to it. Religious men admit all the facts connected with our solar system; all the facts of geology, and of comparative anatomy, and of biology. Ought not this to satisfy scientific men? Must we also admit their explanations and inference? If we admit that the human embryo passes through various phases, must we admit that man was

[36] Ibid., p. 605.

once a fish, then a bird, then a dog, then an ape, and finally what he now is? If we admit the similarity of structure in all vertebrates, must we admit the evolution of one from another, and all from a primordial germ? It is to be remembered that the facts are from God, the explanation from men; and the two are often as far apart as Heaven and its antipode.[37]

In his Systematic Theology, Hodge clearly stated that the issue was whether man was a developed ape, which the Darwinian theory implied, or whether he was created in the image of God, as the Bible indicated.[38]

But the main brunt of Hodge's rejection of Darwinism was the atheistic implication inherent in the denial of design. Here the word implication is important, for Hodge wished to distinguish the man Darwin from the theory. He knew that for Darwin the existence of matter and life admitted a Creator; he knew further that Darwin was not an atheist, but primarily a naturalist and observer.[39] In this sense Darwin differed from Spencer or Haeckel or Huxley, the latter two of whom wanted religion to leave science alone but did not return the courtesy. For Hodge, the problem with Darwin's view was that the Creator had no relation to the world apart from the initial creation of unintelligent matter. From the moment in which matter was created, everything proceeded by a natural as against a supernatural development. Hence, maintained Hodge, teleology and all final causes were rejected. It was said, for example, that " the eye was formed without any purpose of producing an organ of vision."[40] Hodge was aware that much in nature belied design or purpose. But he believed that there was enough design in nature to keep us from letting disorder overwhelm us to such an extent as to deny intelligence in the world.[41] For Hodge the denial of design was virtually the denial of God.

In saying that this system is atheistic, it is not said that Mr. Darwin is an atheist. He expressly acknowledges the existence of God; and seems to feel the necessity of his existence to account for the origin

[37] Charles Hodge, What is Darwinism? (New York, 1874), p. 132.
[38] C. Hodge, Systematic Theology, II, 19.
[39] C. Hodge, What is Darwinism?, pp. 26-27.
[40] Ibid., p. 52.　　　　　[41] C. Hodge, Systematic Theology, I. 170.

of life. Nor is it meant that everyone who adopts the theory does it in an atheistic sense . . . Natural laws are said to be to God what the chisel and the brush are to the artist. Then God is as much the author of species as the sculptor or painter is the author of the product of his skill. This is a theistic doctrine. That, however, is not Darwin's doctrine. His theory is that hundreds or thousands of millions of years ago God called a living germ, or living germs, into existence, and that since that time God has no more to do with the universe than if He did not exist. This is atheism to all intents and purposes, because it leaves the soul as entirely without God, without a Father, Helper, or Ruler, as the doctrine of Epicurus or of Comte. Darwin, moreover, obliterates all the evidences of the being of God in the world. He refers to physical causes what all theists believe to be due to the operations of the Divine mind. There is no more effectual way of getting rid of a truth than by rejecting the proofs on which it rests. Professor Huxley says that when he first read Darwin's book he regarded it as the deathblow of teleology, i.e., of the doctrine of design and purpose in nature.[42]

But Hodge was not interested as such in the arguments from design. He was aware of their inadequacies, and he was concerned with dimensions of faith beyond those exhibited by Paley.

The clue to Hodge's main concern is found in the fact that a theistic interpretation of Darwinism was no more acceptable to him than an atheistic one. Darwinism in its most favourable light was no better than an entirely natural explanation. Theism, as such, was no more compatible with Christianity than naturalism. Hence, he believed that Christians had to fight against scientists and others who were interested in religion apart from its Christian character. Hodge wrote:

The truths on which all religion is founded are drawn within the domain of science, the nature of the first cause, its relation to the world, the nature of second causes, the origin of life, anthropology, including the origin, nature, and destiny of man. Religion has to fight for its life against a large class of scientific men.[43]

[42] C. Hodge, *Systematic Theology*, II, 16. A similar passage is found in *What is Darwinism?*, pp. 173-74.
[43] C. Hodge, *What is Darwinism?*, p. 142.

Hodge could not disengage any Darwinian hypothesis from a direct threat to a total Christian view. That is why the theistic version was as unsatisfactory as the atheistic one. Christianity had a conception of the destiny of man as well as of his origin and life. The denial of design, or even the affirmation of design in a general theistic context, was essentially different from the Christian conception of creation, fall, and redemption. That is why Hodge believed that the abandonment of design and purpose in nature was the final abdication of a Christian view of life. Even a theistic view could not provide a proper context for design and purpose. That demanded the whole Christian understanding of creation, history, and redemption.

Hodge had genuine grounds for maintaining that evolution was a threat of graver import to Christianity than the astronomical changes which had taken place. But he did not see that some new conceptions would have to emerge in biology as well as in astronomy. Instead, he rejected the antiquity of man and attempted to solve the problem of fossils by citing dubious evidence from the lake dwellings of central Europe. Moreover, his view that Scripture was the deposit of scientific fact, however circumscribed, made it impossible for him to come to grips with the problem in a creative way.

But there were those who combined a fairly orthodox Christian conception and the Darwinian theory. Of these, James McCosh of Princeton University was most interesting. Initially, he opposed Darwinism by objecting to natural selection and by affirming the significance of design. But even prior to Darwin's work, McCosh had suggested that God worked through the spontaneous adaptations which apparently occurred in the world. This view demanded a reinterpretation of the traditional concept of design. For McCosh, design was not equivalent to the fitness of an organ to perform its function, as the eye to see. It was rather that adaptations and fitness were manifest through the changes which occurred in response to what appeared to be accidental interferences with events. These events McCosh interpreted to be the direct interference of God. Commenting on McCosh's views of the Darwinian hypothesis, Professor Herbert Schneider rightly says:

Why not interpret the variations which Darwin called spontaneous, chance, or accidental differences, and for which he did not pretend to give an explanation, as supernatural choices of an intervening Designer? Natural selection and divine election amounted to the same thing in practice, or to quote McCosh, " Supernatural design produces natural selection."[44]

McCosh's view was ingenious. It combined, as Professor Schneider further suggests, the attitude toward man held by Calvinists with the concept of struggle found in Darwinism. It affirmed both against the optimistic outlook of the Spencerians. Moreover, it maintained the concept of design, though not in the older traditional sense. But the theory was too ingenious. Not only was it a transformation of Darwinism; it was another instance in which a theological outlook was too closely identified with the particular form of a dated scientific view. When the particular features of Darwinism upon which McCosh's theory was built were no longer acceptable, the theological interpretation also collapsed. In one sense, McCosh was more relevant than Hodge; but in another sense, both were wrong. On the basis of an inadequate view of the Bible, Hodge opposed evolution; on the basis of a too close identification of theological notions with a particular interpretation of science, McCosh's apologetic collapsed with the changes in science and theology.

If Hodge rejected evolution and McCosh interpreted it in a so-called Calvinistic sense, it was Henry Drummond who painstakingly interpreted the relation of Christianity to evolution in a positive, progressive way. Drummond was a preacher, a friend of Moody, a scientist, and amateur theologian. This combination is indicative of a capacity to hold many facets in a creative or eclectic unity, depending on one's perspective of interpretation. Essentially, Drummond was concerned to affirm an analogy between science and religion. But his views were in marked contrast to those of Bishop Butler, for whom the natural world was analogous to Christianity. For Drummond, Christianity was essentially like the world of science. Nature had its

---

[44] H. Schneider, " The influence of Darwin and Spencer on American Philosophical Theology," *Journal of the History of Ideas*, VI (1945), p. 6.

laws; so did Christianity. The laws of Christianity were as exacting and as definite as those of the natural world. Christianity was a process, which had a law of spiritual development. Character, destiny, and life were forged by living in the reality of love. There was a law of causation in the spiritual life just as in nature.[45] Just as there was design in the natural world, so there was design in the spiritual world.

These wonderful adaptations of each organism to its surroundings— of the fish to the water, of the eagle to the air, of the insect to the forest-bed; and of each part of every organism—the fish's swim-bladder, the eagle's eye, the insect's breathing tubes—which the old argument from design brought home to us with such enthusiasm, inspire us still with a sense of the boundless resource and skill of Nature in perfecting her arrangements for each single life . . . Man, too, finds in his Environment provision for all capacities, scope for the exercise of every faculty, room for the indulgence of each appetite, a just supply for every want. So the spiritual man at the apex of the pyramid of life finds in the vaster range of his Environment a provision, as much higher, it is true, as he is higher, but as delicately adjusted to his varying needs . . . It is not a strange thing, then, for the soul to find its life in God. This is its native air.[46]

In this form of analogous thinking, Drummond, like Schleiermacher, emphasized the supportive role of nature, that is, its dependable character. The order of things was more fundamental than any element of disorder. In fact, nothing happened by chance, either in nature or in religion.[47] A proper participation in each was a clue to the meaning of reality.

Drummond's views on miracles and evidences correspond to this orientation. Miracles were not defined in terms of the suspension of nature, but rather as genuine transformations of life. Faith and miracle were identical.

Miracles; but that question is thrown at my head every second day; " What do you say to a man when he says to you, ' Why do you

[45] *The Contribution of Science to Christianity*, in *Henry Drummond, An Anthology*, ed. J. W. Kennedy (New York: Harper & Brothers, 1953), p. 70.
[46] *Henry Drummond, An Anthology*, p. 193.
[47] Ibid., p. 131.

believe in miracles?'" I say, "because I have seen them." He says, "When?" I say, "Yesterday." He says, "Where?" "Down such-and-such a street I saw a man who was a drunkard redeemed by the power of an unseen Christ and saved from sin. That is a miracle." The best apologetic for Christianity is a Christian. That is a fact which the man can not get over. There are fifty other arguments for miracles, but none so good as that you have seen them. Perhaps you are one yourself. But take you a man and show him a miracle with his own eyes. Then he will believe.[48]

In the same way, the traditional evidences were rejected, and the matter put in personal terms.

The evidence for Christianity is not the Evidences. The evidence for Christianity is a *Christian*. The unit of physics is the atom, of biology the cell, of philosophy the man, of theology the Christian. The natural man, his regeneration by the Holy Spirit, the spiritual man and his relations to the world and to God, these are the modern facts for a scientific theology. We may indeed talk with science on its own terms about the creation of the world, and the spirituality of nature, and the force behind nature, and the unseen universe; but our language is not less scientific, not less justified by fact, when we speak of the work of the risen Christ, and the contemporary activities of the Holy Ghost, and the facts of regeneration, and the powers which are freeing men from sin. There is a great experiment which is repeated every day, the evidence for which is as accessible as for any facts of science; its phenomena are as palpable as any in nature; its processes are as explicable, or as inexplicable; its purpose is as clear; and yet science has never been seriously asked to reckon with it, nor has theology ever granted it the place its impressive reality commands.[49]

It is no wonder that Moody's associates wondered about Drummond's orthodoxy, even though they were impressed by his piety.

Drummond not only saw an analogy between science and religion; he believed science, and evolution in particular, to be a key which liberated Christianity, restored the Bible to men, and gave them an-

[48] Ibid., p. 110. [49] Ibid., pp. 69-70.

other one in addition.[50] Evolution, therefore, had not threatened Christianity; it had in fact confirmed Christianity and provided it with a new understanding. Science had put creation through its crucible. It had taken the questions of the theologians from them and attempted to answer them. But—

> they are now handed back, tried, unanswered, but with a new place in theology and a new power with science. Science has attained, after this ordeal, to a new respect for theology. If there are answers to these questions, and there ought to be, theology holds them.[51]

But at the same time, if theologically understood, the doctrine of evolution " fills a gap at the very beginning of our religion," exhibiting a newly acquired view in an extraordinarily beautiful form.

Yet, after all, its beauty is not the only part of its contribution to Christianity. Scientific theology *required* a new view, though it did not require it to come in so magnificent a form. What it wanted was a credible presentation, in view especially of astronomy, geology, and biology. These had made the former theory simply untenable. And science has supplied theology with a theory which the intellect can accept and which for the devout mind leaves everything more worthy of worship than before.[52]

It is only too apparent that this conception of evolution would have been foreign to Darwin. It presupposed design and purpose in the development from the inorganic through the organic to man. For Drummond, the evolutionary process culminated in man, whose particular destiny consisted in discovering the way of love exhibited by Christ. Further, an eschatological hope was confessed, namely, that a new stage in the development of man would be reached through man's increasing concern for others. Evolution dealt, not with the descent of man, but with the ascent of man. Evolution and Christianity were identical in the concern for man's ascent. Moreover, God was at work in both.[53]

> Up to this time no word has been spoken to reconcile Christianity with Evolution, or Evolution with Christianity. And why? Because the two are one. What is Evolution? A method of creation.

[50] Ibid., pp. 76-80.   [51] Ibid., p. 73.   [52] Ibid., p. 75.   [53] Ibid., pp. 218 ff.

What is its object? To make more perfect living beings. What is Christianity? A method of creation. What is its object? To make more perfect living beings. Through what does Evolution work? Through Love. Through what does Christianity work? Through Love . . . The Ascent of Man and of Society is bound up henceforth with the conflict, the intensification, and the diffusion of the Struggle for the Life of Others. This is the Further Evolution, the page of history that lies before us, the closing act of the drama of Man . . . The further Evolution must go on, the Higher Kingdom come—first the blade, where we are today; then the ear, where we shall be tomorrow; then the full corn in the ear, which awaits our children's children, and which we live to hasten.[54]

Drummond represented the wedding of the concepts of evolution and progress. He held these views with the utmost of piety and with a deep conviction that the power of Christ transformed human lives. He admitted that he had ignored many theological problems. But he believed it more important to know the sanctifying power of God in Christ, whom one accepted as leader and as teacher.[55] Christianity affected the lives of people. It included even an element of common sense.[56] While it introduced people into a kingdom unlike other kingdoms, it nevertheless utilized their talents.

He who joins this Society finds himself in a large place. The Kingdom of God is a Society of the best men, working for the best ends, according to the best methods. Its membership is a multitude whom no man can number; its methods are as various as human nature; its field is the world. It is a commonwealth, yet it honours a King; it is a Social Brotherhood, but it acknowledges the Fatherhood of God. Though not a Philosophy the world turns to it for light; though not political it is the incubator of all great laws. It is more human than the State, for it deals with deeper needs; more Catholic than the Church, for it includes whom the Church rejects. It is a Propaganda, yet it works not by agitation but by ideals. It is a Religion, yet it holds the worship of God to be mainly the service of man. Though not a Scientific Society its watchword is Evolution;

[54] Ibid., p. 220.   [55] Ibid., pp. 125-26.   [56] Ibid., p. 152.

though not an Ethic it possesses the Sermon on the Mount. This mysterious Society owns no wealth but distributes fortunes. It has no minutes for history keeps them; no member's roll for no one could make it. Its entry-money is nothing; its subscription, all you have. The Society never meets and it never adjourns. Its law is one word—loyalty; its Gospel one message—love. Verily " Whosoever will lose his life for My sake shall find it."[57]

Drummond represented an evangelical piety which made him a friend of the most conservative theological figures; he elaborated a theological position which defined the Gospel in progressive terms. For Drummond, sanctification was the completion of creation. There was no sense of a chasm which divided creation and redemption. The first ran naturally into the second. Drummond's piety glossed over the fact that, in his thought, Christianity had been too closely identified with a progressive conception of evolution.

C: THE SPECIAL TASK OF PROTESTANT LIBERALISM

Two initial observations must be made about Protestant liberalism. First, the liberal Protestant tradition in America had indigenous roots. Nevertheless, the full development of liberalism occurred in Europe, particularly in Germany. The flowering of the American liberal tradition resulted, in part, from the fact that many of the theological leaders studied in German universities. Second, while the liberal Protestant theologians used evolutionary concepts in their thinking, their concerns were broad in scope and they never identified Christianity and evolution, as had Lyman Abbott or Henry Drummond. They were concerned to maintain a genuine Christological centre in all their thinking. Albrecht Ritschl, the great liberal theologian, intended to return to the New Testament understanding of the Gospel via the Reformers. He appreciated Schleiermacher's notion that theology belonged to the community of faith. But he criticized Schleiermacher for not having an adequate Christological foundation to his thought.

While Protestant liberalism was more diverse than the development

Ibid., p. 159.

represented by Ritschl, he is a master key to the type of problem which the movement generally faced with reference to Darwinism. We should not be misled by the fact that Ritschl, as well as other liberal theologians, seldom directly referred to Darwin and Darwinism. The concern of the liberal tradition with the nature of man stemmed directly out of the final blow that the materialistic interpretation of man—which was implied in Darwinism even if it was not confined to it—had delivered to theology. Some, like Julius Kaftan as late as the early twentieth century, distinguished between Darwin and Darwinism. But the basic problem was not altered by distinguishing between the two.[58] Adolf Schlatter believed that the Darwinian impact was in fact more devastating than was the materialistic philosophy generally. It attacked man's descent, which from Plato to Darwin, had remained about the same. Further, Darwinism reinforced materialism and the rationalism of the Enlightenment by providing scientific undergirding to what was previously only a philosophy.[59] Friedrich Loofs wrote against Ernst Haeckel, accusing the latter of misunderstanding science; even more, he accused Haeckel of plain dishonesty in his use of sources and in his understanding of Christianity.[60] Ritschl himself believed that the scientists were right in pointing to the " mechanical regularity of all sensible things "; but their fundamental mistake was the attempt to explain the organic in terms of a mechanical, materialistic interpretation.

Now the claim of materialism to invalidate the Christian view of the world rests on the belief that it must succeed in deducing the organic from what is mechanical, and similarly the more complex orders of being from those immediately below. The materialistic interpretation of the world busies itself with the pursuit of these empty possibilities. Its scientific character is limited, however, by the fact that it can only suggest chance as the moving force of the ultimate causes of the world, and of the evolution of special realms of being out of those which are more general; for this is really to confess that science

[58] J. Kaftan, Philosophie des Protestantismus (Tübingen, 1917), pp. 361-62, 364.
[59] See A. Schlatter, Die philosophische Arbeit seit Cartesius (Dritte Auflage; Gütersloh, 1923), pp. 269-73.
[60] F. Loofs, Anti-Haeckel (Halle, 1900).

cannot penetrate to the supreme law of things. In all the combinations exhibited by the materialistic theory of the genesis of the world, there is manifest an expenditure of the power of imagination which finds its closest parallel in the cosmogonies of heathenism—which is of itself a proof that what rules in this school is not scientific method, but an aberrant and confused religious impulse. Thus the opposition which professedly exists between natural science and Christianity, really exists between an impulse derived from natural religion blended with the scientific investigation of nature, and the validity of the Christian view of the world, which assures to spirit its pre-eminence over the entire world of nature.[61]

Two things in this passage deserve further comment. First, the Darwinian problem is definitely included in the materialistic interpretation which was attacked. Second, and more important, the theme which runs all through liberal theology was sounded, namely, man's spiritual supremacy over nature. The expression " man over nature " was tantamount to a battle cry among liberal theologians. It explains much about the character of liberal theology. The traditional conceptions of God and of the world had not only been attacked; for many the reality of both God and world was called into question. Now man, as he had understood himself, was also challenged. The last ingredient of theology—man himself—was no longer theologically intelligible. The former dimensions through which God, world, and man, had been conceived, buttressed as they were by overly pictorial conceptions of space, had now been completely destroyed. Not a single element of the God, world, man correlation remained intact.

The greatness of liberal theology lay in seeing that a more adequate conception of man was essential if the theological task was to go on. Liberal theology did not know how much the nature of God and the world also needed attention; it knew it had to fight the battle for man. In this sense, it set the stage for the theological task of the present. Contemporary theologians are still concerned with a proper view of man. Even those who have been concerned most to overcome liberal-

[61] A. Ritschl, *The Christian Doctrine of Justification and Reconciliation* (Edinburgh, 1902), pp. 209-10.

ism's conception of man have not been able to escape its being in the forefront of concern. Liberalism played a creative role.

But liberalism's definition of man, in essentially moral terms, was not adequate to the theological task. The moral man looked too much like the bourgeois man, who was already being attacked by Dostoevsky, Kierkegaard, Marx, and Nietzsche. The liberal man was the personification of an idea, and not sufficiently man in all his powers of good and evil. There was no vibrant life in him, no dimension of height and depth. But the very urgency and desperateness of the liberal task is evident in the fact that nothing less than the divinization of man would do; his divinity was at least proof that he was more than animal. To be sure, the God who was so closely related to man was Himself as domesticated as the man he was meant to rescue from animality.

The Darwinian impact was the final threat to all the vertical and depth dimension within man and the cosmos. It marked the culmination of a period in which no adequate symbols were left for expressing and thinking about the classical Christian heritage. The symbols of this culture enslaved the very Christianity expressed through it. The late nineteenth and early twentieth centuries may have been one of those rare periods in history in which theology was virtually impossible, when the crisis of language and imagination excluded the essential depth of both God and man.

PART TWO

NOTES ON NEW DIRECTIONS

fore a response to the first. Finally, it may be added that in spite of the favourable situation of the present, I believe that the time is not ripe for new, extensive delineations of the interrelations of theology and science; it is rather imperative to point out new dangers and to indicate possible lines of approach to the issues.

In this chapter, attention is focused upon the major revolutions in thought which have taken place in both theology and science during the first half of the twentieth century.

In origin and in conception, the two revolutions were independent of each other. Each revolution was accompanied by a determination to restrict the area of alleged competence to one's own domain and to reject all unwarranted claims concerning areas outside one's own professional concern. In spite of some attempts to relate the two areas to each other, it is far more characteristic that each has affirmed its unique but more limited area of competence. This self-limitation has led to a greater intensity within the respective areas, but paradoxically enough, without the doctrinaire or absolutist claims to which the areas were previously prone. The notion of the unity of all knowledge and truth has become subsidiary to the proper demarcation and integrity of each discipline.

This independence is further evident in that there are few attempts to find a middle ground where mutual problems converge upon each other. Unlike the situation we encountered for the past, there is practically no interest in natural theology as such a point of encounter. The contention is that any relations between the areas must be explored from the standpoint of the uniqueness and strength of each discipline. The mood is that the unity of knowledge is at best an ideal, not a reality which can be attained at any moment of history. The complex and changing patterns of modern science, and the theological conviction that no final system can be formulated, have resulted in an equal suspicion of finality. While differences are maintained, a similar mood is evident in both fields. This has led some interpreters to relate the two areas through a delineation of analogies in method and in procedure, rather than by exploring specific problems.

A: THE THEOLOGICAL REVOLUTION

The beginning of the theological revolution is usually dated from *Barth's Commentary on Romans,* which appeared soon after World War I. Much has been said and written about the theological break-through that this book accomplished over against a liberal Protestantism, which had been formed by the content of the very culture it was trying to transform. More attention could be focused on the way in which this book, its subsequent editions, and indeed, Barth's theological enterprise as a whole, are directed to the overcoming of the issues, as posed in the history which we have sketched in the first part of this volume. In the most immediate sense, Barth considered his task that of overcoming the liberal view of God and of man in the light of the Biblical view of God and man. He wanted to speak of God and His acts on the basis of the Biblical word over against all ideas of God which were no more than man writ largely. But he soon discovered that his own early writing was governed by the anthropological language of existentialism. He found that he had been as bound as his predecessors to the thought forms, and therefore also in some sense to the content, of a culturally conditioned approach. In his subsequent attempt to expunge every sheerly anthropological source from his theology, Barth has affirmed the independence of theological conceptions and of theological communication from all cultural conditioning, whether social, philosophical, or scientific. This does not mean that Barth was unaware of the fact that all words are conditioned; nor does it mean that he had a special regard for the Biblical words. The theological task exists in a context in which human words, for all their inadequacy, are nevertheless the medium for genuine theological communication. In theology, words do not always convey meaning and power through the obviousness of what they say, but frequently " in spite of " what they directly mean. It was on this level that Barth maintained that faith created its own conditions; in short, that the miracle of faith always occurred in the midst of such inadequacies of thought and of language.

tinual crisis of every man before God. In a very real sense, Barth's voluminous theological output to date has the characteristic of a relentless elaboration of the nature and meaning of God's grace in its ramifications. Barth's only significant change has been that his theological method has had to be refined in the light of the single subject with which theology has to deal. However much others may disagree with Barth's method as it has developed, all recognize in Barth the initial prophetic power by which the Gospel was recovered, and by which they themselves were led to see it anew.

While Tillich's theology presents a marked contrast to Barth's, the extent to which Tillich's thinking is addressed to the same problem is not widely recognized. Tillich, like Barth, found it necessary to reconstitute the understanding of " world " as he expounded the contents of the Christian faith. But instead of using the world view of the Bible, he insisted that the only adequate method for theology lay in developing the kerygma or Gospel in correlation to the world and man's situation in it. But he understands " world " and man's place in it quite differently than do the nineteenth-century thinkers. Tillich constructed a conception of the world, not from the world view of the Bible nor from the world view of a particular time, but from motifs of understanding found throughout the history of thought. The most important of these are in the pre-Socratics, Plato, Aristotle, Medieval Realism, Kant, Hegel, Existentialism, depth Psychology, contemporary Naturalism, and Social thought.[4]

This would, undoubtedly, have been Tillich's method, even if he had not found it necessary to reconstruct a view of the world in order to provide more adequate dimensions than those found in the period through which we have just passed. For Tillich, a proper understanding of the world and man's place in it usually demands more than the questions and formulations any particular period provide, even though every period must find its own unique manner of expression. One of Tillich's great contributions has been his ability to bring the history of the past into living relation to the present. Specialists may disagree

---

[4] See my article, " Introduction to Tillich's Theology," *Drew Gateway*, (Autumn, 1951), pp. 17-23.

with the details of Tillich's interpretation of philosophy and history, and even with the substance itself; but no one would deny that, in each instance, Tillich has brought to life for us a man or a movement as he or it lived once before in its own time.

Tillich's use of cultural materials of the present and the past are suggestive rather than normative. It is well to bear in mind that Tillich has no interest in past history as such. It has meaning in terms of his own interests and purposes. An insight which Tillich has gathered from anywhere within the sweep of existence is no longer understood in its previous context alone; it now has a new setting, baptized by his understanding of the world and the Christian base from which he writes. Those who are bothered by so many references to non-Christian writers should note that his reconstruction of an adequate world view demands the use of the things of this world, including its thought structures; for Tillich, the source is irrelevant and the form and content everything.

For such an enterprise, Tillich's broad cultural and philosophical knowledge, as well as his theological training, (Tillich has held chairs both in theology and philosophy) equipped him admirably. His not being a disciple of any particular cultural, historical, or philosophical position is a help, rather than a hindrance, for it frees him to penetrate into the thoughts of others and to utilize what he believes to be of abiding significance. Moreover, it frees him for more adequate philosophical constructions of his own. The criterion for selection is general philosophical adequacy under the norm of its suitability for expressing the kerygma and its implications.

Barth and Tillich are concerned with the same problem. While they are the most divergent theologians in the contemporary revival of theology, they are both concerned with the rediscovery of the Gospel and in thinking about the full compass of its meaning in terms which are more adequate than those of the era from which we have just emerged. But whereas Barth works within the framework of the world view of the Bible, Tillich radically reconstructs a world view from the materials of man's historical questions and answers. But each has had to bring a new world with him in order to speak meaning-

science; it protested wherever men became an object. Further, such protests came from many fronts. In economic terms, Marx protested against man becoming an object in a process, without realizing that his own answer was equally objectifying. Dostoevsky protested against the Euclidian man, the man of reason, and man as animal. Nietzsche protested against the moral man whose character reflected the views of his culture. Kierkegaard protested against all of these forms, including the man who had become an object in the Church. Common to all the protests was that the personal and vital character of man was in jeopardy. Nietzsche, in looking at the Christianity of his day, declared that God was dead; he could have said the same of man. Instead he beckoned him to transform himself, to effect a transvaluation of values in the affirmation of himself.

The emergence of existentialism in the theological renaissance of the twentieth century stands for a recovery of man more congenial to classical theology, than the notion of man as the embodiment of value or as moral personality. The latter notion makes man appear as an idea rather than a person, that is, it makes him into a noble or ideal object. The issue is whether a living sinner is not more human and personal than a walking idea, moral or intellectual. In the latter view, he is at best an " instance of." He is not unique, nor personal, but meets another, not person to person, but always as what he might be or ought to conform to. Essentially, such a man has no heart-beat, no vitality. Diagrammatically, he can only be represented in terms of a flat horizontal line, emulating another line or level of ideas. He does not need to be redeemed. He needs an example to follow. In contrast, the existential man corresponds to a fever chart, with its ups and downs. He is sick, but therefore also gives signs of being alive and of being all too human. He is in need, not of an example, but of redemption; though in non-Christian terms, he can only resign himself to his fate of being sick and affirming his nobility by making the best of it, even by being responsible to his fellow man.

In a world in which depth dimensions disappeared, existentialism stands for their recovery in the depth of man. Whereas the dimensions of the cosmos, as, for example, the tripartite world, once provided a context in which to understand God and man in a convenient reference of space and of time, under the Darwinian impact both the undergirding conception of the cosmos and man himself were lost. Existentialism represents the restoration of the internal dimensions of man. These have taken the place of a cosmos in which such dimensions were once naturally sustained. The very pathos of existentialism is that it cannot naturally speak of man; it speaks of him with an element of descriptive compulsiveness. It cannot assume dimensions; it must fight for them.

Existentialism stands for the affirmation of the vitality and personal nature of man against all that objectifies him. Whether in its Christian or atheistic form, existentialism declares that man is subject, not object. Objectivization, of course, is related to man both as value and as animal. In either case, he becomes " thing." In Heidegger's sense, we must distinguish between authentic and unauthentic existence. On the one side, unauthentic existence is the subjection of man to essentialism, to the realm of ideas. On another side, it is subjection to an objective nature. A situation is unauthentic when science or nature is the last court of appeal.

In Heidegger as in Kierkegaard and Nietzsche, science stands for unauthentic existence. Science is a matter of indifference, of concern with selected objects or items, whether of nature or of history. It conceals man in his totality, in his mystery, by a concern with the multiplication of knowledge essentially indifferent to himself as an existing subject. Although thrown into being, man is a mysterious being whose wholeness must be affirmed. Such affirmation constitutes history, not nature. Where man is an item in the historical process, history has been reduced to nature. Where he lives in the true affirmation of his being, history and meaning are constituted. His being or his freedom is affirmed as he " stands out " from any objective thing which is " over against " him.

While the main terms in the preceding two paragraphs obviously come from Heidegger, the same point is made in different ways by the exponents of existentialism. In every instance, it is the passionate affirmation of man, or of the world of man. Indeed, the real world is

it may be instructive to note that Bultmann has accepted the full impact of the history and philosophy of science. He decided that all conceptions of the world must be abandoned. Like the liberal theologians, he believes that the theological issue lies at the point of the meeting between man and God. But Bultmann, unlike the liberals, has described this encounter in a way which makes the kerygma central and meaningful. Bultmann has clearly articulated that it is God who addresses man, and that in this very fact, a response of one kind or another is inevitable.

While Barth has continued to develop theological statements through a sophisticated reading of the Scripture and the history of the Church, and Tillich has recreated a new world to which the Gospel speaks, Bultmann has frankly abandoned all attempts to define theological concepts in any other way than in their direct meaning for us, that is, in existential terms. For Bultmann, the attempt to speak of " God in Himself " in the light of " God for us " has been abandoned. The question we must ask is whether or not the relevance of theology has been achieved at the expense of shrinking its horizons and concerns.

However, the alternative cannot be found in the rather easy elaboration of Biblical concepts done by Bultmann's conservative opponents, particularly on the continent of Europe. While under the influence of Barth, they are more conservative than Barth. Whereas Bultmann, for example, interprets Cross and Resurrection to be synonymous with what happens when the Word is preached, and assumes that it is inappropriate to ask what lies behind such eventfulness, the more conservative theologians proceed as if science did not exist; or as if the new science now once again made all things possible. They speak of the Resurrection in objective terms. In that direction lies the danger of a new orthodoxy.

Succinctly put, the theological revolution of the twentieth century recovered a conception of man and God more in accord with the Biblical understanding than probably any period since the Reformation itself. This is accomplished while rethinking theological problems in the context of contemporary thought. In that enterprise, existentialist categories played a prominent role, even if they will prove not to be entirely adequate.

The theological revolution once again made the redemptive focus central. Moreover, the redemptive focus incorporated the meaning of the history of Israel. Hence, the concept of the history of salvation became important again. The concern with nature inevitably and justifiably took a secondary role. But the temptation was to act and think as if nature had no place at all, as if it were but an indifferent stage for the drama of history. Be that as it may, it was necessary that God's grace and judgment again become central for Christians and that the historical process take on meaning. Moreover, this new vision took form in its own right; it had meaning for culture and yet was not unduly conditioned by it. The powerful impact of Paul Tillich and Reinhold Niebuhr in America bears testimony to this fact.

Part of the strength of the theological revolution stems from an authentic recovery of integrity and of power, coupled with the capacity to relate its message to other disciplines and areas of life. In Karl Barth, this strength is the power of a consistent, yet somehow relevant, concern with the Biblical message in its own terms. In Paul Tillich, it is the genius of a correlative encounter of the Biblical message with the total cultural scene. In Reinhold Neibuhr, it is the message and power of Christian love in conversation and encounter with the ambiguous stuff of contemporary history. But it must be said that for these theologians, the scientific enterprise, apart from its implications for the social scene, has not come into purview. There is a sigh of relief that the old problems no longer exist and that scientific dogmatism has been overcome. We must certainly agree that the burning theological issues of our time have not lain in the relation between theology and science. But insofar as theology must eventually be related to all the disciplines, the time has come for us to raise the question of what significance the new situation in science has for the theological enterprise. We are still caught, by and large, between those who see no relation between the two and those who see it too readily.

Theoretical physicists are generally unwilling even to say that they deal with aspects of reality. The basis for such a statement is not clear, since a responsible discipline must have some relation to reality. But by this assertion they do mean two things. First, they want to avoid, if at all possible, the mistakes of the past. Second, they believe that even the suggestion of restricting the work of science to an aspect of reality is too unguarded a statement. The character of the scientific enterprise changes with, and affects the scope and character of, alleged aspects of reality. However, can one escape the philosophical problem simply by saying one will lay it aside and restrict oneself to what explains, or more accurately describes, the functioning of certain limited areas of concern?

It is difficult, in any case, for non-scientists to understand or to comprehend what science is about. Classical physics had the luxury of being comprehensible in observable and imaginable images. There is no possibility of imagining or conceiving many aspects of contemporary science; without the specialist's knowledge of mathematics and of energy, there is no way into the mystery. The only available language is that of classical physics stretched beyond its limits. Moreover, even among scientists, a language or frame of reference beyond classical physics has not yet been found. In fact, there is doubt that it can be found; hence, there is a distinct preference for mathematical symbols. But if such a new and unified discourse is found, it may provide unity where there now appear to be contradictory or as yet irreconcilable elements. It will certainly be a frame of reference which is alien to the experience of most of us for whom the traditional classical symbols are more meaningful. This is not simply a matter of changing one's orientation. In terms of the obvious experience of men, the new science of the twentieth century is stranger than that manifested in any previous period. It is, after all, easier to think of the fundamental elements of all things as indivisible material particles than it is to think of energy and electrical charges. It is also easier to conceive of the earth or the sun as the centre of a universe than to realize that no absolute centres can be found. It is precisely for this reason that the man on the street still lives in a Newtonian world.

The development of quantum physics came in various stages through the works of Planck, Bohr, Schrödinger, de Broglie, Einstein, Heisenberg, and others. Light was defined with reference to particle and wave properties. The energy in atomic structures, originally conceived in terms of the emission of waves, was also defined in terms of quanta on the basis of radiation experiments. Mass can be defined in terms of energy and vice versa. The stuff of the world can no longer be said to be composed of inert, hard, particles of matter. The electrical components of all atomic structures, whether the behaviour is in terms of waves or quanta, has provided unheard of possibilities in scientific advance. But no new theory has yet emerged to unify the discordant material.

Two problems, frequently interpreted in philosophical terms, have arisen in this context. The first area of concern is with the so-called microscopic as opposed to the macroscopic level. It involves the meaning of prediction, probability, and the laws of nature. The behaviour of particular electrical particles cannot be predicted with accuracy, in fact, mostly not at all; but aggregate probabilities can be predicted. Consequently, one refers to laws as statistical probabilities. Frequently philosophers, theologians, and a few scientists have drawn the conclusion that strict causal laws are no longer operative in science and have therefore been abandoned. It is said that disorder lies beneath everything, that laws are but the imposition of categories upon chaos. In more moderate terms, it is said that the absence of rigid order leaves room for occasional occurrences outside what we recognize as order. But it is not legitimate to draw either of the above conclusions. The breaking down of the old rigid causal laws once ascribed to nature occurred, of course, through the fact that they could no longer be substantiated in current physics. But in many areas, a circumscribed concept of causality is still helpful.

In any case, the concept or reality of causation in physics does not prove determinism in other realms, unless one already has accepted a materialistic interpretation of life. Nor does the absence of causation in physics necessarily destroy deterministic elements in other aspects of experience. Among physicists, the problem is by no means settled

though predictability and probability remain in the aggregate and on so-called macroscopic levels. Nevertheless, it would appear safer to say that the element of indeterminacy is fundamentally an unresolved problem in physics. Further, it appears that theologians and philosophers should neither try to solve this scientific problem, nor build on it, nor interpret it with the wish being the father to the thought. For the present, at least, the impossibility of simultaneously determining position and velocity has introduced an unbridgeable chasm. Nevertheless, information about either velocity or position is significant.

Nils Bohr has attempted to meet the apparent dichotomy by introducing the principle of complementarity. While the two experiments concerning velocity and position exclude each other, they belong together and form a unity. They are only apparently contradictory and in fact complement each other. The principle of complementarity, here utilized in physics, was actually taken over by Bohr from philosophy and theology. Now it is frequently applied to problems in theology as if it had come originally from physics. But with reference to physics, it would again appear safer to leave open the question whether or not complementarity has a permanent or a temporary role to play.

Popular attention originally centred in Einstein's conception of relativity. In actuality, the concept of relativity belongs to a whole context of experiments and developments which preceded and followed, and should not unduly be singled out for attention. For our purposes, it is important to note that the concept of relativity has conclusively destroyed an absolute centre of reference with respect to the uniform validity of time and space throughout the universe. There is no point at rest from which such secure calculations can be made; any statement on this level necessarily involves a particular co-ordinate of time and space applicable to its own context and not in the same way to others. This does not mean that laws have disappeared. The laws of motion can be said to be precisely identical for the same set of co-ordinates, and applicable for others; but while the experience in another set of co-ordinates may be the same, the actuality may be different. The experience of time, for example, may be similar in different sets of co-ordinates, but the actuality of time may be quite different. Hence, there is the baffling question of what simultaneity means. In principle, clocks moving through space are slower than those at relative rest; and the likelihood is that the measurement of time is relative to speed and position. Time is related to both position and velocity. One could say the same of each of the other terms. This is why one now speaks of a space-time continuum, and why one can no longer think of the universe as a box in which time, space, and position can be determined with the fixity of such a container.

Both in the so-called microscopic and macroscopic levels, the situation is both more complicated than is generally assumed and more impervious to common-sense notions. But the fact that one is involved in the system of co-ordinates, and that this very point of reference leads to different results than other points of reference does not mean that everything is relative, either in science or the other disciplines. According to the present way of thinking, it means that everything is more suspended or set in relational contexts having structures, than the old notions of fixity had warranted. Nor does the relativity concept mean that now we can relate all times to each other by a conception of different time spans, as for example, those of the may-fly, man, and God. Quite apart from the doubtful use of such analogies, it does not follow from the concept of relativity.

When one combines the concept of relativity with the theories concerning the extent and nature of the universe, imagination is lost in an incredible dizziness. Einstein, of course, believed in a finite rather than an infinite universe. But his conception of finiteness dwarfs previous conceptions of infinity, even if one realizes that on one level, the problem of the finite-infinite is not a quantitative but a qualitative problem. But if one associates this conception with the curvature of space, namely, the notion that there are no straight paths through which light travels, but that it would eventually return to the point from which it started, one sees something both of the dimensions of the universe and of what Einstein meant. A beam of light travelling at the rate of 186,000 miles per second would, in terms of a circle,

the older mechanistic theories have continued to receive more attention in biology than in physics and astronomy. But here, too, there has been a trend to an organismic conception, in which life is seen to be made up of structural components in a complex and inexhaustible unity. The late Lecomte du Noüy made much of the complex conic structure of the eye and believed that its development demanded a conception of a Creator. But the question of the conic development of the eye is a matter for biologists to explore, and our present or future ignorance in this field is not an argument for God. Nevertheless, it can be said that biology is moving into concerns more commensurate with the phenomenon which we know as life. In doing so, biologists have had to draw on many of the other sciences, since life is such a complex phenomenon. These two tendencies are present in contemporary biology. On the one side, biology is closely related to chemistry and physics. On the other side, it confronts the necessity of understanding complexities in terms of wholes or directions of development. Such wholes apparently contain mysteries which valid empirical knowledge does not exhaust or perhaps even touch.

X

Theology and Science

A: SUBJECT MATTER AND METHOD

When viewed against the background of our study, the contours of the revolutions in theology and physics are clear enough. But when attention is focused on each field, it is immediately evident that each area is in ferment and in a transitional period. It is not by accident that the problem of method is a matter of direct and self-conscious concern in each field. Questions of methodology arise when the very character of a discipline is under examination. Achievements in both disciplines, including the new habits of thought which have come as a result, have not only been unable to suppress this question; they appear to have created the problem. We may be living in one of those rare moments in history when it is recognized that new accomplishments bring as many problems with them as the breakdown of an old era. Nevertheless, such new problems are generally to be preferred.

In spite of, or precisely because of, the new theological vigour of recent decades, we find that the nature of theology is a persistent problem running through the variety of theological expression. But the situation is not novel. It is not unlike other moments in history when the discipline of theology was at stake. One need only mention such figures as Augustine, Aquinas, Luther, Calvin, and Schleiermacher. They remind us that theological thought has frequently had

283

theoretical science as much as do concrete observation and controlled experiment.

It would be too simple to say that the situations in theology and science are directly parallel. In contemporary theology, there is considerable unanimity concerning the nature of its subject matter and its central concerns.[3] Its one concern is the proper understanding and articulation of the Biblical message in the contemporary church and world; the problem of method arises in that context. In the natural sciences, there is no such circumscribed and normative matrix. In short, the difference in subject matter means that there are limits to which parallels can be seen. Genuine mystery may surround both revelation and the understanding of some observable aspect of science. But revelation has to do with the mystery of *disclosure*, while science deals with the mystery which is associated with *discovery*. They are different in principle, however much the two converge.

The present ferment in theology and in the natural sciences may be followed by a period of greater stability. One need not decide whether or not that would be a more favourable situation; it would have its own kind of problems. But the present situation reminds us that the methodology in the various disciplines is not as different as is usually assumed. The doctrinaire views which combined content and method have had to be abandoned. In each area, the distinctiveness of subject matter and the necessity of positive affirmations are held concurrently with a greater degree of openness to further developments.

B: THE RELATIONSHIP OF THEOLOGY AND SCIENCE

It is singularly important that theologians recognize that the new science is no longer surrounded by metaphysical assumptions detrimental to theology. This new openness in science dare not be misinterpreted, however. It is not a warrant for basing philosophical and religious ideas on specific conceptions in the new science. There is a great danger of filling the gaps in science with theological answers, or of seeing too readily the footprints of God in the world, or of assuming

[3] A scientist looking at theology would probably disagree.

that one is thinking God's thoughts after Him. Few indeed are those who see an argument for free will in the concept of indeterminacy or who follow du Noüy in finding a theistic frame of reference in biology.[4] The bland assumption that contemporary science has destroyed the notion of materialism needs careful scrutiny. If one defines materialism simply as the notion that the fundamental components of reality are hard, solid material particles—as had been the case in both ancient atomists and in their eighteenth- and nineteenth-century equivalents— it no longer obtains. But the abandonment of the older view does not imply a spiritual interpretation of reality, as is frequently assumed, or that we should now believe in a Universal Mind.

Much semi-popular writing on science has fallen into this pitfall. The writings of James Jeans fall into this category. The thesis essentially is that the orderly mysteries of nature can only be understood from something more fundamental, namely, Mind or Spirit. This type of analysis is then set over against the mechanical Newtonian view. But those who associate Mind or Spirit with the new physics find support in physics for a view held on quite independent grounds. The respect for mystery which has emerged in contemporary science does not necessarily imply a spiritual or religious interpretation of the world.

Aloys Wenzel and Bernard Bavinck directly identify aspects of contemporary science with a concept of spirit. Energy or wave theories, as contrasted to the billiard ball conception of atoms, demand a spiritual interpretation of the universe. For Wenzel, free and spontaneous occurrences in nature argue that the world is not a dead or lifeless place. Even the arena of mathematical nature is called a world of the " lower spirits." For Bavinck, the wave theory of matter directly argues for a spiritual interpretation of reality rather than a material one. But in and of itself, the concept of energy or wave is neither more or less materialistic, nor, more or less spiritual. Where such a

[4] Lecomte du Noüy, *Human Destiny*. For an exposition in which concepts of spirit and Spirit are brought into relation to biology, in what to the present writer seems to be quite dubious, see Edmund W. Sinnott, *The Biology of the Spirit* (New York: The Viking Press, 1955).

way. There is no reason for affirming that God is at work any less in the midst of ordered structures than He is in the midst of disorder. Nor is there any reason to define revelation in a way which contradicts the orderly processes which we know. The orthodox theologians, who defined God's breaking into the order of the world as the manifestation of another order, were wrong in accepting the problem in the way in which it was presented to them; but they correctly sensed that God's relation to a world is not to be defined by order or disorder, but by the manifestation and apprehension of His presence and mystery in ways which cannot be defined in terms of these alternatives. It is theologically wrong to define such a concept as the Virgin Birth through contemporary science, and from one perspective, the biological possibility of a virgin birth would produce as many problems as it would solve.[5] In a world which has lost its sense for mystery, theologians are tempted to find support for it in science. But the mystery in science is potentially more open to specific forms of investigation, and hence transformation, than the essential mystery of revelation. The mystery of revelation is of another order, even if the mysteries present in scientific achievements do not abate.

A more fruitful and less dangerous way of relating theology and science is through analogy. In a broad sense, the comparison of methods in the two fields is an exercise in analogy. Such comparative analysis is a most helpful way of breaking down the feeling that a widely different way of going about things obtains between theology and science. The likenesses and differences between the two fields, with a due recognition of the different levels, have been suggestively set forth by Dean Harold Schilling in various articles. They should do much in the American scene to dispel the notion that the procedures in both disciplines are fundamentally different.[6] The question of presuppositions or post-presuppositions, as some of the guiding

[5] For a theological defence of a biological virgin birth in the light of the new science, see E. L. Mascall, *Christian Theology and Natural Science* (New York: Longmans, Green and Co., 1956), pp. 310-11, and A. F. Smethurst, *Modern Science and Christian Beliefs* (New York: Abingdon Press, 1955), pp. 215-17.

[6] See, for instance Harold K. Schilling, *Concerning the Nature of Science and Religion, A Study of Presuppositions*, published by the School of Religion at the State University of Iowa, 1958.

principles are called by Schilling, is, however, the clearing ground for undertaking subsequent work in the area. It is not a substitute for it.

The analogy most frequently employed is that of complementarity. Just as the concept of complementarity is used by Bohr and others to describe the apparently distinct and yet probably related aspects of wave and particle with reference both to light and matter, so it is affirmed that religion and science must be complementary. This may be true; but the interesting question will be to show wherein this complementarity consists. Within the field of science, as well as between science and theology, it is apparent enough that a certain parallelism exists at this juncture in history. We simply do not know how certain diverging and converging aspects fit together. Perhaps the introduction of some new concept will provide the key for overcoming the apparent contradictions in such a way as to make the concept of complementarity unnecessary. At present, however, the concept is extensively used by a German scientist who is also an amateur theologian, Günter Howe. He is particularly impressed by the similarity between the concept of complementarity as used by Bohr and the way in which the attributes of God are developed in Karl Barth's theology.[7] Assuming that the analogy is true, we are still left with the question whether it is significant.

A more fruitful analogy, it would seem to me, is the apparent combination of randomness and pattern in so many realms of thought. It is believed that there is an apparent random movement and yet a definite pattern in many areas of study. It can be said to be true in sub-atomic physics, in astronomical patterns, in history itself, and in the life of any individual man. But certain difficulties inhere in putting the matter this way. If the analogical nature between these areas were taken hypothetically, one could abandon it the moment there was evidence to the contrary. But the difficulty is that analogical thinking inevitably shifts ground toward an analogy of being. One cannot so easily abandon that. If the analogy of randomness and pattern were

[7] Günter Howe, "Parallelen zwischen der Theologie Karl Barths und der heutigen Physik," in *Antwort, Festschrift zum 70. Geburtstag von Karl Barth am 10. Mai 1956; Der Mensch und die Physik*, Jugenddienst-Verlag (Wuppertal, 1958).

true, one could oppose Pascal and say that man did bear a proportion to nature. This would not imply a different conception of God or man than that held by Pascal; it would only mean that Pascal had to save man in his time by declaring that the relation between man and nature was essentially disproportionate. Today, we have a more congenial conception of nature. Further, since man's transcendence of nature can be guaranteed by a proper delineation of history, including the drama of redemption, man can safely be said to bear proportion to nature. But to make this point is in fact to state that the theological point of man's relation to nature is not dependent on any analogy, such as randomness and pattern.[8] Further, in the light of the fact that all previous analogies have broken down, it is exceedingly doubtful that this one should be pursued. In any case, the theological assertion of man's relation to nature is not dependent on the analogy.

The almost totally negative comments on the existing attempts to relate theology and science would seem to call either for a total division of spheres, as in the case of Karl Barth, or for an attempt to relate the two in ways quite different from those we have discussed. The perspective of history would seem to call for the careful separation of disciplines for the sake of their integrity. But history has also shown that it is impossible to maintain such integrity either by separating the disciplines or by positively relating them to each other. The former leads to irrelevance in theology and frequently also to rearguard action; the latter leads to the distortion of one discipline by another. But we can hope that integrity will be struggled for and that creative attempts will be made to relate the disciplines to each other. In our time, we have recovered the integrity of the disciplines; we have also been confronted by the sheer complexity and incredible increase in knowledge in all areas. Even if we affirm that truth is one, human pretensions and the sheer vastness and transitional nature of knowledge make it impossible for us to achieve such unity. But we shall still need to relate what we can.[9]

[8] Protestant thought responds more directly to scientific currents than does Roman Catholicism inasmuch as the philosophical assumptions of an *analogia entis* do not exist. In this sense, Pascal was a Protestant in his thought.

[9] See J. Robert Oppenheimer's address, *Daedalus*, Winter, 1958, p. 76.

We must be extremely cautious in any positive interrelating of theology and science. The scientist in one sense does more fully open to us the wisdom of God; but he can also open to us the terror of hell. The scientist may also describe processes which to the theological mind are evidences of purposes; but for others, purpose may not be apparent or if it is, it may fall in a totally different context than a Christian one. Scientific processes do not in themselves give theological meaning.

Those who separate the disciplines of theology and science with respect to subject matter are basically more correct than those who too easily find relations between them. But the difficulty with those who completely divorce the disciplines is that they act and think as if nothing happened in the other disciplines which affects them in any way. The distinctiveness of subject matter does not mean that implications in one area can be ignored in another. It means only that what happens in one area cannot become *normative* for the essential content of another. Some have gone so far as to say that modern science shows us that the Bible is correct after all, that the traditional problems of resurrection or miracle can, with sophistication, be defined as before. But a miracle, for example, should not be defined as a factual possibility, once denied, but now again possible in the light of contemporary science. The only gain in the contemporary scene is that the transforming power of God's presence is no longer automatically excluded by what scientists claim to be true of the world. But this is no justification for defining miracles as the invasion of the natural by the supernatural, nor as God's manipulation of electrons or the latest scientific equivalent. Miracles occur in the totality of the natural—directing, fulfilling, transforming it. Miracles are not disjunctive with science as science. We can affirm that levels of reality meet and intersect; but they do not create gaps or do violence to each other. Hence, neither area should essentially be defined in terms of the other, either positively or negatively. For this reason, theologians should exercise extreme care in the way they formulate theological problems. The history of science *does* mean that the old ways of putting things are no longer viable. It *does not* mean that the essential content of theology is thereby changed. A degree of demythologizing is inescapable, however essential symbols and myths may be. Put in minimum terms, a more imaginative use of traditional rational language is essential.

There are areas where the achievements in science do not directly affect theological thought but where they ought, nevertheless, to be taken into account. It has been evident throughout this study that the historical side of the Christian claim was always in danger of being swallowed by a conception of nature. It is not by accident that the recent theological revolution is centred in the conception of history. While the understanding of history continues to be debated, it is definitely the unique and unrepeated, which has given substance to the contemporary understanding of history and also to the Christian claim of a redemptive event in an historical matrix. But the question is whether the unique is unrepeated because it is the unpredictable dropped into the orderly world, or whether the unrepeated is the special characteristic of something which in all other respects does not appear to be decisively different. If the latter is true, providence should not be connected with chance, or the unique with being empirically unique.[10] It seems to me that the qualitatively different is genuinely different; but from the standpoint of natural science it cannot be shown to be essentially different. Its effects and characteristics may of course be described from a sociological perspective.

The Christian understanding of the world rests in a special history and in a special event in that history, Jesus Christ. But the uniqueness of this event cannot be certified by maintaining that it is a special, providential, and perplexing history in an empirical sense. It is genuinely unique only as it is appropriated. Empirically speaking, the history of Israel and of Jesus Christ can be interpreted positively or negatively, either as a glorious history or as a history of calamity and misfortunes. Both aspects may be present but transformed by the

[10] It seems to me that Mr. Pollard is very close to this way of putting it in his recent book, *Chance and Providence* (New York: Charles Scribner's, Sons, 1958). Nor does it seem to me that one can say that quantum physics has introduced history into nature, as he suggests at one point.

context of their appropriation. Where that happens, Biblical history is a special and unique history.

In maintaining that the historical drama is central to Christian understanding, it must not be forgotten that there are other planets which may have life in forms not dissimilar from ours. This notion has had a long history, and we must be open to it. Certainly, God's creative relation to a cosmos which, for all practical purposes, borders on infinity is more extensive than the parochial imagination of many Christians. But it must be recognized that the statement that God is related to the world in such comprehensiveness follows, for the Christian, from his conception of God the Creator. But it was precisely this situation which tempted both scientists and theologians to stress the Creator rather than the Redeemer, and to return again to nature rather than to history for the clue to theological understanding. It is, however, just as plausible to speak of God's relation to the history of other worlds as it is to speak of His relation to them as Creator. Further, God's relation to our world may be no less or more unique among other worlds than God's particular relation to the revealing history in Israel and in Jesus Christ.

Most of the concepts in theology, such as creation and resurrection, are border or boundary symbols. The " prior " of creation and the " beyondness " of life and destiny are beyond imagination. Science sheds no light on the fundamental theological issues here. But theological statements should be made neither in contradiction to, nor on the basis of, what we know from science. The same methodological implications apply with reference to creation and resurrection, as, for example, to incarnation and miracle. The latest on creation from a scientific standpoint will not help; it will only make the context of reference different.[11] Neither creation of time or in time, nor continuous creation, will change the fundamental theological problem of the world's dependence on its creator; but it will affect or exclude certain ways of expressing that relation. Nor will entropy or the continuous rejuvenation of the world in some rhythmic pattern basically

[11] For a very suggestive but nevertheless dubious analysis of the relation of light and depth in Genesis to contemporary science, see The Christian Scholar (September, 1958), pp. 359-60.

affect the concept of resurrection or destiny. Resurrection stands for the reality of the new life which is known in the present, and which in Christ is trusted for the future. But the symbols for expressing this are less adequate in our culture than in certain other periods of history. Certainly the future cannot be defined as the extension of the present. Paul's symbolism in the Letter to the Corinthians remains as useful as any. In the reality of the newness of life in Christ, in the power already of His resurrection, we live in the present toward the future. We have a foretaste but no vision; in faith we stand before darkness.

In the history of the Western world, the old pictures and symbols have disappeared. Most of our study has been devoted to an analysis of this development. In our contemporary world, new symbols and analogies may well arise, and many of them may again be more adequate than those in the more recent past. But at the present juncture of history, we are in a far greater transitional stage than has usually been the case. It is therefore particularly important to work carefully and slowly. It is tempting to build absolute fences or to establish premature analogies or relations. But it will be wise to work patiently and circumspectly. Along that road it may be possible to move ahead without repeating some of the tragic mistakes of the past. On that road, it may also be possible to reinstate philosophy in new dimensions.

SELECT BIBLIOGRAPHY

Select Bibliography

(Additional literature, and all references to primary sources in Part I, will be found in the footnotes. The bibliography here presented has been selected primarily with reference to additional literature on the total history, special areas, or problems.)

I. ORIENTATION TO THE HISTORY OF SCIENCE

General History

Burtt, E. A. *The Metaphysical Foundations of Modern Physical Science,* Routledge, 1951.

Butterfield, H. *The Origins of Modern Science,* G. Bell, 1949.

Dingle, H. *The Scientific Adventure: essays in the history and philosophy of science,* London: Sir Isaac Pitman & Sons, Ltd., 1952.

Whitehead, A. N. *Science and the Modern World,* Cambridge University Press, 1936.

(For older and dated general literature, see the works of B. W. Dampier, J. W. Draper, J. L. E. Dreyer, J. Singer, A. D. White.)

Specific Areas

De Santillana, Giorgio. *The Crime of Galileo,* Chicago: The University of Chicago Press, 1955.

Dreyer, J. L. E. *Tycho Brahe,* Edinburgh: A. & C. Black, 1890.

Kuhn, T. S. *The Copernican Revolution,* Cambridge, Mass.: Harvard University Press, 1957.

Pemberton, H. *A View of Sir Isaac Newton's Philosophy,* London, 1728.

Maclaurin, C. *An Account of Sir Isaac Newton's Philosophical Discoveries,* London, 1775.

More, L. T. *Isaac Newton, A Biography*, New York: Charles Scribner's, Sons, 1934.

Rosen, E. (Introd. and ed.) *Three Copernican Treatises*, New York: Columbia University Press, 1939.

Stimson, D. *The Gradual Acceptance of the Copernican Theory of the Universe*, New Hampshire, 1917.

2. THEOLOGY AND SCIENCE IN THE CONTINENTAL REFORMATION PERIOD

Bornkamm, H. *Luther's World of Thought*, St. Louis: Concordia Publishing House, 1958.

Elert, W. *Morphologie des Luthertums*, I. München, 1931.

Hirsch, E. *Die Theologie des Andreas Osiander und ihre geschichtlichen Voraussetzungen*, Göttengen, 1919.

Williams, Arnold. *The Common Expositor: an account of the Commentaries on Genesis*, 1527-1633, Chapel Hill: University of North Carolina Press, 1948.

3. THE PROTESTANT ORTHODOX PERIOD AND THE PROBLEM OF PHILOSOPHY

Althaus, P. *Die Prinzipien der deutschen reformierten Dogmatik im Zeitalter der aristotelischen Scholastik*, Leipzig, 1914.

Bohatec, J. *Die cartesianische Scholastik in der Philosophie und reformierten Dogmatik des 17. Jahrhunderts*, Leipzig, 1913.

Dibon, P. *La philosophie néerlandaise au siècle d'or*, Tome I, Amsterdam, 1954.

Maier, Anneliese. *Die Mechanisierung des Weltbilds im 17. Jahrhundert*, Leipzig, 1938.

——. *Zwei Grundprobleme der scholastischen Naturphilosophie*, Roma, 2. Auflage, 1951.

Ong, Walter J. *Ramus: Method, and the Decay of Dialogue*, Cambridge, Mass.: Harvard University Press, 1958.

Petersen, P. *Geschichte der aristotelischen Philopsohie im protestantischen Deutschland*, Leipzig, 1921.

Pünjer, G. CH. B. *History of the Christian Philosophy of Religion from the Reformation to Kant*, Edinburgh, 1887.

Troeltsch, E. *Vernunft und Offenbarung bei Johann Gerhard und Melanchthon*, Göttingen, 1891.

Weber, E. *Die philosophische Scholastik des deutschen Protestantismus im Zeitalter der Orthodoxie*, Leipzig, 1907.

Weber, Hans Emil. *Reformation, Orthodoxie und Rationalismus*, I and II, Gütersloh, 1937-1951.

Wundt, M. *Die deutsche Schulmetaphysik des 17. Jahrhunderts*, Tübingen, 1939.

4. ENGLISH AND AMERICAN SCENE

Kocher, P. H. *Science and Religion in Elizabethan England*, San Marino, California: The Huntington Library, 1953.

Merton, R. K. " Science, Technology and Society in Seventeenth Century England," *Osiris* 4 (1938) (Book length).

Miller, P. and Johnson, T. H. *The Puritans*, New York: American Book Company, 1938.

Westfall, R. S. *Science and Religion in Seventeenth-Century England*, New Haven: Yale University Press, 1958.

White, E. A. *Science and Religion in American Thought*, Stanford: Stanford University Press, 1952.

5. TOWARD THE ENLIGHTENMENT AND AFTER

Aner, Karl. *Die Theologie der Lessingzeit*, Halle, 1929.

Cassirer, E. *The Philosophy of the Enlightenment*, Oxford University Press, 1948.

Pascal, Roy. *The German Sturm und Drang*, Manchester University Press, 1953.

Philipp, Wolfgang. *Das Werden der Aufklärung in theologiegeschichtlicher Sicht*, Göttingen, 1957.

Wernle, Paul. *Lessing und das Christentum*, Tübingen, 1912.

Wundt, M. *Die deutsche Schulphilosophie im Zeitalter der Aufklärung*, Tübingen, 1945.

6. EVOLUTION AND ITS AFTERMATH

Barnett, S. A. *A Century of Darwin*, Cambridge, Mass.: Harvard University Press, 1958.

Bergson, H. L. *Creative Evolution*, London: Macmillan, 1954.

Carter, G. S. *A Hundred Years of Evolution*, New York: The Macmillan Co., 1957.

Furniss, N. F. *The Fundamentalist Controversy*, New Haven: Yale University Press, 1954.

Gillispie, C. C. *Genesis and Evolution*, New York: Harper Torch-books, 1959.

Morgan, C. L. *Emergent Evolution*, London: Williams and Norgate, 1923.

Persons, S. (ed.) *Evolutionary Thought in America*, New York: George Braziller, Inc., 1956.

Simonsson, T. *Face to Face with Darwinism*, Lund, 1958.

Simpson, G. G. *The Meaning of Evolution*, London: Muller, 1953.

7. AREAS OF SCIENCE AND THE CONCEPTIONS OF SCIENCE

Nature of Science

Bridgman, P. W. *The Nature of Physical Theory*, New York: Dover Publications, Inc., 1936.

Reflections of a Physicist, New York: Philosophical Library, Inc., 1955.

Caldin, E. F. *The Power and Limits of Science*, London: Chapman and Hall, 1949.

Campbell, N. *What is Science?* New York: Dover Publications, Inc., 1952.

Conant, J. B. *On Understanding Science*, London: Muller, 1956.

Frank, P. *Modern Science and Its Philosophy*, Oxford University Press, 1949.

Philosophy of Science, Englewood Cliffs, N. J.: Prentice-Hall, Inc., 1957.

Heisenberg, W. *Philosophic Problems of Nuclear Science*, London: Faber, 1952.

The Physical Principles of the Quantum Theory, Chicago: The University of Chicago Press, 1930.

Physics and Philosophy, New York: Harper & Brothers, 1958.

Margenau, H. *The Nature of Physical Reality*, New York: Mc-Graw, 1950.

Oppenheimer, J. Robert. *Science and the Common Understanding*, Oxford University Press, 1954.

Planck, M. *Scientific Autobiography and other Papers*, New York: Philosophical Library, Inc., 1949.

Poincaré, H. *Science and Hypothesis*, New York: Dover Publications, Inc., 1952.

Reichenbach, H. *Atom and Cosmos*, London: Allen & Unwin.

Sullivan, J. W. N. *The Limitations of Science*, New York: A Mentor Book, 1949.

Toulmin, S. *The Philosophy of Science*, London: Hutchinson University Library, 1953.

Waddington, C. H. *The Scientific Attitude*, London: Pelican Book, Second and Revised Edition, 1948.

Von Weizsäcker, C. F. *The History of Nature*, London: Routledge, 1951.

Areas of Science

Bondi, H. *Cosmology*, Cambridge University Press, 1952.

Cassirer, E. *Substance and Function and Einstein's Theory of Relativity*, New York: Dover Publications, Inc., 1953.

D' Abro, A. *The New Physics*, New York: Dover Publications, Inc., 1939.

De Broglie, Louis. *Physics and Microphysics*, New York: Pantheon Books, Inc., 1955.

Gamow, G. *The Birth and Death of the Sun*, London: Muller, 1956.

The Creation of the Universe, London: Macmillan.

Hoyle, Fred. *Frontiers of Astronomy*, London: Heinemann, 1955.

The Nature of the Universe, New York: Harper & Brothers, 1950.

Jammer, M. *Concepts of Space*, Oxford University Press, 1954.

Jones, G. O., Rotblat, J., Whitrow, G. J. *Atoms and the Universe*, Eyre & Spottiswoode, 1956.

Jordan, P. *Physics of the Twentieth Century*, New York: Philosophical Library, Inc., 1944.

Lenzen, V. F. *Causality in Natural Science*, Oxford: Blackwell Scientific Publications, 1954.

Sinnott, E. *The Biology of the Spirit*, London: Gollancz, 1956.

Von Weizsäcker, C. F. *The World View of Modern Physics*, London: Routledge, 1952.

Whyte, L. L. *Accent on Form*, London: Routledge, 1955.

8. SCIENTIFIC AND PHILOSOPHICAL CONCEPTIONS OF SCIENCE
AND RELIGION

Alexander, S. *Space, Time and Deity*, London: The Macmillan Company, Ltd., 1920.

Compton, Arthur H. *Religion of a Scientist*, New York: Jewish Theological Seminary of America, 1938.

Conant, J. B. *Modern Science and Modern Man*, Oxford University Press, 1952.

du Noüy, Pierre Lecomte. *Human Destiny*, Longmans, Green & Co., 1947.

Eddington, A. *The Nature of the Physical World*, Cambridge University Press, 1932.

Jeans, J. H. *The Mysterious Universe*, Cambridge University Press, 1931.

Long, Edward LeRoy. *Religious Beliefs of American Scientists*, Philadelphia: The Westminster Press, 1952.

Löwith, K. *Wissen, Glaube und Skepsis*, Göttingen, 1956.

Needham, J. *The Great Amphibian*: SCM Press, 1931.

Oppenheimer, J. Robert. *Science and the Common Understanding*, Oxford University Press, 1954.

Polanyi, M. *Personal Knowledge*, Chicago: The University of Chicago Press, 1958.

Randall, Jr., J. H. *The Role of Knowledge in Western Religion*, Boston: Starr King Press, 1958.

Schrödinger, E. *What is Life?*, Cambridge University Press, 1944.

Sinnott, Edmund W. *Two Roads to Truth*, New York: The Viking Press, Inc., 1953.

Dixon, W. T. *Religion and the Modern Mind*, London: Macmillan, 1953.

9. THEOLOGY AND SCIENCE

Baillie, J. *Natural Science and the Spiritual Life*, New York: Charles Scribner's, Sons, 1952.

Balthasar, Hans Urs von. *Science, Religion and Christianity*, London: Burns and Oates, 1958.

Coulson, C. A. *Science and Christian Belief*, Oxford University Press, 1955.

Dilschneider, Otto. *Das christliche Weltbild*, Gütersloh, 1951.

Dolch, Heimo. *Kausalität im Verständnis des Theologen und der Begründer der neuzeitlichen Physik*, Frieburg, 1954.

Evangelische Theologie, see 1947–1948 for many articles on European conversations.

Gilkey, Langdon. *Maker of Heaven and Earth*, New York: Doubleday & Company, Inc., 1959.

Hartshorne, M. Holmes. *The Promise of Science and the Power of Faith*, Philadelphia: The Westminster Press, 1958.

Heim, K. *Christian Faith and Natural Science*, London: SCM Press, 1953.

Horton, W. M. *Theism and the Scientific Spirit*, New York and London: Harper & Brothers, 1933.

Howe, Günter. *Der Mensch und die Physik*, Wuppertal, 1958.

Mascall, E. L. *Christian Theology and Modern Science*, London: Longmans, Green & Co., 1956.

Milne, E. A. *Modern Cosmology and the Christian Idea of God*, Oxford: The Clarendon Press, 1952.

Pollard, W. *Chance and Providence*, New York: Charles Scribner's, Sons, 1958.

Raven, C. *Natural Religion and Christian Theology*; I. *Science and Religion*, II. *Experience and Interpretation*, Cambridge University Press, 1953.

Schilling, H. *Concerning the Nature of Science and Religion* (pamphlet), School of Religion at the State University of Iowa, 1958.

Schrey, Heinz-Horst. *Weltbild und Glaube im 20. Jahrhundert*, Göttingen, 1955.

Smethurst, A. P. *Modern Science and Christian Belief*, London: Nisbet, 1955.

Titius, A. *Natur und Gott*, Göttingen, 1926.

Whitehouse, W. A. *Christian Faith and the Scientific Attitude*, London: Oliver and Boyd, 1952.

(For readings in contemporary theology and related philosophical writings in which the area of science is indirectly but inescapably relevant, see, for example, the writings of Karl Barth, Paul Tillich, Emil Brunner, Reinhold Neibuhr, Rudolph Bultmann, Karl Jaspers, Gabriel Marcel, Martin Heidegger, Friedrich Gogarten.)

10. SUPPLEMENTAL LITERATURE (Philosophical and Literary)

Barfield, O. *Saving the Appearances*, London: Faber and Faber, 1957.

Carré, M. H. *Phases of Thought in England*, Oxford: The Clarendon Press, 1949.

Collingwood, R. *The Idea of Nature*, Oxford: The Clarendon Press, 1946.

Heidegger, M. *Holzwege*, Frankfurt am Main: Klostermann, 1952.

Hesse, M. *Science and the Human Imagination*, SCM Press, 1954.

Jones, R. F. *Ancients and Moderns*, St. Louis: Washington University Studies, 1936.

Langer, S. *Philosophy in a New Key*, Oxford University Press, 1951.

Mitchell, B. (ed.). *Faith and Logic*, London: George Allen and Unwin, 1957.

Nicolson, M. *Science and Imagination*, Ithaca, New York: Great Seal Books, 1956.

Stebbing, S. L. *Philosophy and the Physicists*, London: Methuen and Co., Ltd., 1937.

Whitehead, A. *The Concept of Nature*, Cambridge University Press, 1930.

Willey, B. *The Seventeenth Century Background*, London: Chatto and Windus, 1950.

————. *The Eighteenth Century Background*, London: Chatto and Windus, 1950.

————. *Nineteenth Century Studies*, London: Chatto and Windus, 1950.

Wood, Herbert G. *Belief and Unbelief since* 1850, Cambridge University Press, 1955.

INDEX

Index of Names

Index of Subjects